Geography Militant

Cultures of Exploration and Empire

Felix Driver

Royal Holloway, University of London

B BLACKWELL
Publishers

First published 2001

2 4 6 8 10 9 7 5 3 1

2 4 6 8 10 9 7 5 3 1

Blackwell Publishers Ltd
108 Cowley Road
Oxford OX4 1JF
UK

Blackwell Publishers Inc.
350 Main Street
Malden, Massachusetts 02148
USA

British Library Cataloguing in Publication Data
A CIP catalogue record for this book is available from the
British Library

Library of Congress Cataloging-in-Publication Data
Driver, Felix.
    Geography militant : cultures of exploration and empire / Felix Driver.
        p. cm.
    Includes bibliographical references (p.).
    ISBN 0-631-20111-4 (hc : alk. paper) — 0-631-20112-2 (pb : alk. paper)
        1. Geography—Philosophy. 2. Geography—Great Britain—History—19th century. 3.
    Explorers—Great Britain—History—19th century. I. Title.

G70 .D75 2000
910'.941'09034—dc21

                                                                    00-025855

This book is printed on acid-free paper.

Geography Militant

WITHDRAWN

UCP Marjon

Contents

Acknowledgements

In the process of writing and rewriting this book, I have learned much from discussions and debates with friends, colleagues and students, and I must begin by thanking them for their patience and persistence: the final product may not be what they expected, but then it is not what I expected either. In particular, I would like to thank Charles Withers, whose critique of a first draft made me start all over again, and Denis Cosgrove, Catherine Hall, Dorothy Helly, David Livingstone, Luciana Martins, Miles Ogborn and Andrea Zemgulys, for their comments on earlier versions of specific chapters. I must also acknowledge the help of the large number of people who provided guidance and advice on particular points, including Tim Barringer, Michael Bravo, James Cameron, Jonathan Crush, Derek Gregory, Peter Hansen, Michael Heffernan, Jane Jacobs, Dane Kennedy, Jeremy Krikler, John MacKenzie, Dorinda Outram, David Pinder, Teresa Ploszajska, James Ryan, James Sidaway and the late Raphael Samuel. I am very grateful to Andrew David, Alice Clareson and Arthur Reade for making their own collections of books and family papers available to me. I must also thank colleagues at Royal Holloway, University of London, for providing a supportive and stimulating environment for learning and research, and the regulars at the London historical geography seminars for much else besides.

I have troubled legions of archivists, librarians and curators in the course of my research. I would particularly like to thank Rachel Rowe, Janet Turner, Joanna Scadden and Andrew Tatham at the Royal Geographical Society (with the Institute of British Geographers) and Peter Funnell at the National Portrait Gallery. I also gratefully acknowledge the help of staff at the British Library, Cambridge University Library, the Geological Society of London, the Huntington Library,

Imperial College, Kings College Cambridge, the Museum of Mankind, News International, the Oxford Museum of Natural History, the Public Records Office, Rhodes House Oxford, the Royal Botanic Gardens, Royal Holloway, St Mary's Medical Hospital, Southampton city archives, Unilever, University College London, the Wellcome Institute, West Sussex Records Office and Yale University Divinity School.

The research for three of the chapters in this book was conducted during a period of research leave funded by the Humanities Research Board of the British Academy, which I gratefully acknowledge. Preliminary versions of several chapters were presented at the North American Conference on British Studies in Washington, the Gibellina Colloquium on Geographical Representations, a Symposium on Display and the Victorians at the Victoria & Albert Museum, a Summer School on Imperialism at Essex University, the Conference on Scientific Instructions to Travellers at the Gabinetto G. P. Vieusseux in Florence, the IGU Symposium on the Circulation of Ideas in the History of Geographical Thought in Lisbon and an AAG Session on Spaces of Geographical Knowledge in Boston. Thanks to the organizers and participants on these occasions for numerous helpful comments and suggestions.

It is a pleasure to acknowledge the help I have received from the editorial staff at Blackwell: especially John Davey, who commissioned the book and has been marvellously supportive ever since, and Sarah Falkus and Joanna Pyke, who have patiently seen it through to publication. I am also grateful to Justin Jacyno and Sue May at Royal Holloway for preparing the illustrations. An earlier version of chapter 4 appeared in *David Livingstone and the Victorian Encounter with Africa*, published by the National Portrait Gallery in 1996. Chapter 6 is a substantially revised version of a paper which appeared in *Past and Present*, no. 133 (1991). A preliminary outline of the argument in chapter 3 was presented as a paper at an IGU Symposium in Lisbon, since published in *Finisterra: Revista Portuguesa de Geografia*, 33, 65 (1998).

Chapter 1

Geographical Knowledge, Exploration and Empire

'I hate travelling and explorers.' So begins *Tristes Tropiques*, Claude Lévi-Strauss's reflections on anthropological fieldwork, first published in 1955. The book continues with a stern rebuke to modern consumers of tales of adventure: 'Nowadays, being an explorer is a trade, which consists not, as one might think, in discovering hitherto unknown facts after years of study, but in covering a great many miles and assembling lantern-slides or motion pictures, preferably in colour, so as to fill a hall with an audience for several days in succession.' The calling of the anthropologist was something altogether more noble, precisely because it was more modest: considered observation instead of superficial stories, reflection not judgement. 'Adventure has no place in the anthropologist's profession ... The truths which we seek so far afield only become valid when they have become separated from this dross.' For Lévi-Strauss, the modern cult of exploration was a relatively recent phenomenon, associated with the cinema and the glossy picture-book: the craving for fantasies of the exotic went hand-in-hand with the inexorable advance of technological and commercial modernity across the globe. The anthropologist too was caught up in this new world, from which there was no escape: Lévi-Strauss himself attributed the fifteen-year delay between his departure from Brazil and the publication of *Tristes Tropiques* to his 'shame and repugnance' at the very idea of the exotic travel narrative.[1]

The distinction between the adventurous explorer and the scientific traveller, presented by Lévi-Strauss as the product of twentieth-century modernity, in fact had a much longer history. Anxieties about the relationship between sober science and sensational discovery,

1. C. Lévi-Strauss, *Tristes Tropiques* (London, 1973), pp. 1–2.

'professional' fieldwork and 'popular' travel, have characterised writings on anthropology (and geography) for at least two hundred years. Indeed, one might say that the history of the field sciences during this period is a history of constant efforts to differentiate between, and within, the categories of travel, exploration and discovery. Rather than simply assume a neat distinction between the discourses of adventurous travel and scientific exploration, historians of geography ought to focus precisely on the unsettled frontier between them.[2] During the eighteenth and nineteenth centuries, as much as the twentieth, the idea of exploration was freighted with multiple and contested meanings, associated variously with science, literature, religion, commerce and empire. The business of the scientific explorer was not always, or easily, distinguished from that of the literary *flâneur*, the missionary, the trader or the imperial pioneer. In this sense, the ambivalent anthropologist who writes a book of travels despite himself, the explorer who hates explorers, was already a familiar figure.

This book is about the relations between geographical knowledge and the cultures of exploration in a largely, though not exclusively, British context. While all the sciences were shaped, to some extent, by practices of exploration – the voyage, the survey, the mapping of the earth, the seas and the stars – the field of geography more than any other came to be associated with the figure of the explorer. I say 'field' here because of the heterogeneous nature of geographical knowledge before the formation of modern disciplines at the end of the nineteenth century. During the eighteenth century, geography was a large and diffuse body of knowledge, encompassing aspects of cartography, topography, surveying and navigation, all of which provided vital information for allied sciences such as astronomy and natural history.[3] While the conceptual basis for geography was to undergo a significant shift during the nineteenth century, geography remained a remarkably diverse field throughout the period. Even if one adopts a narrow definition of 'geographical knowledge' as concerned simply with the mapping of locations on the earth's surface – a science of position – it is evident that this knowledge was far from the sole property of a single scientific community. Geographical knowledge in this restricted sense

2. The difficulty of distinguishing 'adventurous' exploration from 'scientific' travel is acknowledged in N. Broc, *La Géographie des philosophes: géographes et voyageurs français au XVIIIe siècle* (Paris, 1974), p. 9.
3. R. Sorrenson, 'The ship as a scientific instrument in the eighteenth century', in H. Kuklick and R. Kohler (eds), *Science in the Field* (Chicago, 1996), esp. pp. 222–4; C. Withers, 'Geography, natural history and the eighteenth-century Enlightenment: putting the world in place', *History Workshop Journal*, 39 (1995), pp. 137–63.

was an adjunct to many different forms of practice – scientific, scholarly, technical, commercial and military, for example. Moreover, the range of work done throughout this period in the name of 'geography', as reflected in the writings of philosophes or the proceedings of geographical societies, for example, extended well beyond topographical mapping. Geographers increasingly described their subject as one of synthesis, drawing together a range of different kinds of knowledge in order to construct accounts of particular places, regions or landscapes. Where these places were unknown, or at least unfamiliar, then the knowledge of the explorer entered the field of geography. In this sense, the explorer was the foot-soldier of geography's empire; a pioneer of Geography Militant.

Conquerors of Truth: on Geography's History

The term 'Geography Militant' comes from a late essay by Joseph Conrad, reprinted in 1924 in the pages of the *National Geographic*. Under the ostensibly modest title 'Geography and some explorers', Conrad charted three epochs in the history of geographical knowledge. The first, Geography Fabulous, he described as a 'phase of circumstantially extravagant speculation which had nothing to do with the pursuit of truth', an age when medieval cartographers crowded their maps 'with pictures of strange pageants, strange trees, strange beasts, drawn with amazing precision in the midst of theoretically-conceived continents'.[4] Geography Militant, in contrast, exemplified a more worldly quest for empirical knowledge about the geography of the earth, marked by voyages of exploration by sea and land; according to Conrad, Captain Cook was its perfect embodiment. During the nineteenth century, in search of 'exciting spaces of white paper', Cook's successors turned from the navigation of the oceans to the mapping of the continents: they are described by Conrad as 'adventurous and devoted men, . . . conquering a bit of truth here and a bit of truth there, and sometimes swallowed up by the mystery their hearts were so persistently set on unveiling'.[5] As the white spaces succumbed to the dominion of science, Conrad laments, the mystique of geographical

4.   J. Conrad, 'Geography and some explorers', *National Geographic*, 45, no. 3 (March 1924), reprinted in R. Curle (ed.), *Last Essays* (London, 1926), pp. 1–31 [quote from p. 3]. The essay was originally published in 1923, under the title 'The romance of travel'. This brief summary is based on F. Driver, 'Geography's empire: histories of geographical knowledge', *Environment and Planning D: Society and Space*, 10 (1992), 23–40 [23–4].
5.   Conrad, 'Geography and some explorers', pp. 19–20.

exploration slowly faded; and Geography Militant gave way to Geography Triumphant.

For Conrad, the romance of exploration led inexorably to disenchantment: the passage from Geography Militant to Geography Triumphant marked the irreversible closure of the epoch of open spaces, the end of an era of unashamed heroism. The modern traveller, he wrote, was 'condemned to make his discoveries on beaten tracks';[6] or worse, to find his romantic dreams shattered by mere opportunists and fortune-hunters. Conrad pictures this sense of loss while on his own journey up the Congo River in 1890: 'there was no shadowy friend to stand by my side in the night of enormous wilderness', he recalls, 'no great haunting memory, but only the unholy recollection of a prosaic newspaper "stunt" and the distasteful knowledge of the vilest scramble for loot that ever disfigured the history of human conscience and geographical exploration'.[7] In alluding to perhaps the most famous of all episodes in the history of modern exploration – 'Dr Livingstone, I presume?' – and the unholy scramble which followed it, Conrad appears to suggest that Livingstone was the last of the heroic explorers, and Stanley the first of a new breed; modern men, hell-bent on worldly gain.

'Geography and some explorers' offers a nostalgic lament for the spirit of heroic exploration represented by Geography Militant, a spirit which had apparently been extinguished in modernity's wake. Its singular confidence in the nobility of the true explorer contrasts markedly with the multiple tellings and murky impressionism of Conrad's novels, which so unsettled – even as they mimicked – the conventions of Victorian adventure fiction.[8] Yet this late essay does serve a purpose, by drawing our attention to the wider cultural meanings of geography and its history. Conrad knew that the business of exploration involved more than simply the mundane collection of geographical facts: that it required and sustained the mobilization of a range of material and emotional resources, in both its conduct and its representation. The explorers of Geography Militant might well be characterized as 'conquerors of truth', to adapt Conrad's telling phrase, and not simply because their maps and charts crafted a new way of seeing the worlds beyond Europe, for the same process involved the construction of heroic myths about the explorers themselves. The most influential of these myths represented the explorer as a missionary of science, extending the frontiers of (European) geographical knowledge. Such images were

6. Conrad, 'Travel', in *Last Essays*, pp. 121–34 (p. 134).
7. Conrad, 'Geography and some explorers', p. 25.
8. A. White, *Joseph Conrad and the Adventure Tradition: Constructing and Deconstructing the Imperial Subject* (Cambridge, 1993).

inevitably partial; indeed, they were in a sense designed to resolve imaginatively what could not be resolved in other ways. For the business of exploration could be profoundly unsettling, as much for the explorers as for the explored. The status and purpose of exploration were matters of contention throughout the nineteenth century.

Conrad's sketch of the history of geographical exploration struck a melancholy note. His childhood obsession with the blank spaces of unexplored continents (also reflected in the famous map-pointing scene in *Heart of Darkness*) had become an anachronism; the bewildered traveller in search of the exotic found only the mundane.[9] In 'Geography and some explorers', Conrad projects the contrast between his own youthful faith in the ideals of enlightened exploration and his disenchantment with their worldly effects on a larger historical plane. In these terms, his tale has two turning points, represented by Cook and Stanley respectively: the one encapsulates the era of Geography Militant, the other brings it to a close. Of course we must be sceptical of this sort of history, with its narratives of innocence corrupted, though it is remarkable how faithfully these same turning points are reproduced in many histories of exploration and travel, whether orthodox or critical in intent. Nostalgia for an age of genuine exploration in unmapped territory was nothing new even in Conrad's time: his distrust of modern tourism in the age of steam travel and popular guidebooks was utterly conventional. But in this sense so too are those more radical critiques of the effects of global modernity that seek after some Edenic age of cultural encounter before the Fall. Here, for example, is Lévi-Strauss again, lamenting the passing of an age of true voyaging:

> Journeys, those magic caskets full of dreamlike promises, will never again yield up their treasures untarnished. A proliferating and overexcited civilization has broken the silence of the seas once and for all. The perfumes of the tropics and the pristine freshness of human beings have been corrupted by a busyness with dubious implications, which mortifies our desires and dooms us to acquire only contaminated memories.

Lévi-Strauss, like Conrad before him, finds in the Third World a reflection of the corruption of the West: 'The first thing we see as we

---

9. On Conrad's melancholia, see C. Gogwilt, *The Invention of the West: Joseph Conrad and the Double-Mapping of Europe and the Empire* (Stanford, 1995), ch. 5; on the disorientation of the 'bewildered traveller', see J. W. Griffith, *Joseph Conrad and the Anthropological Dilemma* (Oxford, 1995), ch. 1.

travel round the world is our own filth, thrown into the face of mankind.'[10]

The notion of a 'great divide' between an epoch of pure exploration and an epoch of corrupted travel (another word for modern tourism?) would be regarded by many historians today as unsustainable; though they took different forms at different times, the associations between exploration, modernity and empire stretch back as far as we care to look. We might perhaps redeem the contrast between Geography Militant and Geography Triumphant by treating it symptomatically rather than sequentially, as the expression of an inescapable tension within projects of European exploration since the eighteenth century. But this is necessarily to take a more critical view of the history of exploration than Conrad or his contemporaries could provide. 'There can be no question', asserted Clements Markham a century ago, 'that a study of the heroic deeds of explorers, [and] the contemplation of their high qualities ... excite a feeling of sympathy which is ennobling to those who are under their influence, and is an education in itself.'[11] These words, uttered in celebration of the achievements of the Hakluyt Society during the nineteenth century, have today lost much of their innocent charm. At the beginning of the twenty-first century, such names as Columbus, Cook and Livingstone, not to mention Hakluyt, are as likely to evoke troubling memories of empire as ennobling feelings of sympathy. Voyages and travels, 'those magic caskets full of dreamlike promises', have been opened to far more critical scrutiny.

In the wake of decolonization, it was the partiality of triumphal narratives of European exploration that attracted critical attention, both within and beyond the academy: what was once regarded as noble because universal – the conquest of truth, the idea of progress, the heroism of exploration – was now tainted with particularity. Critical reappraisals of the relationship between geographical knowledge and imperial power have subsequently taken many different forms.[12] One

10. Lévi-Strauss, *Tristes Tropiques*, pp. 37–8, 43. See also P. Brunt, 'Clumsy utopians: an afterword', in N. Thomas and D. Losche (eds), *Double Vision: Art Histories and Colonial Histories in the Pacific* (Cambridge, 1999), pp. 257–74 (pp. 257–8).
11. R. Bridges and P. Hair (eds), *Compassing the Vaste Globe of the Earth: Studies in the History of the Hakluyt Society, 1846–1996* (London, 1996), p. 25 n. 1.
12. These reappraisals in some respects (though not all) anticipated current interest in postcolonial theory. See, for example, B. Hudson, 'The new geography and the new imperialism', *Antipode*, 9 (1977), pp. 12–19; R. Stafford, *Scientist of Empire: Sir Roderick Murchison, Scientific Exploration and Victorian Imperialism* (Cambridge, 1989); Driver, 'Geography's empire'; A. Godlewska and N. Smith (eds), *Geography and Empire* (Oxford, 1994); M. Bell, R. Butlin and M. Heffernan

of the distinctive features of recent work from a postcolonial perspective, for example, is the treatment of the European literature of travel and exploration as an exemplary site of imperial vision.[13] While academic debates over postcolonialism are becoming increasingly sterile, especially when framed in terms of an essential antagonism between history and theory,[14] one thing at least is clear. The idea of Europe and the West as self-contained entities, whose self-generated 'expansion' shaped the modern world, has been shown for what it was: a powerful fiction. This, it seems to me, was the single most important message of Edward Said's *Orientalism*, a book which has been widely treated, not unproblematically, as the founding text of contemporary postcolonial criticism. This critical attitude towards the idea of a self-sufficient Europe or the West (and the correspondingly essentialised versions of its Others) has significant implications for historians of geographical knowledge, as it asks how such fictions came to be established, which voices were heard and which were silenced, and how else we might conceive the geographical tradition.[15] Yet, as Said has himself argued, the academic literature of postcolonialism has too often effected a narrowing of perspective, especially, I would add, in the context of the history of exploration and travel. If the promise of path-breaking works like Peter Hulme's *Colonial Encounters* has not been realised, it is partly because the effort of interpretation has too often been restricted

(eds), *Geography and Imperialism, 1820–1940* (Manchester, 1995); D. P. Miller and P. H. Reill (eds), *Visions of Empire: Voyages, Botany and Representations of Nature* (Cambridge, 1996); M. Edney, *Mapping an Empire: The Geographical Construction of British India* (Chicago, 1997); D. Clayton, *Islands of Truth: The Imperial Fashioning of Vancouver Island* (Vancouver, 1999).
13. See especially M. L. Pratt, *Imperial Eyes: Travel Writing and Transculturation* (London, 1992); also, P. Hulme, *Colonial Encounters: Europe and the Native Caribbean, 1492–1797* (London, 1986); P. Carter, *The Road to Botany Bay: An Essay in Spatial History* (London, 1987); D. Spurr, *The Rhetoric of Empire: Colonial Discourse in Journalism, Travel-writing and Imperial Administration* (Durham, NC, 1993); A. Blunt, *Travel, Gender and Imperialism* (New York, 1994); T. Youngs, *Travellers in Africa: British Travelogues, 1850–1900* (Manchester, 1994); S. Ryan, *The Cartographic Eye: How Explorers Saw Australia* (Cambridge, 1996); J. Duncan and D. Gregory (eds), *Writes of Passage: Reading Travel Writing* (London, 1999).
14. J. MacKenzie, *Orientalism: History, Theory and the Arts* (Manchester, 1995); D. Kennedy, 'Imperial history and post-colonial theory', *Journal of Imperial and Commonwealth History*, 24 (1996), pp. 345–63; 'Colonial desire' (roundtable discussion), *Journal of Victorian Culture*, 2 (1997), pp. 113–52.
15. 'Geographical traditions: re-thinking the history of geography' (feature), *Transactions of the Institute of British Geographers*, 20 (1995), pp. 403–22; J. Sidaway, 'The (re)making of the western "geographical tradition"', *Area*, 29 (1997), pp. 72–80. On Said's conception of geography, see D. Gregory, 'Imaginative geographies', *Progress in Human Geography*, 19 (1995), pp. 447–85.

to the analysis of finished texts and partly because these texts have been too quickly reduced to a sort of imperial will-to-power. Postcolonial criticism has frequently given way to an essentialized model of 'colonial discourse' which obscures the heterogeneous, contingent and conflictual character of imperial projects.[16] While the textual analysis of published travel narratives can yield valuable insights into the culture which produced and interpreted them, it is also important to consider other sorts of text – and indeed other sorts of evidence – in order to situate these narratives historically. The published narrative was the end-product of a sequence of stages in the writing of travel, a process through which the explorer in the field was translated into the published author.[17] Instead of interpreting texts as projections of colonial discourse or productions of an imperial eye, it might therefore be more useful to construe them as articulations of practices, an approach which I believe offers a more complex and provisional sense of the textual with which we can work historically.[18] In this book, I am in fact concerned less with exploration narratives themselves than with the ways in which they were produced and consumed.

Cultures of Exploration

In this book, exploration is understood as a set of cultural practices which involve the mobilization of people and resources, especially equipment, publicity and authority. This approach enables us to situate the travels and narratives of individual explorers in a wider context. The idea of 'cultures of exploration' is offered here as no more than a short-hand term, denoting the wide variety of practices at work in the production and consumption of voyages and travels. This usage complements recent work by historians of science, as for example in a recent

16. For similar arguments, see N. Thomas, *Colonialism's Culture: Anthropology, Travel and Government* (Oxford, 1994); B. Schwarz, 'Conquerors of truth: reflections on postcolonial theory', in B. Schwarz (ed.), *The Expansion of England: Race, Ethnicity and Cultural History* (London, 1996), pp. 9–31.
17. See especially I. MacLaren, 'Exploration/travel literature and the evolution of the author', *International Journal of Canadian Studies*, 5 (1992), pp. 39–68.
18. For parallel arguments about the interpretation of the visual archive of travel, see L. Martins, *O Rio de Janeiro dos Viajantes: O Olhar Britânico* (Rio de Janeiro, 2000); L. Bell, 'To see or not to see: conflicting eyes in the travel art of Augustus Earle', in J. F. Codell and D. S. Macleod (eds), *Orientalism Transposed: The Impact of the Colonies on British Culture* (Aldershot, 1998), pp. 117–39.

collection of essays on *Cultures of Natural History.*[19] The various practices associated there with natural history have their counterparts in the wider field of exploration, for example: material practices concerned with the making and handling of things (in the case of exploration knowledge, these would include the organization of expeditions, the gathering and transport of baggage, equipment and personnel, the making and distribution of publications and exhibitions); social practices involving all kinds of social relations and negotiations (including the relations within an expedition party, the conventions associated with the presentation of exploration reports, the codes of conduct in scientific societies); literary practices raising issues of representation and genre (including conventions associated with the writing of exploration narratives); bodily practices of self-presentation and experience (including conventions of conduct both in the field and within those institutions where exploration knowledge was sanctioned); and what Jardine and Spary term 'reproductive' practices, those concerned with the transmission of knowledge (including in the present context both the formal and informal means by which exploration knowledge was imparted).

Projects of exploration self-evidently involved the movement of bodies into and through 'the field', which may be thought of here as both a material and an imaginative space. In the period I am concerned with, exploration was conceived of as a particular kind of travel associated with the sight of new landscapes, peoples, plants and animals. To lay eyes upon a lake, a peak, a species, for the first time, was the dream of every aspiring explorer. Crucially, however, the explorer's search for a reputation depended on social relationships at 'home' as well as in the 'field', with patrons, publishers, editors and image-makers acting as vital mediators. The fame of the most celebrated explorers of the eighteenth and nineteenth centuries, no less than that of their successors, depended upon more than their own labours. (In this sense, Lévi-Strauss's complaints about the twentieth-century popular culture of exploration greatly underestimated its longevity.) The part played by editors and other intermediaries in shaping the literary output and public reputation of figures such as Captain Cook or David Livingstone is well established; and it is also evident in the process by which countless less well-known narratives of exploration were transmitted into the public domain, via institutions such as the Royal Geographical

19. N. Jardine and E. Spary, 'The natures of cultural history', in N. Jardine, J. Secord and E. Spary (eds), *Cultures of Natural History* (Cambridge, 1996), pp. 3–13.

Society and publishers such as Blackwood or Murray.[20] In the last third of the nineteenth century, moreover, the business of exploration was profoundly influenced by the transformation of popular journalism.[21] Henry Morton Stanley's expeditions, for example, required substantial funds, obtained partly from the press, as well as from fund-raising campaigns. His commission to 'find Livingstone' was conceived by James Gordon Bennett of the *New York Herald* as a scoop; indeed, without Livingstone it seems that Stanley might even have found himself on a mission to find the Dalai Lama. Throughout his career as an explorer, Stanley used his experience as a journalist to maximize the impact of his reports, and the controversies which surrounded him indicate that the alliance between the new journalism and sensational exploration was far from uncontested (see chapter 6).

Far from being a homogeneous field, then, the culture of exploration was riven with differences over the style, methods and function of the explorer: the quest for geographical truth took many forms. This was partly a matter of audience, for what might be acceptable in one context (a tale of adventure, for example) was not necessarily credible in another (a scientific meeting). It is worth noting here that many of the explorers of the nineteenth century wrote fiction as well as exploration narratives: frequently, they intended the stories for women and children and the narratives for a masculine public. As this suggests, the culture of exploration was profoundly gendered: the man of science was no mere figure of speech. Yet it would be wrong to overemphasize the solidity of the boundary between adventure fiction and exploration narratives: with Stanley, for example, these genres were so blurred that it was difficult to say where one ended and the other began. More generally, the idea of exploration, of travel across the blank spaces, provided a common vehicle for very different forms of practice and different kinds of knowledge, and it is precisely the tensions between them that provide the focus for several of the following chapters. These tensions became visible in moments of controversy: methodologically, such episodes offer the historian a particularly fruitful way to open up the archive of exploration and travel, exposing the contested nature of the field.

In a sense, the business of exploration posed as many problems as it

---

20. See I. MacLaren, 'From exploration to publication: the evolution of a nine-teenth-century Arctic narrative', *Arctic*, 47 (1994), pp. 43–53; B. Smith, 'Cook's posthumous reputation', in R. Fisher and H. Johnston (eds), *Captain James Cook and His Times* (Vancouver, 1979), pp. 159–85; Youngs, *Travellers in Africa*; D. Helly, *Livingstone's Legacy: Horace Waller and Victorian Myth-making* (Athens, Ohio, 1987).
21. B. Riffenburgh, *The Myth of the Explorer* (Oxford, 1993).

solved. As Dorinda Outram has argued in the context of the Enlightenment, voyages and travels raised troubling questions about authority (can the explorer be trusted?) and identity (might exploration change our selves?).[22] The problematic status of exploration knowledge is tellingly illustrated in Outram's account of the response of Georges Cuvier, professor of comparative anatomy at the Museum of Natural History in Paris, to the work of Alexander von Humboldt, the archetypal scientific explorer of the New World. For Cuvier (writing in 1807), the field naturalist (*naturaliste-voyageur*) experiences nature in the raw, in all its abundance, but he cannot grasp the whole; it is the sedentary naturalist who has the task of providing a more reliable overview. Commenting on Humboldt's journey along the Orinoco, Cuvier insists that 'the traveller can only travel one road; it is only really in one's study (*cabinet*) that one can roam freely through the universe, and for that, a different sort of courage is needed'.[23] Outram suggests that this opposition between two ways of doing natural history is structured not only by contrasting models of science and masculinity, but also by two different experiences of space. In Cuvier's view, the scientific mastery of nature depends not on the bodily experience of movement into new spaces, but on the observer's very distance from a particular field site. 'For the eye of the field naturalist, seduced by the dazzle of passing events, Cuvier's sedentary naturalist substitutes an observation which is distanced, and thereby dominating in its control over the whole range of the natural order.'[24] As Outram notes, Cuvier was undoubtedly attempting to protect his authority against the rising reputation of Humboldt, and it must also be remembered that Humboldt was no ordinary field naturalist. Nevertheless, the episode serves as a reminder that the geography of knowledge mattered.

Spaces of Knowledge

Outram's essay 'New spaces of natural history' considers a number of different sites in which natural science was produced at the beginning of the nineteenth century, from the natural history museum to the tropical forest, each of them associated with different kinds of knowl-

22. D. Outram, 'On being Perseus: new knowledge, dislocation and Enlightenment exploration', in D. Livingstone and C. Withers (eds), *Geography and Enlightenment* (Chicago, 1999), pp. 281–94.
23. D. Outram, 'New spaces in natural history', in Jardine, Secord and Spary, *Cultures of Natural History*, pp. 249–65 [p. 261].
24. Outram, 'New spaces in natural history', p. 263.

edge, ethics and authority. This concern with the spaces of knowledge is a notable feature of several other recent works by geographers and historians of science.[25] In this book, I too approach the culture of exploration from a variety of different sites where knowledge about exploration was produced and consumed, including the Royal Geographical Society in London, the space of the popular exhibition, the narrative of exploration and the various 'field' locations through which explorers travelled. Differences over the nature and purpose of the geographical knowledges produced in these various sites could give rise to heated controversy: the relation between observation in the field and reflection in the study was particularly fraught with difficulty.

In this context, it is worth noting that historians of geography have paid far less attention to the subject of fieldwork than to geographical ideas or institutions, despite the evident significance of notions of the 'field' and practices of 'fieldwork' for the development of the discipline: recent work by feminist geographers makes a notable departure in this respect, though much more remains to be done.[26] If we think of geographical knowledge as constituted through a range of embodied practices – travelling, seeing, collecting, recording, mapping and narrating – the subject of fieldwork becomes difficult to escape.[27] The field in this sense is not just 'there'; it is always in the process of being constructed, through both physical movement – passage through a

25. R. Cooter and S. Pumfrey, 'Separate spheres and public places: reflections on the history of science popularization and science in popular culture', *History of Science*, 32 (1994), pp. 237–67; D. Livingstone, 'The spaces of knowledge: contributions towards a historical geography of science', *Environment and Planning D: Society and Space*, 13 (1995), pp. 5–34; A. Ophir, 'The place of knowledge: a methodological survey', *Science in Context*, 4 (1991), pp. 3–21; S. Shapin, 'Placing the view from nowhere: historical and sociological problems in the location of science', *Transactions of the Institute of British Geographers*, 23 (1998), pp. 5–12; C. Smith and J. Agar (eds), *Making Space for Science: Territorial Themes in the Shaping of Knowledge* (London, 1998); C. Withers, 'Towards a history of geography in the public sphere', *History of Science*, 36 (1998), pp. 45–78.

26. M. Domosh, 'Towards a feminist historiography of geography', *Transactions of the Institute of British Geographers*, 16 (1991), pp. 95–104; G. Rose, *Feminism and Geography: The Limits of Geographical Knowledge* (Cambridge, 1993); H. Nast, 'Women in the field', *Professional Geographer*, 46 (1996), pp. 54–66; M. Sparke, 'Displacing the field in fieldwork: masculinity, metaphor and space', in N. Duncan (ed.), *Bodyspace: Destabilizing Geographies of Gender and Sexuality* (London, 1996), pp. 212–33; C. McEwan, 'Gender, science and physical geography in nineteenth-century Britain', *Area*, 30 (1998), pp. 215–223.

27. The notion of fieldwork as a spatial practice is developed in the context of the discipline of anthropology in J. Clifford, *Routes: Travels and Translation in the Late Twentieth Century* (Cambridge, Mass., 1997), esp. pp. 52–91.

country – and other sorts of cultural work in other places.[28] It is produced locally by the spatial practices of fieldwork, and discursively through texts and images, including publications like the Royal Geographical Society's *Hints to Travellers* (which provides the focus for chapter 3). Such an approach to fieldwork prompts many further questions, only some of which are addressed in this book: questions about the relationships between travelling, seeing and knowing, about the means by which geographical skills are transmitted and reproduced, and about the embodiment of these skills in the figure of the geographer, both in and out of the 'field'. As Gillian Beer shows in a fascinating essay on Darwin's *Beagle* voyage, nineteenth-century field observation was embodied in a variety of ways; and far from being the self-evident source of empirical knowledge, observation in the field could be deeply problematic.[29]

The contrast between the knowledges of the field and of the study is not of course new to historians of geography. In his influential account of eighteenth-century French geography, for example, Numa Broc identified two very different kinds of knowledge: the scholarly geography of the cabinet, essentially concerned with the compilation of maps, and the adventurous geography of the *voyageur* in search of new knowledge.[30] Yet, while this distinction was certainly familiar to contemporaries, it was far from being a fixed boundary, across which it was impossible to travel: as well as addressing the meaning of the boundary itself, we must therefore consider the ways in which it was bridged. Attempts to reconcile the knowledges of the field and the study took many forms, from the publication of instructional literature for travellers to the development of new ideas about the relationship between the observer and the empirical world. In the context of natural history, Outram suggests that the tension between the knowledge of the cabinet and the knowledge of the field – which she argues was sharpened rather than settled by Cuvier's critique of Humboldt – remained

---

28.   Cf. A. Cooper, 'From the Alps to Egypt (and back again): Dolomieu, scientific voyaging and the construction of the field in eighteenth-century natural history', in Smith and Agar, *Making Space for Science*, pp. 39–63; Kuklick and Kohler, *Science in the Field*; J. Camerini, 'Remains of the day: early Victorians in the field', in B. Lightman (ed.), *Victorian Science in Context* (Chicago, 1997), pp. 354–77; T. Ploszajska, 'Down to earth? Geography fieldwork in English schools, 1870–1944', *Environment and Planning D: Society and Space*, 16 (1998), pp. 757–74.
29.   G. Beer, 'Four bodies on the *Beagle*: touch, sight and writing in a Darwin letter', in G. Beer, *Open Fields: Science in Cultural Encounter* (Oxford, 1996), pp. 13–30. Cf. D. Stoddart, 'Darwin and the seeing eye: iconography and meaning in the Beagle years', *Earth Sciences History*, 14 (1995), pp. 3–22.
30.   Broc, *La Géographie des philosophes*, p. 475ff.

in evidence throughout the nineteenth century. Whether this argument holds for other sciences is an open question, although the enduring tendency of explorers in the field to define their projects in opposition to those of armchair geographers, geologists or anthropologists is certainly striking. While publications such as *Hints to Travellers* represented the scientific explorer as the travelling eye of metropolitan science, it is important to recognize that the nature of this science was itself undergoing significant change: Jonathan Crary has argued, for example, that the image of perception exemplified by the camera obscura was giving way to more mobile, and more embodied, models of vision.[31] In this context, Humboldt's writings can themselves be conceived of as an attempt to reformulate rather than reiterate the conventional opposition between field science and theoretical knowledge. Certainly, his reputation as a scholar more than matched his fame as an explorer. Indeed, on his return to Paris from South America in 1804 he was hailed as the very embodiment of the idea of philosophical travel: 'that man is a complete walking academy', observed one leading chemist.[32] For Humboldt, the study of nature was more than simply a matter of describing or mapping what was visible to the eye in the field: as Massimo Quaini points out, it also required a scholarly knowledge of history and myth, a knowledge primarily obtained through the reading of ancient and modern texts.[33]

Further evidence of efforts to reconcile the knowledge of the field with that of the cabinet is provided in many contemporary portraits of scientific explorers. Eduard Hildebrandt's portrait of the venerable Humboldt philosophizing in his library (figure 1.1) is a well-known example of a larger genre of portraits of scientific explorers situated in the cabinet, often accompanied by books, maps, specimens or instruments.[34] Here knowledge is represented not merely as a matter of exploring the outer world, but rather as the accumulated product of hours of contemplation within the private space of the study, the place where the raw material of nature is imaginatively but patiently trans-

31. J. Crary, *Techniques of the Observer: On Vision and Modernity in the Nineteenth Century* (Cambridge, Mass., 1992). For a development of this argument in the context of Humboldtian fieldwork, see D. Poole, *Vision, Race and Modernity: A Visual Economy of the Andean Image World* (Princeton, NJ, 1997), pp. 67–82.
32. D. Botting, *Humboldt and the Cosmos* (London, 1973), p. 178.
33. M. Quaini, 'Alexander von Humboldt: cartografo e mitografo', in C. Greppi (ed.), *Alexander von Humboldt: L'Invenzione del Nuovo Mondo* (Firenze, 1992), pp. ix–xxix.
34. Cf. J. Browne, 'I could have retched all night: Charles Darwin and his body', in C. Lawrence and S. Shapin (eds), *Science Incarnate: Historical Embodiments of Natural Knowledge* (Cambridge, 1998), pp. 240–87.

1.1 *Alexander von Humboldt in seiner Bibliothek* (1856), lithograph by Storch & Kramer from a watercolour by Eduard Hildebrandt. By permission of the Stadtmuseum, Berlin.

formed into ideas, theories, arguments. Humboldt's own inscription on a lithograph of the Hildebrandt portrait (now held at the Royal Geographical Society) draws our attention to the role of intellectual labour, of the compilation and comparison of the fruits of travel with the written archive of science. It is in the study, writes Humboldt, that the scientific mind can finally master 'the accumulated mass of empirical experience'. This is not to suggest that the cabinet was represented as a disembodied space in contrast to the field; rather, it was inhabited in a different way, as evidenced in countless portraits of men of science depicted book-in-hand. In the present case, given what is known about Humboldt's life during the 1850s, the space of the cabinet represented in Hildebrandt's portrait might be described as domestic rather than private: visitors to his residence in Berlin's Oranienburger Strasse were received by his long-time companion and housekeeper Johann Seifert, who had joined Humboldt on his travels. It was in fact Seifert who presented the lithograph to an American scientist shortly after Humboldt's death, having added a touching inscription of his own: 'Honoured Herr Professor, may you always remember, when you look at this portrait, the house of Alexander von Humboldt which you visited shortly after his passing. Johann Seifert (the travelling

1.2 Eduard Ender, *Alexander von Humboldt und Aimé Bonpland im Urwald* (1856), oil on canvas. By permission of the Berlin–Brandenburgische Akademie der Wissenschaften.

companion for many years of this great man), Berlin, August 24, 1859.'[35]

Of course scientific explorers were also commonly pictured in the field, as for example in Eduard Ender's famous portrait of Humboldt and Bonpland in the South American jungle, painted in the same year as Hildebrandt's, though representing a scene supposed to have taken place nearly sixty years earlier (figure 1.2). Significantly, however, such portraits often represented the explorer as the embodiment of scientific reason, a more or less 'complete walking academy' confronting a riotous natural world, bolstered by the accoutrements of scientific exploration – books, instruments, baggage and so on. It is interesting to note that the aged Humboldt himself expressed some disquiet about

35. Thanks to Rachel Rowe, the RGS librarian, for allowing me a closer look at the lithograph: a rough translation of Humboldt's inscription is provided in the *Geographical Journal*, 136 (1970), pp. 162–3. See also Botting, *Humboldt*, pp. 279–80.

1.3 William J. Burchell, *Inside of My African Waggon* (1820), watercolour, By permission of Oxford University Museum of Natural History.

Ender's evidently staged composition. The painting was clearly more studio than jungle.[36]

The prominence of the instruments of European science within such images of field exploration was more than incidental: they signified the extension of the knowledge of the cabinet into, and through, the field. This process is strikingly represented in William Burchell's portrait of his own collecting wagon, in which he travelled across southern Africa between 1810 and 1815; this was exhibited at the Royal Academy in 1820 (figure 1.3). The first volume of Burchell's *Travels in the Interior of Southern Africa* includes a painstaking description of the design of the wagon, which he regarded as perfectly suited to the terrain he had to negotiate, and which he had especially fitted up so as to enable him to transport the tools of his trade (figure 1.4).[37] His portrait of the wagon was intended as a measured record of his life as a travelling naturalist: typically, Burchell made a precise record of the time it took to complete the painting, just as he did when arranging and labelling

36. H. von Kügelgen and M. Seeberger, 'Humboldt und Bonpland in Enders "Urwaldatelier"', in *Alexander von Humboldt: Netzwerke des Wissens* (exhibition catalogue, Haus der Kulturen der Welt, Berlin, 1999), p. 157.
37. W. J. Burchell, *Travels in the Interior of Southern Africa*, vol. i (London, 1822), pp. 108–11, 118–20.

1.4 William Burchell's collecting wagon: cross section (*Travels in the Interior of Southern Africa*, 1822, vol. i, p. 108).

his specimens.[38] The small image (only 50 cm by 36 cm) was crammed with instruments of all kinds – including compass, telescope, thermometer, weighing scales, writing and drawing materials, maps, bottles, specimen cases, plant press, rifle and pistols – as well as numerous botanical and zoological specimens, an ethnographic portrait, the flag he had raised above his wagon on Sundays while beyond the territory of the Cape colony, the flute he had played to amuse himself and the hammock he had slept in. (A large book of astronomical charts, its brilliant pages lying open amid the debris, rested above Burchell's travelling library of natural history, fifty volumes in all.) Burchell's sextant is notably absent from the picture, and the absence is more than incidental: in the first volume of his published narrative, he carefully notes that he packed the most delicate instruments in his bedding during the hours of travel, in order to avoid damage from the motion of the wagon on the rough roads of the veld; while in the second, he comments that the sextant was too 'showy and attractive' to be seen by the so-called hottentots, and he took it out only under cover of darkness.[39]

Burchell's wagon itself was perhaps the most important instrument of all: it functioned both as a mobile laboratory, in which he could simultaneously travel and read, write, draw, weigh, measure, dissect and skin, and as an instrument itself, the rotations of its wheels providing Burchell with a means of calculating the distances he travelled across the

38. E. B. Poulton, *William John Burchell* (London, 1907), p. 40.
39. Burchell, *Travels in the Interior of Southern Africa*, vol. i, p. 120; vol. ii, p. 351.

landscapes of southern Africa. Of course, like the cabinets of Europe, the space of the wagon was not as self-sufficient as it appeared: Burchell depended throughout his travels on the labours of his numerous servants, on the health of his oxen, on his constant negotiations with Boer farmers and black Africans. His search for antelopes, hippopotami and rhinoceros, indeed all his copious verbal and visual depictions of the fauna, flora and peoples of the areas he explored, were accomplished through relationships and exchanges of one kind or another. The porcelain beads in the painting presumably signify the gifts he took with him on his travels in order to enrol the support of local peoples; the black, white and blue, he noted, were more sought after than the red or transparent.[40] Yet the picture itself presents an enclosed view, looking in, not out: it is an interior space, the space of the cabinet transposed to the field.

The space of the field is more directly acknowledged in a later image of African exploration – Henry Wyndham Phillips's portrait of James Grant and John Hanning Speke, which was exhibited at the Royal Academy in 1864 (figure 1.5). The two explorers are depicted contemplating a map of the lakes region of East Africa, Speke with dividers in hand and Grant sketching, while in between them leans a deferential and passive Timbo, described as 'a young native from the country of the Upper Nile'.[41] Viewers of the painting would have known nothing of Timbo, in contrast to the information which was disseminated about the guides who had accompanied the British explorers on their journey, eighteen of whom (including Bombay, Speke's assistant) were awarded medals by the RGS.[42] His role here was to be a specimen of his race rather than a knowing subject, though he was potentially also a source of clues to the mystery of the Nile sources – clues, that is, rather than finished knowledge.[43] In contrast, the two white explorers are pictured as reflective and determined men, engaging their powers of reason and imagination in the search for the source of the Nile: insight as well as survey. They are depicted as upright British gentlemen, suitably dressed

40. Burchell, *Travels in the Interior of Southern Africa*, vol. i, p. 119; vol. ii, p. 400.
41. Royal Academy Catalogue, entry no. 324 (1864). I am very grateful to Peter Funnell for this reference and for further information about the portrait.
42. Speke's *Journal of the Discovery of the Source of the Nile* (London, 1863) contains a list of men engaged on the expedition. See also H. Honour, *The Image of the Black in Western Art*, vol. 4, part 1: *Slaves and Liberators* (Cambridge, Mass., 1989), pp. 278–9; D. Simpson, *Dark Companions: The African Contribution to the European Exploration of East Africa* (London, 1976), pp. 25–38.
43. On the racialized distinction between 'native hearsay' and European knowledge, see C. Barnett, 'Impure and worldly geography: the Africanist discourse of the Royal Geographical Society, 1831–1873', *Transactions of the Institute of British Geographers*, 23 (1998), pp. 239–51.

1.5 Henry W. Phillips, *Captain Speke and Captain Grant with Timbo, a young native from the Upper Nile* (1864), oil on canvas. By permission of P. G. H. Speke.

and posed somewhat incongruously beneath a straw roof and African skies. The surrounding props – the rifle, union flag and botanical specimens – gesture to the manifest spirit and purpose of their expedition. But the image alone cannot resolve the problem of correspondence between various forms of knowledge – represented here by the map, the sketch-book, botanical specimens and native testimony. Speke's claim to have settled the controversy over the Nile sources was in fact to be brought into question: his maps were ridiculed, and his guarded defence of the use of oral testimony was challenged.[44]

* * *

44. A. Maitland, *Speke and the Discovery of the Source of the Nile* (London, 1971), pp. 187–99, 221–3. These controversies were fuelled by the antagonism of Richard Burton to his former companion. Burton did not discredit native testimony *per se*, but regarded Speke's ignorance of Arabic, Swahili and Hindi as fatal to any accurate communication about the geography of the river systems of East Africa: 'Bombay, after misunderstanding his master's ill-expressed Hindostani, probably

This book considers a variety of contexts in which geographical knowledge was produced and consumed. The Royal Geographical Society in London came to be a notably authoritative site for the production of geographical knowledge during the nineteenth century, though it certainly did not have a monopoly on the business of exploration. Chapter 2 provides an account of the Society's attempt to co-ordinate the production of geographical knowledge across the globe, by situating its emergence and development in the wider context of the histories of scientific exploration and empire. The argument here is that the Society was less a centre of calculation than an information exchange, an arena in which different kinds of knowledge were accommodated without necessarily being reconciled. Differences over the nature and purpose of geographical knowledge could give rise to heated controversy, especially where exploration was concerned: the relationship between observation in the field and reflection in the study was particularly fraught with difficulty. The question of the credibility of field observation is addressed in chapter 3, which provides an account of the burgeoning literature devoted to instructing travellers on what and how to observe. *Hints to Travellers*, first published by the RGS in 1854, provides the focus for this chapter: far from being a confident assertion of a geographical way of seeing in the field, however, the text is portrayed here as an ambivalent and unsettled intervention in the culture of exploration.

The contested nature of exploration knowledge is emphasized throughout this book. Much of the aura of controversy which surrounded the claims of individual explorers boiled down to questions of credibility: in this context, portraits such as those discussed above bestow just one kind of authority on their subjects. The image of the explorer as a maker of pathways through unknown country, or passages through uncharted waters, was adaptable to a variety of purposes. It could serve the scientific community as a model of enlightened reason: to map the earth was in this sense to know it.[45] But it could also serve to sustain more directly colonial and imperial projects: to explore unknown country was in this sense also to subdue it (though explorers

---

mistranslated the words into Kisawahili to some travelled African, who in turn passed on the question in a wilder dialect to the barbarian or barbarians under examination. During such a journey to and fro words must be liable to severe accidents'. See R. Burton, *The Lake Regions of Central Africa* (London, 1860), vol. ii, p. 208.

45. M.-N. Bourguet, 'The explorer', in M. Vovelle (ed.), *Enlightenment Portraits* (Chicago, 1997), pp. 257–315. See also A. Godlewska, 'Map, text and image: the mentality of enlightened conquerors: a new look at the *Description de l'Égypte*', *Transactions of the Institute of British Geographers*, 20 (1995), pp. 5–28.

differed in the degree of their reliance on the language of conquest). And it clearly drew on religious imagery, as did the idea of Geography Militant itself; not only the idea of the crusade in the earthly sphere, but also the idea of cultivating the field, of rendering it productive as a garden. These different aspects of the image of the explorer found perhaps their most famous expression in the figure of David Livingstone, the subject of chapter 4, who was represented as simultaneously a scientific explorer, a missionary and an imperial pioneer. No other British explorer met with such unalloyed fame: though he had many critics during his lifetime, after his death Livingstone was virtually beyond reproach. More commonly, however, explorers were represented as controversial figures who challenged rather than defended orthodoxy. In the struggle for a reputation, success was rare: the paths to the source of the Nile or the North-West Passage were littered with failures. Chapter 5 provides a study of one of the casualties in this struggle, the author and traveller Winwood Reade. The story of Reade's negotiation of the worlds of metropolitan science and literature affords a different perspective on the culture of exploration, not simply because Reade failed where Livingstone succeeded, but also because it sheds light on the very different purposes that exploration could serve. Reade found in the figure of the martyred explorer a means of cultivating his own marginality, eventually casting it on the larger stage in his book *The Martyrdom of Man*, a quasi-Darwinian study of world history.

The next three chapters focus explicitly on the contested nature of the culture of exploration, in the context of the new era heralded by Stanley's encounter with Livingstone in 1871. For many of his critics, as I argue in chapter 6, Stanley embodied a distinctly modern approach to exploration. Within the geographical establishment, his sensational style was seen as a threat to the conventions of gentlemanly science; for his liberal and socialist critics, Stanley's methods amounted to nothing less than 'exploration by warfare'. These controversies provide an opportunity to consider the ways in which the culture of exploration intersected with contemporary anxieties about class, race, gender and empire. Chapter 7 considers yet another site for the production of exploration knowledge, a popular show (the Stanley and African exhibition) held in London in 1890. Here, the problem of representing Africa was revealed as exactly that – a problem – in the course of legal proceedings brought by the Anti-Slavery Society against the self-appointed guardians of two African boys on show at the exhibition. The archive of the court case offers the possibility of unsettling the narrative of exploration constructed at the exhibition, drawing our attention to the instabilities and tensions within the very idea of representation. If this chapter achieves anything like a deconstruction of the exhibition, it is a form of deconstruction effected as much through contextual interpretation as through a close textual reading. This method of interpretation also involves a distinctly geographical manoeuvre, joining the exhibition space in the West End, the High Court in the Strand, and the spaces of colonialism in South-East Africa.

Chapter 8 is concerned with the appropriation of narratives of exploration in the context of social investigation in British cities during the late nineteenth and early twentieth centuries. As is well known, William Booth's *In Darkest England* of 1890 drew directly on the model that Stanley had provided with the publication of *In Darkest Africa* earlier in the same year; what is less often recognized, however, is that the critical response to Booth's methods mimicked almost exactly the critical response to Stanley's. The key term in both cases was 'sensationalism', and in this respect William Booth appears a much more modern figure than is sometimes recognised. To his critics, Booth represented something new and dangerous, perhaps Americanized philanthropy, perhaps the methods of modern advertising applied to religion, perhaps the spectre of the demagogue exploiting the potential of the new journalism for his own ends. As this chapter shows, the mapping and colonization of 'Darkest England' took many forms, including for example the more sober social surveys of Charles Booth and the idea of the labour colony. The language and politics of exploration abroad were recycled in the context of debates over social policy at home as the frontiers of geographical knowledge were mapped onto the heart of empire.

The story of Geography Militant does not come to an end with the passing of what the geographer Halford Mackinder called the 'Columbian era' of European expansion and exploration: on the contrary, it is regenerated in a wide variety of places, from the playground to the auction-house. Chapter 9 traces the worldly after-life of Geography Militant in the realms of public culture, from the end of the nineteenth century to our own time. In order to understand the contemporary significance of images of exploration, I argue, it is necessary to think more expansively about what geographical traditions are and how they are sustained. Beyond the confines of the cabinet, in so many theatres of memory, the culture of Geography Militant is alive and well.

Chapter 2

The Royal Geographical Society and the Empire of Science

The Royal Geographical Society occupies a unique place in the cultural history of exploration. Founded in 1830, the Society came to be associated in the public mind with many of the most celebrated expeditions of the nineteenth century, and its representatives were keen to capitalize on the publicity which surrounded them. While its resources permitted relatively meagre direct support to expeditions, especially when compared with the role of the Royal Society or the Admiralty in the late eighteenth and early nineteenth centuries, the RGS played a pivotal part in mid-Victorian debates over the conduct and significance of exploration. Its publications reported the results of exploration around the globe; its officers advised prospective explorers about the best ways to explore unknown territories; and its leading figures claimed to exert considerable influence in the corridors of Whitehall. This high public profile during the mid-Victorian years was reflected in a substantial membership, making the RGS the largest scientific society in London by 1870. Some critics within the scientific and scholarly communities found fault in this very success, regarding with growing scepticism the Society's attempt to court publicity. These anxieties reflected a more fundamental feature of the Society's history: for, from the moment of its inception, the RGS was a hybrid institution, seeking simultaneously to acquire the status of a scientific society and to provide a public forum for the celebration of a new age of exploration. That these roles were not easily reconciled is evident from the many controversies which punctuated its subsequent history, including (for example) anxieties about the sensationalism of its 'African nights', repeated calls for a greater emphasis on scientific training for explorers and the controversy over the admission of women as Fellows.[1]

1. The first two episodes are discussed in this chapter and the next; on the third,

Historians of science have paid relatively little attention to the work of the RGS. This neglect may perhaps reflect continuing uncertainty over the 'scientific' status of geography in general and the heterogeneous character of geographical exploration in particular. Moreover, the patently hybrid character of the Society itself – part social club, part learned society, part imperial information exchange and part platform for the promotion of sensational feats of exploration – may have had the effect of diminishing the significance attached to it by those historians seeking 'purer' lines of descent for modern scientific endeavour. The task of narrating the Society's history has been left until recently to 'official' histories, with all their attendant characteristics: an intimate knowledge of the inner workings of the organization combined with a somewhat sketchy attempt to contextualize its historical development. The orthodox narrative of the history of the RGS has been a story of progress, one in which geographical science gradually triumphs over the mysteries of the earth: the Society is thus represented as becoming increasingly modern, increasingly scientific and increasingly successful in the years since its foundation in 1830 to the present day.[2] This approach has attracted predictable charges from critics of Whiggish histories, and in recent years more attention has been paid to the social and intellectual contexts in which the RGS operated during the nineteenth century.[3] Much depends, however, on the way in which these contexts are conceived: in particular, it is important to avoid portraying context as an inert background for the otherwise disinterested pursuit of knowledge.

In this chapter, I situate the foundation and subsequent history of the RGS in the wider context of a developing culture of exploration. The argument here, as elsewhere in this book, is that this culture extended well beyond the frontiers of science, and, moreover, that these frontiers were constantly being renegotiated and even redefined. In this perspective, conventional accounts of the genealogy of modern scientific

---

see M. Bell and C. McEwan, 'The admission of women fellows to the Royal Geographical Society, 1892–1914', *Geographical Journal*, 162 (1996), pp. 295–312.

2. Of all the 'official' histories, the centenary volume edited by Hugh Mill, in collaboration with Douglas Freshfield, is the most informative. In tone and content, the book clearly belongs to another age; yet it does at least make an effort to situate the Society in the context of wider social and scientific developments. See H. R. Mill, *The Record of the Royal Geographical Society* (London, 1930); I. Cameron, *To the Farthest Ends of the Earth: The History of the Royal Geographical Society* (London, 1980); J. Keay (ed.), *The Royal Geographical Society History of World Exploration* (London, 1991).

3. D. R. Stoddart, *On Geography and Its History* (Oxford, 1986); D. Livingstone, *The Geographical Tradition* (Oxford, 1992).

exploration – tracing a line of descent from Cook, through Forster and Humboldt, to Darwin – are evidently partial. The image of the enlightened and disinterested explorer, pursuing science in a sober spirit of inquiry, was undoubtedly both powerful and enduring: it cannot simply be dismissed as rhetorical, if by that term we understand something superficial or secondary.[4] Equally, to reduce the history of exploration to such a singular figure necessarily obscures the material and imaginative relations which sustained scientific exploration, notably (in this context) the search for status amongst men of science, the commercial culture of adventure and the relations between scientific knowledge and empire. Even the purest aspirations of the scientific avant-garde, encapsulated by the term 'Humboldtian science', were necessarily implicated in these wider contexts: indeed, nowhere are they clearer than in the campaign to promote the science of terrestrial magnetism, widely regarded by historians of science as an exemplar of the Humboldtian programme.[5] The observation of magnetic variations over the earth's surface might today be regarded as a more properly scientific project than the quest for the North-West Passage; yet both involved the mobilization of symbolic and political resources which extended well beyond the realm of disinterested knowledge. It is perhaps significant in this context that after the Rosses returned from their privately funded four-year voyage in the Arctic in 1833, the RGS presented a medal to Captain John Ross rather than to his nephew, James Clark Ross, who claimed to have actually located the magnetic North Pole. Voyages of Arctic exploration provided ample opportunity for spectacular celebrations of British prowess: the season of entertainments at Vauxhall Gardens thus opened on 30 May 1834 (the King's birthday) with a 'Grand Scenic Representation' of the Ross expedition. The theatrical proceedings of the evening, set against vast images of polar landscape, concluded with what was described as a 'grand allegorical display, complimentary to British enterprise'. 'In this scene', visitors were promised, 'an imitation will be given of one of those awful thunder storms which visit the Northern Regions: and at the close, a gigantic Image of

---

4. M.-N. Bourguet, 'The explorer', in M. Vovelle (ed.), *Enlightenment Portraits* (Chicago, 1997), pp. 257–315.
5. S. Cannon, *Science in Culture: The Early Victorian Period* (New York, 1978), pp. 73–110; J. Cawood, 'The magnetic crusade: science and politics in early Victorian Britain', *Isis*, 70 (1979), pp. 493–518; J. Morrell and A. Thackray, *Gentlemen of Science: Early Years of the British Association for the Advancement of Science* (Oxford, 1981), pp. 353–70, 523–31. The mapping of terrestrial magnetism had a longer but no less imperial history, outlined by Patricia Fara in *Sympathetic Attractions: Magnetic Practices, Beliefs and Symbolism in Eighteenth-century England* (Princeton, NJ, 1996), 91–117.

Captain Ross will appear in his Polar Costume, rising from amidst the Icebergs.'[6]

This chapter situates the RGS in two interrelated contexts: the history of scientific exploration and the history of empire. The first part considers the extent to which the RGS may be understood, in the context of the history of scientific exploration, as a 'centre of calculation'; the second addresses the imperial setting within which the RGS emerged and developed during the nineteenth century, paying particular attention to the promotion of geography as a science of empire. While there are merits in seeing the Society as a kind of imperial information exchange, it is important to recognize the heterogeneity of the RGS as it developed in the mid-nineteenth century. This argument is developed in chapter 3 through a discussion of *Hints to Travellers*, the Society's celebrated guide for prospective explorers, which is portrayed less as the product of a masterful vision of geographical knowledge than as an attempt to exert authority on a field that was already too large and diverse to be mastered.

The Royal Geographical Society: a Centre of Calculation?

The immediate origin of the Royal Geographical Society lay in a resolution passed at a meeting of the Raleigh Travellers' Club, chaired by John Barrow, permanent secretary at the Admiralty, on 24 May 1830. The aim of the new Society was described as 'the promotion and diffusion of that most important and entertaining branch of knowledge, Geography'. These terms anticipated some of the diverse ways in which geographical knowledge was to be promoted by the new Society. Geography was 'important' because it was useful, both to science and to government; and it was 'entertaining' because it provided a form of rational enjoyment to those equipped to study it. Drawing attention to the 'scattered and dispersed' nature of existing geographical information, the prospectus for the new Society enumerated six more specific objectives: first, to 'collect, register and digest, and to print . . . such new, interesting and useful facts and discoveries as the Society may have in its possession'; second, to 'accumulate gradually a library of the best books on Geography . . . [and] a complete collection of Maps and

---

6.   For an account of the public reception and subsequent recriminations surrounding this expedition, see M. J. Ross, *Polar Pioneers: John Ross and James Clark Ross* (Montreal, 1994), pp. 165–91. James Clark Ross was closely involved in the 'the magnetic crusade' and was awarded an RGS medal in 1842 for his own Antarctic expedition.

Charts'; third, to 'procure specimens of such instruments as experience has shown to be most useful'; fourth, 'to prepare brief instructions for such as are setting out on their travels'; fifth, to 'correspond with similar societies that may be established in different parts of the world'; and sixth, to 'open a communication with all those philosophical and literary societies with which Geography is connected'.[7] Together, these aims provided the rationale for the establishment of an institution which would co-ordinate the collection, storage and dissemination of geographical knowledge in a rational manner.

The foundation of the new Geographical Society must be seen in the context of a burgeoning discourse on geographical exploration since the mid-eighteenth century, especially in the wake of Cook's voyages in the Pacific. Knowledge about exploration was transmitted during this period through a wide range of different channels: formal reports (in the shape of narratives, maps, charts and tables) presented to government departments such as the Admiralty or the Foreign Office; papers given to an increasing number of specialist scholarly, scientific, missionary and philanthropic societies; books describing and illustrating voyages and travels, intended for a wider audience; journal and magazine articles reviewing, and sometimes promoting, the work of exploring expeditions; and imaginative literature of all kinds, including adventure stories and juvenile fiction. Such an inventory provides some indication of the breadth and diversity of the literary and graphic representation of exploration in eighteenth- and nineteenth-century Britain.[8] The field of exploration knowledge was traversed in different ways, and for different purposes, by a wide range of figures, including naval officers, soldiers, naturalists, artists, surveyors, missionaries, novelists and journalists. Indeed, many of the most well-known explorers performed several of these roles at once. David Livingstone, as we shall see, simultaneously acted as a missionary, a roving consul and an explorer; and whether Henry Morton Stanley was primarily a journalist, a conquistador or a geographer was very much an open question. The wider point here is that the culture of exploration was heterogeneous,

---

7. Raleigh Club Minute Book, 24 May 1830 (RGS Archives, Additional Papers no. 115, AR28). The main features of this prospectus may also be identified in earlier proposals, including one said to have been presented to Sir Joseph Banks in 1807: see S. Lee to R. Brown, 20 October 1829, British Library, Add. MSS 32,441, ff. 97–100.
8. P. Marshall and G. Williams, *The Great Map of Mankind: British Perceptions of the World in the Age of Enlightenment* (London, 1982), pp. 45–63; N. Rennie, *Far-fetched Facts: The Literature of Travel and the Idea of the South Seas* (Oxford, 1995); A. White, *Joseph Conrad and the Adventure Tradition* (Cambridge, 1993), pp. 8–38.

and the knowledge it produced took a great variety of forms. In this context, what constituted legitimate knowledge was always a matter of contention.

The task the Royal Geographical Society set itself in 1830 was to co-ordinate the geographical knowledge produced within this rapidly expanding discourse of exploration. This co-ordinating role had three essential features: the construction of guidelines for the recording of topographical and other geographical information in the field, according to standardized observational procedures and rules of measurement; the establishment of a centralized archive of authoritative geographical information, available to legitimate explorers and others to whom such knowledge would be useful (most notably, departments of government); the diffusion of geographical knowledge in a rational and educative manner. In all three respects, the rhetoric of the Society's founding document appears at first sight to correspond with what one would expect of a 'centre of calculation'.[9] In his account of the history of scientific observation, Latour places particular emphasis on the role of technologies of inscription – writing, mapping and other forms of visual representation. Such inscriptions, he argues, prove powerful only in so far as they are mobile (i.e. they can be transported from one place to another), immutable (i.e. they remain constant over space and time), and combinable (i.e. they can be translated into other forms of inscription). 'Centres of calculation', according to Latour, function as pivots in flows of information, co-ordinating ever larger networks of communication, diffusing standard techniques of observation and centralizing the results of data collection. Journeys of exploration are of use to such 'centres' only if they actually bring information home, in a reliable form, and in the shape of observations or specimens which can readily be combined with other observations and specimens.

Latour's account has been criticized for placing too much emphasis on the role of instruments in the translation of knowledge from place to place, and too little on the continuing significance of the negotiation of trust. (This becomes especially significant in the context of instructions to prospective travellers: see chapter 3). More generally, it has been argued that notions of accuracy, calculation and information are themselves far from self-evident, but rather are negotiated in a variety of contingent, situated ways.[10] None the less, the centralization of the

9. B. Latour, *Science in Action: How to Follow Scientists and Engineers Through Society* (Milton Keynes, 1987), ch. 6; B. Latour, 'Visualisation and cognition: thinking with eyes and hands', *Knowledge and Society*, 6 (1986), pp. 1–40.
10. See especially S. Shapin, 'Placing the view from nowhere: historical and sociological problems in the location of science', *Transactions, Institute of British*

rules, means and products of scientific observation – understood as a particular historical project rather than as an inexorable process – is clearly an important theme for historians of geographical exploration. In this respect, the RGS programme might plausibly be seen in the context of earlier efforts to secure a more systematic and centralized approach to information collection. The career of Joseph Banks, 'a sort of presiding genius of exploration' during the late eighteenth and early nineteenth centuries, is a case in point.[11] Banks, who accompanied Cook on his first voyage to the South Seas in 1768, occupied a commanding position within the London scientific community for the next fifty years. He was President of the Royal Society (from 1778 until his death in 1820) and an important figure at Kew Gardens, the British Museum, the Linnean Society and the Board of Longitude for much of this period. From his bases at Soho Square and Kew Gardens, Banks co-ordinated the collection of botanical and zoological specimens from around the world and encouraged the transplantation of species (including cotton, vegetable dyes, medicinal drugs, tea and coffee) between different parts of the empire.[12] Adapting Latour's terminology, David Miller has suggested that the Banksian learned empire was an effective centre of calculation, overseeing the production of accurate maps of longitude and latitude, visual encyclopaedias of botanical species and museum collections of well-preserved specimens of plants and animals.[13] In an age before the establishment of government departments responsible for co-ordinating the gathering of such information, Joseph Banks helped to establish a collecting network of truly global scope.

Joseph Banks's legacy is thus of considerable significance for the development of a centralized approach to scientific exploration, and indeed for the subsequent emergence of the RGS itself. However, recent historians of geography (drawing on a passing comment in Mill's

---

Geographers, 23 (1998), pp. 5–12; M. Bravo, 'Ethnographic navigation and the geographical gift', in D. Livingstone and C. Withers (eds), *Geography and Enlightenment* (Chicago, 1999), pp. 199–235.

11. J. C. Beaglehole, *The Life of Captain James Cook* (Stanford, 1974), p. 291. See also D. MacKay, 'A presiding genius of exploration: Banks, Cook and empire, 1767–1805', in R. Fisher and H. Johnston (eds), *Captain James Cook and his Times* (Vancouver, 1979), pp. 21–39; J. Gascoigne, *Science in the Service of Empire: Joseph Banks, the British State and the Uses of Science in the Age of Revolution* (Cambridge, 1998).

12.   D. MacKay, 'Agents of empire: the Banksian collectors and the evaluation of new lands', in D. P. Miller and P. H. Reill (eds.) *Visions of Empire: Voyages, Botany and Representations of Nature* (Cambridge, 1996), pp. 38–57. See also D. MacKay, *In the Wake of Cook* (London, 1985).

13.   D. P. Miller, 'Joseph Banks, empire and "centers of calculation" in late Hanoverian London', in Miller and Reill, *Visions of Empire*, pp. 21–37.

Record of the Royal Geographical Society) have portrayed him more as an obstacle to the emergence of a new geographical society.[14] While this emphasis on Banks's personal resistance to the formation of rival organizations to his own power base in the Royal Society is echoed by other historians of science, it rather obscures the considerable parallels between the Banksian project and that of the RGS, which in many respects represented an attempt to continue the geographical dimension of Banks's project – the centralization of accurate geographical knowledge – by other means. (Indeed, Mill himself suggested at one point that Banks's appointment to the *Endeavour* expedition set in train a process 'that led without a break to the formation of the Royal Geographical Society sixty-three years later').[15] In this context, it should be emphasized that Banks's sponsorship of exploration was not limited to maritime voyages of discovery; indeed, he played an important role in the establishment (in 1788) of the African Association, one of the most important forerunners of the RGS; it was absorbed into the Society in 1831.[16]

Several of the most influential founders of the RGS, including John Barrow (second secretary at the Admiralty between 1804 and 1845) and the botanist Robert Brown (Banks's librarian and a key figure in the Linnean Society)[17] had been close associates of Banks during his lifetime. Barrow himself has been described as the 'heir of Banks in the field of geographical exploration'.[18] His dual role at the Admiralty and at the Royal Society gave him considerable influence over scientific exploration in various parts of the globe. Like his superior at the Admiralty between 1809 and 1830, the arch-Tory John W. Croker, he was a regular contributor of articles to the *Quarterly Review*, which he used to promote both geographical exploration (notably in Africa and the Arctic) and his particular 'imperial vision'.[19] Barrow was undoubtedly an important gate-keeper in the field of geography and exploration;

14. Stoddart, *On Geography*, pp. 18–19; Livingstone, *Geographical Tradition*, p. 159; Mill, *Record of the Royal Geographical Society*, p. 7.
15. Mill, *Record of the Royal Geographical Society*, p. 4.
16. R. Hallett (ed.), *Records of the African Association, 1788–1831* (London, 1964).
17. D. J. Mabberley, *Jupiter Botanicus: Robert Brown of the British Museum* (Braunschweig, 1985).
18. C. Lloyd, *Mr Barrow of the Admiralty: A Life of Sir John Barrow, 1764–1848* (London, 1970), p. 157; Gascoigne, *Science in the Service of Empire*, pp. 126–7, 196.
19. J. Cameron, 'Sir John Barrow as a *Quarterly* Reviewer', *Notes and Queries*, 241 (1996), pp. 34–7; J. Cameron, 'Agents and agencies in geography and empire: the case of George Grey', in M. Bell, R. Butlin and M. Heffernan (eds), *Geography and Imperialism, 1820–1940*, (Manchester, 1995), pp. 13–35.

challenges to his authority, such as that of the young explorer Thomas Bowdich (who described Barrow's contemptuous review of his *Mission from Cape Coast Castle to Ashantee* as 'the slanderous inventions of an ignorant man'), were rarely effective.[20] His role as an intermediary between the Admiralty and the world of scientific exploration was to have a lasting influence on the character and composition of the RGS.

Although the founders of the RGS in many respects shared the aspirations of Joseph Banks, they operated in a quite different institutional milieu. From the early nineteenth century, substantial sections of the Banksian empire had been colonized by departments of government, a process evident in the establishment of the Admiralty Hydrographic Office and the Ordnance Survey, and ultimately to incorporate Kew Gardens itself.[21] At the same time, the scientific world was undergoing a significant transformation, witnessed by a proliferation of specialist societies, including the Geological Society (1807), the Astronomical Society (1820), the Royal Asiatic Society (1823) and the Zoological Society (1826). The hegemony of the *ancien régime* represented by Banks at the Royal Society was under attack from without; and its methods were to be reformed from within following Banks's death in 1820.[22] By the 1830s, there was a wealth of new periodicals for both the general reader and the specialist (the term 'scientist' was first coined in 1834), a range of new universities and colleges, a new national organization for the promotion of science (the British Association for the Advancement of Science) and the beginnings of a movement for diffusing the principles of scientific investigation to a much wider audience. These developments signalled not so much the creation of a new public sphere for science as its proliferation and fragmentation.[23]

20. Bowdich addressed his angry response to the 'Geographer of the Quarterly Review', though the identity of his protagonist was clear. See T. Bowdich, *A Reply to the Quarterly Review* (1820 ms., British Library); for attribution of the original review to Barrow, see H. Shine and H. C. Shine, *The Quarterly Review under Gifford* (North Carolina, 1949), p. 68.
21. The Hydrographic Office deserves far more attention from historians of the RGS than it has received hitherto: for an administrative history, see A. Day, *The Admiralty Hydrographic Service, 1795–1919* (London, 1967).
22. D. P. Miller, 'Between hostile camps: Sir Humphry Davy's Presidency of the Royal Society of London, 1820–1827', *British Journal for the History of Science*, 16 (1983), pp. 1–47.
23. Morrell and Thackray, *Gentlemen of Science*; I. Morus, S. Schaffer and J. Secord, 'Scientific London' in C. Fox (ed.), *London: World City, 1800–1840* (New Haven, Conn., 1992), pp. 129–42; R. Yeo, *Defining Science: William Whewell, Natural Knowledge and Public Debate in early Victorian Britain* (Cambridge, 1993), pp. 28–48; C. Withers, 'Towards a history of geography in the public sphere', *History of Science*, 36 (1998), pp. 45–78.

The world of British science in 1830 contained many different institutional sites, and they did not always work in harmony.

The dissolution of the Banksian empire, the ensuing political machinations within the Royal Society and the expansion of maritime exploration after the end of the Napoleonic wars provided fertile ground for those seeking to establish a new forum for geographical science. The establishment of Geographical Societies in Paris and Berlin provided a further rationale for innovation, an argument from national honour routinely resorted to by scientific reformers of the day. During the 1820s, John Barrow was a significant player in the successive crises over the leadership of the Royal Society, portraying himself as the defender of the Banksian legacy against radicals and democrats. (In 1827, he urged Sir Robert Peel to stand for election to the Presidency in order to restore the prestige of the Society.)[24] While Barrow played a conservative role within the Royal Society, others who were to be prominent in the new Geographical Society took the side of the reformers.[25] During the celebrated contest for the election of a new Royal Society President in 1830, for example, Roderick Murchison and Robert Brown supported the astronomer John Herschel – indeed Murchison claimed that they 'had been his two most zealous supporters' – while Barrow himself supported the Duke of Sussex.[26] If Barrow regarded the formation of a new geographical society as a continuation of the Banksian project by other means, others saw it as an opportunity for the development of a more specialized and less dilettante approach to the practice of science. And agitation for the formation of a new society was not confined to the world of gentlemanly science: the journalist William Jerdan, editor of the *Literary Gazette*, later claimed to have been responsible, together with the antiquarian John Britton, for the original idea which led ultimately to the formation of the RGS.[27]

While a variety of rival schemes for a new geographical society were canvassed during the late 1820s, Barrow's involvement proved a

24. J. Barrow to R. Peel, 21 November, 23 November 1827, British Library, Add. MSS 40,394, ff. 256–7, 274–7.

25. Miller, 'Between hostile camps', pp. 30, 40; Lloyd, *Mr Barrow of the Admiralty*, p. 154.

26. Murchison later recalled that 'all the real men of science' had supported Herschel, while 'the Royal toadies were . . . flattering the worthy good Duke (who really had not a grain of science in him)'. Murchison's account of the dispute was clearly partial – both camps were actually much more diverse – and he himself was later to turn 'royal toadying' into something of an art form. See Murchison Journals, vol. 7, 'Scientific Life: Alps, London, Silurian, 1826–1838', pp. 238–9, Murchison Papers, Geological Society of London.

27. *The Autobiography of William Jerdan*, vol. 4 (London, 1853), pp. 266–72, 405–11. See also Mill, *Record of the Royal Geographical Society*, pp. 12–22.

decisive influence on the character of the Society that eventually emerged. The Admiralty presence in the new Society was certainly substantial: Barrow was joined on the first Council by three senior naval officers, W. H. Smyth, Basil Hall and Francis Beaufort, and the first issues of the Society's *Journal* were dominated by reports of naval exploration and hydrographic survey. During the 1830s, the RGS itself sponsored several maritime expeditions, including Captain George Back's voyage to the Arctic and John Biscoe's circumnavigation of the Antarctic; and among the first recipients of its awards were John Ross in 1834, for his Arctic exploration, and Robert Fitzroy in 1837, following his return from the *Beagle* voyage. Francis Beaufort's position as Hydrographer at the Admiralty was particularly significant in the early years of the new Society: he too acted as an influential intermediary between the world of science (including geographers, astronomers, oceanographers, geodesists and meteorologists) and the imperial government. 'Wearing one hat, that of a Fellow of a learned society', writes his biographer, 'Beaufort could enlist himself, or be enlisted, in the course of one or another scientific enterprise; thereupon, wearing a second, official hat, he was in a position to forward it by furnishing ships, officers, equipment, instruments and, most important, finance.'[28] Beaufort's work in the preparation of maps and charts at the Hydrographic Office has largely been forgotten; if he is remembered at all today, it is for his role in the appointment of Charles Darwin to assist Fitzroy on the *Beagle*.[29]

The presence of military and naval personnel within the new Society does not necessarily signify intellectual conservatism: indeed, David Miller has argued that 'scientific servicemen' like Beaufort played a significant, if largely unsung, role within the reformulation of the physical sciences during the first half of the nineteenth century.[30] The founders of the RGS also included the astronomer Francis Baily and the geologist Roderick Murchison, both of whom belonged to an inner coterie of scientific reformers within the British Association for the Advancement of Science, established in 1831.[31] Beaufort, Baily and Murchison were active in campaigns for scientific and institutional innovation, most notably the 'magnetic crusade' of the 1830s.[32] Susan

28. A. Friendly, *Beaufort of the Admiralty: The Life of Sir Francis Beaufort, 1774–1857* (London, 1977), p. 289.
29. J. Browne, *Charles Darwin: Voyaging* (London, 1995), pp. 149–51.
30. D. P. Miller, 'The revival of the physical sciences in Britain, 1815–1840', *Osiris*, n.s. 2 (1986), pp. 107–34. While Miller does not mention the RGS, this important paper does provide a context for understanding some of the research programmes with which a section of the Society was associated in its early years.
31. Morrell and Thackray, *Gentlemen of Science*, pp. 24–8.
32. Cawood, 'The magnetic crusade'.

Cannon has coined the term 'Humboldtian science' to characterize the intellectual programme represented by such ventures.[33] Its principal features, according to Cannon, included an emphasis on the need for ever more precise observation in the field, using the latest advances in portable instrumentation (Humboldt himself travelled with an awesome collection of chronometers, sextants, horizons, barometers and other instruments), the urge to visualize numerical data in the form of graphs and maps, reflecting Humboldt's own obsession with the isometric mapping of all sorts of natural phenomena and, finally, a particular concern with the spatial relations between geology, biology and meteorology and with their role in determining the geography of plants and animals. Cannon suggests that the model of Humboldtian fieldwork inspired the scientific *avant-garde* across early nineteenth-century Europe: in comparison, 'the study of nature in the laboratory or the perfection of differential equations was old-fashioned, was simple science concerned with easy variables'. It is worth emphasizing here that numerical sophistication was only one aspect of the Humboldtian scientific temper: just as significant were Humboldt's vision of scientific exploration as a sublime venture and his emphasis on geographical analysis as a means of scientific reasoning. In both respects, Humboldt was a model for Darwin. Controlling Darwin's thought, Cannon concludes, was 'a *topographical vision* of the world, its organisms, and its history, like that of Humboldt'.[34]

The extent to which the founders of the RGS shared a similar 'topographical vision' is open to question. Topographical mapping was one of the essential features of geographical science in this period, and as Michael Bravo points out in the case of James Rennell (the leading British geographer of the late eighteenth and early nineteenth centuries) its products could be readily combined with other forms of geographical knowledge, including descriptions of 'customs and manners' as well as numerical data of various kinds.[35] Yet as the example of Rennell indicates, the construction of a reliable topographical map was as likely to require the compilation of maps in the office as it was to rely on an accurate instrumental survey in the field, even after the adoption of

33. S. Cannon, 'Humboldtian science', in her *Science in Culture*, pp. 73–110. See also M. Dettelbach, 'Humboldtian science', in N. Jardine, J. Secord and E. Spary (eds), *Cultures of Natural History* (Cambridge, 1996), pp. 287–304; M. Dettelbach, 'Global physics and aesthetic empire: Humboldt's physical portrait of the tropics', in Miller and Reill, *Visions of Empire*, pp. 258–92.
34. Cannon, 'Humboldtian science', p. 105, p. 92 (emphasis in original).
35. M. Bravo, 'Ethnological encounters', in Jardine, Secord and Spary, *Cultures of Natural History*, pp. 347–8.

trigonometric methods.[36] The wider point here is that the 'information' routinely collected by geographers and other scientific explorers did not necessarily take a numerical form, nor did it necessarily provide the basis for theoretical discussion of the sort favoured by Humboldt. In this context, Cannon's model of 'Humboldtian science' is better understood as a retrospective synthesis of the principles of the scientific *avant-garde* rather than as a description of the actual conduct of men of science generally; still less as the character of the RGS as a whole. If we leave aside the question of whether it understates the aesthetic and philosophical components of Humboldt's own vision,[37] Cannon's model is clearly more applicable in some fields, such as terrestrial magnetism, than in others, such as ethnology. While some geographers' concerns were genuinely Humboldtian, a large proportion of the founders of the RGS were interested in collecting information, collating travellers' descriptions, producing regional surveys or writing narratives of voyages: hardly the sort of knowledge that constituted 'Humboldtian science' in Cannon's interpretation of the term.

The establishment of the RGS was represented by its founders as an attempt to co-ordinate the production of geographical knowledge in all its diverse forms. Nevertheless, it would be wrong to overstate the degree of institutional and intellectual control this implied: the new society effectively represented a coalition of interests, including not only representatives of the new scientific societies and 'scientific servicemen' but also antiquarian scholars, imperial diplomats and travellers, such as the Foreign Office diplomat William R. Hamilton and the surveyor turned scholar Lieutenant-Colonel Leake, both of whom served as Vice-Presidents of the RGS alongside Barrow, and the orientalist George Renouard, appointed as Foreign Secretary. Their scholarly and antiquarian interests, and the model of polite learning they espoused, were also reflected in the newly formed Royal Society of Literature and the Royal Asiatic Society. The heterogeneous character of the geographical knowledge pursued at the RGS provides a marked contrast with more specialist scientific societies founded during this period; perhaps the closest comparison in this respect is with the Zoological Society.[38] For these reasons, it would be more appropriate to describe the RGS as an

36.   See especially M. Edney, *Mapping an Empire: The Geographical Construction of British India, 1765–1843* (Chicago, 1997).
37.   Humboldt's aesthetic vision was celebrated as much as his embrace of quantification: see W. H. Brock, 'Humboldt and the British', *Annals of Science*, 50 (1993), pp. 365–72, and the discussion of Humboldt as a scholar in chapter 1 above.
38.   A. Desmond, 'The making of institutional zoology in London, 1822–1836', *History of Science*, 23 (1985), pp. 153–85, 223–50.

information exchange than as a centre of calculation in the strict Latourian sense. However we characterize the project of the founders of the Society, though, its success is altogether a different matter; after all, neither information exchanges nor centres of calculation can be willed into existence at the stroke of a pen. The faltering development of the Society during the first twenty years of its existence suggests that before 1850, at least, it occupied a relatively insignificant position both in the world of science and within society at large. The collection of information proceeded slowly, through the establishment of a library and map collection; its diffusion was largely the task of its *Journal*, which appeared somewhat spasmodically before the 1850s. Under the influence of Sir Roderick Murchison, as we shall see, the Society grew considerably in size, but this too was the cause of some anxiety within the scientific community. For by the 1860s it had become clear that the RGS was not just another scientific institution; its concerns and its membership were much larger, and far more diverse, than those of Societies like the Geological or the Linnean. Moreover, under Murchison it established a prominence in the wider public culture of exploration which no other society could match. It is at this point that the language of 'centres of calculation' is found especially wanting, for the kind of science conducted at the RGS was rarely as pure as specialists wanted it to be. To put it another way, the domain of exploration was evidently not the sole preserve of geographical savants and scholars.

Imperial Science

The significance of empire for the development of British science in the eighteenth and nineteenth centuries has been understood in a variety of ways. From the perspective of orthodox histories of exploration, voyages and travels provided an ever increasing volume of information for metropolitan science: in this sense, imperial expansion was part of a larger process of European 'out-thrust', which yielded an unprecedented volume of data from the newly discovered worlds of the 'periphery'.[39] Empire is conceived of here in a more or less enabling role, allowing room for debate over the extent to which travellers and explorers were influenced by 'imperial' designs. Yet the diffusionist logic implicit in such accounts can obscure the extent to which empire

39. R. Bridges and P. Hair, 'The Hakluyt Society and world history', in R. Bridges and P. Hair (eds), *Compassing the Vaste Globe of the Earth: Studies in the History of the Hakluyt Society* (London, 1996), pp. 225–39.

shaped the development of European science itself.[40] The infrastructure of the British Empire was certainly significant for scientific exploration in the field: the imperial state's material resources and geographical reach provided unrivalled opportunities for scientific explorers to pursue their interests on a genuinely global scale. The expeditions of Cook and Banks, or Fitzroy and Darwin, patently depended on the active support of the Admiralty; indeed, in both the *Endeavour* and *Beagle* voyages scientific projects of mapping (of both the heavens and the earth) were intertwined with the more worldly interests of the imperial state. The collection of scientific information relied on a set of institutions closely allied to imperial government, including the Admiralty, the Hydrographer's Office, the East India Company, the Royal Engineers, the Ordnance Survey and the Geological Survey.[41] The role of Kew Gardens at the heart of these collecting networks is well established: according to one historian, it functioned as a 'control center which regulated the flow of botanical information from the metropolis to the colonial satellites, and disseminated information emanating from them'.[42] The imperial context was also vital to the development of scientific programmes ostensibly inspired by more cosmopolitan, even Humboldtian, concerns. The establishment of a chain of geomagnetic and meteorological observatories across the colonies during the 1830s and 1840s, for example, relied heavily on military and naval personnel, as well as government funding.[43] The campaign for official backing for this programme – the 'magnetic crusade'- illustrates the ways in which empire could also become a source of legitimacy even for the most exact sciences: although part of an international collaborative venture, the scheme was also justified in terms of imperial prestige. In the words of the astronomer John Herschel, 'Great physical theories, with their chains of practical applications, are pre-eminently national objects.'[44]

40.   P. Palladino and M. Worboys, 'Science and imperialism', *Isis*, 84 (1993), pp. 94–102; R. Drayton, 'Science and the European empires', *Journal of Imperial and Commonwealth History*, 23 (1995), pp. 503–10; B. Hunt, 'Doing science in a global empire: cable telegraphy and electrical physics in Victorian Britain', in B. Lightman (ed.), *Victorian Science in Context* (Chicago, 1997), pp. 312–33.

41.   J. Browne, 'Biogeography and empire', in Jardine, Secord and Spary, *Cultures of Natural History*, pp. 305–21. See also J. Camerini, 'Remains of the day: early Victorians in the field', in Lightman, *Victorian Science*, pp. 354–77.

42.   L. Brockway, *Science and Colonial Expansion: The Role of the British Royal Botanic Gardens* (New York, 1979), p. 7.

43.   A. Savours and A. McConnell, 'The history of the Rossbank Observatory, Tasmania', *Annals of Science*, 39 (1982), pp. 527–64.

44.   Herschel, cited in Cawood, 'The magnetic crusade', p. 518. The influence of Herschel's work in the Cape on the development of his science is discussed in E. Musselman, 'Swords into ploughshares: John Herschel's progressive view of astro-

However, the empire did not merely provide an infrastructure for scientific exploration, or a means of its legitimation: it also helped to shape the cognitive content of the field sciences. As Robert Stafford puts it in his biography of Roderick Murchison, the imperial scientist *par excellence*, 'the content of science, like the style of an empire, is shaped by its cultural context. British geology and geography, as well as other sciences . . . were significantly influenced by Britain's possession of a colonial empire. Imperial concepts, metaphors, data and career opportunities informed the development of these disciplines, and their institutions in varying degrees expressed this ideological matrix.'[45] Perhaps the most important cognitive link between imperialism and science in the case of the field sciences was provided by territorial mapping, as both metaphor and practice. In the case of Murchison's own work in geology and geography, territorial metaphors enabled imperial and military themes to filter into the heart of scientific debate.[46] In biogeography, the mapping of natural regions into kingdoms, provinces and colonies reflected in part the territorial language of empire.[47] Alfred Russel Wallace's efforts to map species boundaries in the Malay archipelago, so important to the development of his ideas about natural selection, depended on a dense network of relationships – with London naturalists, colonial officials and indigenous peoples – which cannot be understood without reference to their imperial context. Wallace's concern with mapping has also been traced back to his training as a surveyor in the Welsh hills; in this case, the very practice of survey shaped a scientific vision.[48] The topographical mapping of the empire itself was represented as a device for exercising power: as Michael Bravo puts it, 'Reading signs on the surface of the landscape (the sources of rivers, oases, cloud patterns) provided the key for piecing together the landscape's inner propensities, for imperial commerce – the direction and flow of its waters, the moral qualities of its populations

---

nomical and imperial governance', *British Journal for the History of Science*, 31 (1998), pp. 419–35.

45. R. Stafford, *Scientist of Empire: Sir Roderick Murchison, Scientific Exploration and Victorian Imperialism* (Cambridge, 1989), p. 223.

46. J. Secord, 'King of Siluria: Roderick Murchison and the imperial theme in nineteenth-century British geology', *Victorian Studies*, 25 (1982), pp. 413–42.

47. Browne, 'Biogeography and empire', pp. 314–19. See also J. Camerini, 'Evolution, biogeography, and maps: an early history of Wallace's line', *Isis*, 84 (1993), pp. 700–27.

48. J. Camerini, 'Wallace in the field', in H. Kuklick and R. Kohler (eds), *Science in the Field* (Chicago, 1996), pp. 44–65; J. Moore, 'Wallace's Malthusian moment: the common context revisited', in Lightman, *Victorian Science*, pp. 290–311. See also Camerini, 'Evolution, biogeography and maps'.

and the caravan routes for the traffic in humans.'[49] While the efficacy of topographical mapping as an instrument of imperial rule is open to question, the equation between geographical knowledge and imperial power was a powerful component of the rhetoric of cartography.[50]

For many of the founders of the Royal Geographical Society, the notion that scientific exploration might serve some purpose beyond the acquisition of knowledge for its own sake was thus not just an afterthought: it was its *raison d'être*. The Society's initial prospectus made pointed reference to the 'decided utility' of geographical knowledge 'in conferring just and distinct notions of the physical and political relations of our globe'. Its advantages were not simply 'of the first importance to mankind in general', but 'paramount to the welfare of a maritime nation like Great Britain with its numerous and extensive foreign possessions'.[51] Addressing the first meeting of the new Society, in July 1830, John Barrow singled out the role of maritime surveying in the development of global commerce: 'Every accession . . . to hydrographical knowledge – a real danger discovered – a fictitious one demolished – or a peculiarity ascertained – must be of great importance to navigation, and a fit object for promulgation by the Society.'[52] Although he denied the new Society would be 'hostile to theory', Barrow's agenda was utilitarian and empirical: true geographical knowledge was a source of power as well as pleasure.

Such claims for the utility of geographical knowledge were unexceptional: indeed, they would be a staple feature of successive presidents' annual addresses to the RGS. The conception of geography as a tool of European expansion was to remain of service throughout the nineteenth century, as is readily apparent from John Scott Keltie's contribution to the 1893 edition of the Society's *Hints to Travellers*. As far as 'uncivilised or semi-civilised countries' were concerned, Keltie advised his readers, the most important geographical questions were those of resources, wants and accessibility: '(1) What are the available resources of the country that may be turned to industrial or commercial account? (2) What commercial products can find an available market in the country? (3) What are the facilities for or hindrances to intercourse

49. Bravo, 'Ethnological encounters', p. 347.
50. Edney, *Mapping an Empire*; K. Raj, 'La Construction de l'empire de la géographie', *Annales Histoire, Sciences Sociales*, 52 (1997), pp. 1153–80; P. Hansen, 'Vertical boundaries, national identities: British mountaineering on the frontiers of Europe and the Empire, 1868–1914', *Journal of Imperial and Commonwealth History*, 24 (1996), pp. 48–71.
51. Raleigh Club Minute Book, 24 May 1830 (RGS Archives, Additional Papers no. 115, AR28).
52. *Journal of the RGS*, 1 (1831), p. viii.

between the country and the rest of the world?'[53] While historians of geography have connected such pronouncements to the requirements of the 'new imperialism' of the late nineteenth century, it should be emphasized that the conception of geography as an instrument of empire had a much longer history. In 1842, for example, W. R. Hamilton had addressed the RGS thus:

> Geography is the mainspring of all the operations of war, and of all the negotiations of a state of peace; and in proportion as any one nation is the foremost to extend her acquaintance with the physical conformation of the earth, and the water which surrounds it, will ever be the opportunities she will possess, and the responsibilities she will incur, for extending her commerce, for enlarging her powers of civilizing the yet benighted portions of the globe, and for bearing her part in forwarding and directing the destinies of mankind.[54]

The first two presidents of the RGS were government colonial ministers, and many of their successors were career diplomats. Moreover, army and naval officers constituted around one-fifth of the 460 founding members of the RGS, and this proportion was to remain remarkably stable throughout the next seventy years.[55] Formal and informal lines of communication with government departments were taken for granted: leading Fellows like Henry Bartle Frere or Henry Rawlinson were active in both geographical and political circles.[56] Indeed, according to the Society's historian, most of the papers laid before Council in the early years were supplied directly by the Admiralty, the Colonial Office, the India Office and the Foreign Office.[57]

53. J. S. Keltie, 'Industry and commerce', *Hints to Travellers* (1893), p. 411. On the role of geographical societies in the later nineteenth century, see B. Hudson, 'The new geography and the new imperialism', *Antipode*, 9 (1977), pp. 12–19; W. H. Schneider, 'Geographical reform and municipal imperialism in France, 1870–1880', in J. MacKenzie (ed.) *Imperialism and the Natural World* (Manchester, 1990), pp. 90–117; A. Godlewska and N. Smith (eds), *Geography and Empire* (Oxford, 1994); Bell, Butlin and Heffernan, *Geography and Imperialism*.
54. Livingstone, *The Geographical Tradition*, p. 168.
55. D. Stoddart, 'The RGS and the "new geography"', *Geographical Journal*, 146 (1980), p. 191. For an account which emphasizes the role of a larger imperial 'service class' in the RGS, see R. Bridges, 'Europeans and East Africans in the age of exploration', *Geographical Journal*, 139 (1973), pp. 220–32.
56. F. Emery, 'Geography and imperialism: the role of Sir Bartle Frere (1815–84)', *Geographical Journal*, 150 (1984), pp. 342–50; J. L. Duthie, 'Sir Henry Creswicke Rawlinson and the art of great gamesmanship', *Journal of Imperial and Commonwealth History*, 11 (1983), pp. 253–74.
57. Mill, *Record of the Royal Geographical Society*, p. 42. See also Cameron, 'Agents and agencies'.

2.1 Sir Roderick Murchison, chairing the Geographical Section at the British Association, 1864 (detail from *Punch*, 1865, p. 113).

The imperial scope and character of mid-Victorian geography is nowhere clearer than in the career of Sir Roderick Murchison, President of the RGS for much of the period between 1850 and 1870; indeed, his concerns with empire and geography were so intertwined, that it is difficult to say where one ended and the other began (figure 2.1). In this respect, the parallels between Murchison and Joseph Banks are compelling, although one historian suggests that Murchison operated 'within a narrower, more specialized, more institutionally constrained environment than his predecessor'.[58] Yet Murchison was adept at exploiting his formal and informal influence over geographers and statesmen alike; as Robert Stafford has shown, he used his pre-eminent positions at the RGS, the Geological Society, the British Association and the Geological Survey to advance not only the cause of scientific exploration but also

58. Miller, 'Joseph Banks, empire and centers of calculation', p. 33.

the commercial and geopolitical interests of empire. Murchison constantly promoted the RGS as a base for imperial science, securing for the Society an annual government subsidy for its map room (in 1854) and a royal charter (in 1859). He was always ready to proclaim the utility of both geology and geography to the imperial cause, seeing exploration and reconnaissance as the natural prerequisites of the expansion of British influence world-wide. While this emphasis on utility had been evoked by his predecessors, Murchison's contribution was to turn their ambition into practical effect, through his formal and informal influence upon the various arms of government with which he was associated. 'By the late 1850s', Stafford concludes, 'the RGS more perfectly represented British expansionism in all its facets than any other institution in the nation.'[59]

The growth of the Society's reputation during the middle decades of the nineteenth century, making it one of the most fashionable of scientific societies by 1870, owed much to Murchison's labours. Throughout the 1850s and 1860s, he energetically promoted both public and official interest in exploration, most notably in his patronage of David Livingstone (see chapter 4). His intermediary role between geographical science and the imperial state is perhaps best illustrated by a single example: the association of the RGS with the British military expedition to Abyssinia in 1867. The Abyssinian force, totalling thirteen thousand men from Britain and India under the command of Sir Robert Napier, was despatched to force the release of British consular officials and other Europeans held captive at Magdala by the Abyssinian King, and more generally to restore British influence both in the region and beyond.[60] Murchison used his political influence to secure the appointment of a scientific team to accompany the expedition, including a botanist, a meteorologist, a geologist and a geographer, Clements Markham (then working in the India Office). The significance of Abyssinia to the geographers was three-fold: firstly, it had been the site of expeditions (such as Samuel Baker's) exploring the eastern tributaries of the Nile; secondly, its history had long preoccupied scholars interested in the religious and linguistic geographies of the continent; and last, but not least, it occupied a strategically significant position in relation to the pattern of British power in East Africa and the Indian

---

59. Stafford, *Scientist of Empire*, pp. 211–22.
60. For two recent accounts, focusing on visual and literary aspects of the representation of the campaign respectively, see J. Ryan, *Picturing Empire: Photography and the Visualization of the British Empire* (London, 1997), pp. 83–98; T. Youngs, *Travellers in Africa: British Travelogues, 1850–1900* (Manchester, 1994), pp. 24–39.

Ocean. In 1867 and 1868, Murchison encouraged discussion of geographical aspects of the campaign at meetings of the RGS, including questions relating to the army's route, logistics and water supply. He hailed the storming of Magdala not only as a triumph of military might, but also as confirmation of Britain's scientific and imperial supremacy:

> When has Europe marched a scientifically organised army into an unknown intertropical region, and urged it forward as we have done, for hundreds of miles over chain after chain of Alps amidst the grandest scenery? And all to punish a dark king ... This truly is a fine moral lesson which we have read to the world; and . . .; in addition, we reap good scientific data.[61]

Murchison was not alone in emphasizing the virtues of this alliance between science and empire. Given Markham's own efforts to associate the RGS with a long and noble history of British exploits abroad, reflected both in his role within the Hakluyt Society and in his subsequent promotion of polar exploration as RGS President, it is unsurprising to find him celebrating the expedition in just these terms: 'There was something in it that recalled the exploits of that heroic age when dawning science enabled men who were still actuated by the spirit of knight errantry to achieve apparent impossibilities.'[62] Yet the heavily rhetorical character of such claims needs to be acknowledged. In this context, it is significant that Murchison's enthusiastic involvement of the RGS in the Abyssinian campaign met with some resistance from those who were more cautious about associating science with popular imperialism. The discussion of political matters at the RGS 'Abyssinian nights', when Samuel Baker and Henry Rawlinson bullishly advocated the annexation of all or part of Abyssinia, were openly criticized by Viscount Strangford, son-in-law of Francis Beaufort.[63]

The Abyssinian campaign marked an important moment for the RGS, for it confirmed the extent to which the Society had become popularly associated with military ventures undertaken in an imperial spirit well before the onset of the scramble for Africa.[64] For example, in a guide to *Scientific London*, published in 1874, it was claimed that 'the military

61. Ryan, *Picturing Empire*, p. 95.
62. C. Markham, *A History of the Abyssinian Campaign* (London, 1869); A. Savours, 'Clements Markham', in Bridges and Hair, *Compassing the Vaste Globe of the Earth*, pp. 165–99.
63. E. Strangford (ed.), *A Selection from the Writings of Viscount Strangford on Political, Geographical and Social Subjects*, vol ii (London, 1869), pp. 332–9. See also Stafford, *Scientist of Empire*, pp. 184–5.
64. On the wider political context, see F. Harcourt, 'Disraeli's imperialism, 1866–1868: a question of timing', *Historical Journal*, 23 (1980), pp. 87–109.

and civil servants of Her Majesty well appreciate the value of the Society's map-room'. For this author, at least, the RGS had become virtually an arm of the imperial state: 'No sooner does a squabble occur – in Ashanti, Abyssinia or Atchin – than Government departments make a rush to Savile Row, and lay hands on all matter relating to that portion of the world which happens to be interesting for the moment'.[65] However, we should be cautious about treating such pronouncements – especially those with an avowedly rhetorical purpose, including the annual Presidential Addresses – as a *description* of the extent of the Society's actual role in informing imperial policy. It was, after all, part of the job of the RGS president to claim for geography an important place in the conduct of national affairs. Furthermore, the differences over the Abyssinian episode draw our attention to significant differences of opinion within the geographical establishment itself. From the beginning, as we have seen, the RGS was run by a Council which represented a wide variety of social, political and scientific interests. While Murchison sought to represent it as a distinct lobby, in reality the RGS was a far more heterogeneous body than this would suggest. Some indication of this diversity is provided in the appointments of Francis Galton and Thomas Hodgkin as Honorary Secretaries of the Society during the 1850s.[66] While both men boasted respectable credentials in the worlds of geography and ethnology, they held radically different views on the science and politics of race. Galton's account of his expedition to South West Africa in 1850–2 exhibits a degree of contempt for black Africans that encourages comparison with the most racist anthropologists of the period. His profoundly hierarchical view of cultural difference and his insistence on the existence of innate differences between white and black were eventually to find expression in the concept of 'eugenic worth'.[67] Such ideas were far removed from those of the Quaker Thomas Hodgkin, the leading figure in the Aborigines Protection Society, whose motto 'Ab Uno Sanguine' symbolized its faith in the unity of the human race. Through the Society's journal, the *Colonial Intelligencer or Aborigines' Friend*, Hodgkin sought to publicize stories of maltreatment and exploitation of aboriginal peoples throughout the

65. B. Becker, *Scientific London* (London, 1874), pp. 332–3.
66. Hodgkin served as Honorary Secretary between 1851 and 1862; Galton served alongside him from 1857.
67. R. Fancher, 'Francis Galton's African ethnography and its role in the development of his psychology', *British Journal of the History of Science*, 16 (1983), pp. 67–79. For a somewhat different view, see M. Banton, 'Galton's conception of race in historical perspective', in M. Keynes (ed.), *Sir Francis Galton, FRS: The Legacy of his Ideas* (London, 1993), pp. 170–9.

empire and beyond.[68] A Society which could count Hodgkin and Galton, not to mention Bates and Burton, among its leading figures during the 1860s could hardly be said to speak with one voice (see chapter 5).

The difference between Galton and Hodgkin exemplifies the heterogeneity of political and intellectual perspectives represented within the RGS. To understand the nature of this diversity, and its expression in both public and private controversies, it is necessary to look beyond the official record of the Society's deliberations; indeed, the job of such publications was precisely to present a coherent account of the activities of the Society, papering over any cracks which might undermine its credibility. To be sure, the boundaries of these controversies were circumscribed, both by the conscious manipulation of influential Fellows on Council and by the conventions of gentlemanly science. However, the growing size and extent of the Society's activities increasingly brought such differences into public view. By the 1870s, it is possible to identify a number of factions even within the Society's inner circles. Although it is difficult to map these factions precisely (by social class, scientific interest, profession or status, for example), it is clear that by this time the RGS was a much more diverse institution than is sometimes acknowledged. To emphasize this point is not simply to make a plea for a more detailed history. Rather, it is to suggest that, in the wider context of the relations between exploration, science and empire, the RGS was as much an *arena* as an interest group, a site where competing visions of geography were debated and put into practice.

Conclusion

The Royal Geographical Society's founding programme – the co-ordination of the production of geographical knowledge and its application in the service of the imperial state – can in some respects be interpreted as a continuation of the Banksian project by other means. From their powerful positions within both the scientific and the political establishments, figures like Barrow and Murchison promoted geography as an imperial science. While they may have operated within a more restricted field of operations than had been the case under the Banksian regime, one should not overstate the influence of modern notions of expertise and professionalism on either science or the state for much of the

---

68. In 1859, Hodgkin arranged for the African-American Martin Delaney to speak at the RGS: see A. M. Kass and E. Kass, *Perfecting the World: The Life and Times of Dr Thomas Hodgkin, 1798–1866* (Orlando, 1988), pp. 480–1.

nineteenth century: the channels of influence open to gentlemanly science were informal as much as they were formal.[69] Once we look beyond the founding statements and Presidential Addresses, however, the language of 'imperial science' and 'centres of calculation' seems to lose some of its purchase. It is indeed difficult to characterize a body which finds room for missionaries, anti-slavery campaigners, roving explorers, mountaineers, antiquarians, geologists and naturalists under its umbrella as a coherent 'centre' at all. In the mid-Victorian period, it is possible to identify a number of informal networks attempting to use the Society for their own ends, including for example groups associated with the Hakluyt Society, the British Museum and the Anti-Slavery Society.[70] Meanwhile, the emergence of distinct inner circles at the heart of the Society (represented for example by the Geographical Club and the Kosmos Club founded in the 1850s) appears to be one response to the growth of membership, enabling small coteries within the Society to maintain distinct spaces for their self-fashioning. In contrast to other, better-known fraternal organizations, these dining clubs appear to represent a conservative response to change, rather than a challenge to the scientific establishment.[71]

Although the Royal Geographical Society brought together a variety of different interests under the common title FRGS, it could not unify their points of view. In particular, the expansion of the Society under Murchison's influence highlighted some basic uncertainties over the role and status of geographical knowledge. During the 1860s, when public interest in African exploration reached new heights, the Society became so fashionable that it was described by one would-be explorer as 'one of the wonders of London'.[72] Yet this very success raised questions about the nature and limits of RGS authority. On the one hand, there were influential critics within the scientific community, who complained

69.   In this respect, I think the distinction between the Banksian regime and its successors can be overstated: cf. Gascoigne, *Science in the Service of the Empire*, pp. 199–204.
70.   T. Campbell, 'R. H. Major and the British Museum' in Bridges and Hair, *Compassing the Vaste Globe of the Earth*, pp. 81–140; D. Helly, 'Informed opinion on tropical Africa in Great Britain, 1860–1890', *African Affairs*, 68 (1969), pp. 195–217; chapter 4, below.
71.   Cf. H. Gay and J. Gay, 'Brothers in science: science and fraternal culture in nineteenth-century Britain', *History of Science*, 35 (1997), pp. 425–53. The Geographical Club (a successor to the Raleigh Club) was founded in 1854, while the smaller Kosmos Club was founded in 1859. Both were exclusive dining clubs, and their members formed the inner elite of the RGS: see J. Marshall-Cornwall, *History of the Geographical Club* (London, 1976).
72.   W. Reade, 'English scientific societies', *The Galaxy*, 3 (1867), pp. 733–41 (quote from p. 738).

that the name of science was being tainted by the craving for sensation. Joseph Hooker, director of Kew Gardens, expressed such anxieties in a letter in 1864: 'I hate the claptrap and flattery and flummery of the Royal Geographical, with its utter want of Science and craving for popularity and excitement, and making London Lions of the season of bold Elephant hunters and Lion slayers, whilst the steady, slow and scientific surveyors and travellers have no honour at all.'[73] On the other, there were the scholars and antiquarians, a significant proportion of the Society's membership during the 1840s and 1850s, many of whom found themselves derided by some explorers as mere 'armchair geographers'. Among this group were William Cooley and Henry Yule, prominent members of the Hakluyt Society, who were openly critical of the methods of leading explorers such as Livingstone and Stanley.[74] In some respects, these controversies echoed wider tensions between the knowledges of the cabinet and the field, alluded to in chapter 1, which will be considered further in the context of the RGS itself in the next chapter. In its efforts to capitalize on the sensational publicity surrounding African exploration, the RGS extended its operations well beyond the boundaries of both science and scholarship, and in the process – according to these critics – its authority had been compromised. Such differences over the role and purpose of the Society are an almost constant feature of its history, right up to the present day. They throw into relief both the hybrid composition of the RGS and the diversity of the interests it attempted to represent. For all its efforts, the RGS could not operate as just another scientific institution: the culture of exploration was simply too heterogeneous to be contained within a centre of calculation.

73.   Quoted in Stafford, *Scientist of Empire*, p. 59. Hooker's reservations did not prevent him from accepting a Founder's Medal from the RGS in 1883. The doubts of other scientists, including Darwin and Wallace, are alluded to in Mill, *Record of the Royal Geographical Society*, p. 80.
74.   On Yule and Stanley, see below, chapter 6. On Cooley and Livingstone, see R. Bridges, 'W. D. Cooley, the RGS and African geography in the nineteenth century', *Geographical Journal*, 142 (1976), pp. 27–47, 274–86.

Chapter 3

Hints to Travellers: Observation in the Field

The collection of reliable geographical information was one of the principal concerns of the founders of the Royal Geographical Society in 1830. This was not merely a matter of constructing an authoritative archive of books, journals, maps and charts, a record of the progress of exploration, but also of instructing travellers on what remained to be done. The prospectus of the new Society anticipated the preparation of 'brief instructions' for travellers, 'pointing out the parts most desirable to be visited; the best and most practicable means of proceeding thither; the researches most essential to make; phenomena to be observed; the subjects of natural history most desirable to be procured; and to obtain all such information as may tend to the extension of our geographical knowledge'.[1] Such concerns were eventually to find expression in the Society's *Hints to Travellers*, first published in 1854. This text was part of a wider European discourse on field observation, evident in a range of instruction manuals advising travellers how to observe a variety of aspects of the world beyond the study or the laboratory, by means of such devices as questionnaires, tables for the recording of data, and advice on instruments and other equipment. These manuals might perhaps be regarded as attempts to promote an authoritative 'way of seeing' in the field, differentiating the view of scientific explorer from that of ordinary traveller. Yet we ought not to treat this too literally, if only because this disciplinary project extended beyond the traveller's eye: a range of mental and physical faculties were to be exercised in the process of observation. Moreover, subjected to a closer reading, such texts may tell more than one story. In this chapter, I shall portray *Hints to Travellers* less as a confident assertion of a geographical way of

1. *Journal of the Royal Geographical Society*, 1 (1831), p. vi.

seeing than as an unsettled attempt to resolve some fundamental dilemmas: how was field observation to be trusted? What were the limits of 'geographical' knowledge? And, above all, what attitude should the scientific community have towards the untrained traveller?

Observation in the Field

Instruction manuals for the traveller were not in themselves new; indeed, their history stretches back at least as far as the sixteenth century. The distinction between the purposeful traveller (*peregrinari*) and the aimless rambler (*vagari*) was evident in the early modern literature on the art of travel, though its primary goal then was the education of the cultivated self. In the seventeenth and eighteenth centuries, according to Justin Stagl, the emphasis of this instructional literature 'shifted from the improvement of the personality of the traveller to the gathering of knowledge', a process hastened by the institutionalization of knowledge in the European scientific academies.[2] The first number of the Royal Society's *Philosophical Transactions*, published in 1665, thus included Robert Boyle's 'General heads for the natural history of a country great or small drawn out for the use of travellers and navigators', a text which was republished as a manual in 1692. John Woodward's 'Brief instructions for making observations in all parts of the world' appeared shortly afterwards, in 1696. While the Royal Society was not generally in a position to organize expeditions of its own, it sought to direct the gaze of scientific travellers by means of such publications: for the fruits of travel to be useful, they had to be instructed on what and how to observe.[3] It has been suggested that this instructional literature reflected the 'scientization' of travel during the eighteenth century, a process in which travellers became information-gatherers for metropolitan science.[4] Yet we should not overstate the power of institutions such as the Royal Society to direct the manner in which 'philosophical' travel was undertaken. Styles of scientific travel continued to vary widely, from the local tours of country gentlemen to

2. J. Stagl, 'The methodising of travel in the sixteenth century', *History and Anthropology*, 4 (1990), pp. 303–38 (p. 324).
3. D. Carey, 'Compiling nature's history: travellers and travel narratives in the early Royal Society', *Annals of Science*, 54 (1997), pp. 269–92; S. Collini and A. Vannoni, *Viaggere per le Conoscere: Le Istruzioni per Viaggiatori e Scienziati tra Sette e Ottocento* (Florence, 1995).
4. S. Sörlin, 'National and international aspects of cross-boundary science: scientific travel in the eighteenth century', in E. Crawford, T. Shinn and S. Sörlin (eds), *Denationalizing Science* (Dordrecht, 1993), pp. 43–72.

the organised expeditions of Cook or La Pérouse; and while an increasing number of manuals on scientific travel were published in the eighteenth century, 'little consensus had in fact been forged by [the] century's end on how to distinguish the truly scientific fieldworker from the dilettante, let alone on what the proper methods for voyaging – beyond the standard injunction to "observe nature" – might actually be'.[5] The proliferation of instruction manuals for travellers in the nineteenth century – in the context of new techniques of observation, new scientific institutions and challenges to existing models of gentlemanly science – can be seen as both a response to, and a reflection of, this lack of consensus.[6]

In the world of nineteenth-century science, the credibility of claims to empirical knowledge was said to depend on accurate observation, above all else. Observation was more than a matter of simply looking: in order to see properly, one had to observe methodically, to follow a rule. This applied especially to the observation of the traveller. In *What to Observe* (1841), for example, Colonel Julian Jackson (the newly-appointed secretary of the RGS) represented travel as a necessary but insufficient means of acquiring geographical knowledge; it would become truly useful, he insisted, 'only when travellers shall have learnt how and what to observe'.[7] Knowledge gathered in the field had to be put on a secure footing: as Harriet Martineau put it in *How to Observe: Morals and Manners*, 'the powers of observation must be trained, and habits of method in arranging the materials presented to the eye must be acquired before the student possesses the requisites for understanding

5. A. Cooper, 'From the Alps to Egypt (and back again): Dolomieu, scientific voyaging and the construction of the field in eighteenth-century natural history', in C. Smith and J. Agar (eds), *Making Space for Science: Territorial Themes in the Shaping of Knowledge* (London, 1998), pp. 39–63 (p. 44).
6. For comparable studies of nineteenth-century instructional manuals, see A. Larsen, *Not Since Noah: The English Scientific Zoologists and the Craft of Collecting, 1800–1840* (PhD thesis, Princeton University, NJ, 1993), chs 4–5; L. Kury, 'Les instructions de voyage dans les expéditions scientifiques français, 1750–1830', *Revue d'Histoire des Sciences*, 51 (1998), pp. 65–91; J. Urry, 'Notes and Queries on Anthropology and the development of field methods in British anthropology, 1870–1920', *Proceedings of the Royal Anthropological Institute* (1972), pp. 45–72; C. Blanckaert (ed.), *Le Terrain des sciences humaines, XVIIIe-XXe siècle* (Paris, 1996).
7. J. R. Jackson, *What to Observe; Or the Traveller's Remembrancer* (London, 1841), pp. iii–iv. Compare Rousseau (writing in 1762): 'To become informed, it is not sufficient to roam through various countries. It is necessary to know how to travel. To observe, it is necessary to have eyes and to turn them towards the object one wants to know': J.-J. Rousseau, *Émile: Or, On Education* (Harmondsworth, 1981), p. 458.

what he contemplates'.[8] An observer was in this sense never merely a passive spectator, but 'more importantly one who sees within a pre-scribed set of possibilities, one who is embedded in a system of conventions and limitations'.[9] The precise nature of these 'conventions and limitations', however, was open to question. Manuals for the scientific traveller commonly held that all observations had to be written down on the spot, rather than entrusted to memory. Darwin's advice to the would-be field geologist was symptomatic: 'He ought to remember Bacon's aphorism, that "Reading maketh a full man, conference a ready man, and *writing an exact man*." '[10] Yet opinions varied on the actual manner and moment in which a traveller's observations should be recorded, in note-book, diary or journal. Harriet Martineau, for example, specifically warned observers of morals and manners against writing down conversations as they occurred. Such apparently trivial details reflected different assumptions about the nature and purpose of the knowledge gained by travel. Indeed in some contexts, as in the travel narratives of the European literary tourist, the truth of a traveller's observation consisted less in precise description of what was observed – in short, the recording of information – than in creative reflection upon the impressions generated by the experience of travel. 'The observer who instantly jots down every object he sees, never, properly speaking, saw an object in his life', complained one reviewer in *Blackwood's Magazine* in 1827. 'What are all the jottings that ever were jotted down in his jot-book, by the most inveterate jotter that ever reached a raven age, to the Library of Useful Knowledge, that every man – who is a man – carries within the Radcliffe – the Bodleian of his own breast?'[11]

The distinction between scientific travel and literary tourism, which is simply taken for granted in many orthodox accounts of the history of exploration, can also be detected in the instructional manuals for scientific travellers produced in the eighteenth and nineteenth centuries. The Baconian injunction to study nature through direct observation, not via the authority of books, licensed a way of seeing that privileged the recording of verifiable facts, freed as it were from the contingencies of subjectivity. Yet the notion that the truth, indeed the manliness, of the

8.   Harriet Martineau, *How to Observe: Morals and Manners* (London, 1838), p. 1.
9.   J. Crary, *Techniques of the Observer: On Vision and Modernity in the Nineteenth Century* (Cambridge, Mass., 1992), p. 6.
10.   C. Darwin, 'Geology', in J. Herschel (ed.), *A Manual of Scientific Enquiry: Prepared for the Use of Officers in Her Majesty's Navy; and Travellers in General* (London, 1849), p. 163 (emphasis in original).
11.   'The traveller's oracle', *Blackwood's Magazine*, October 1827, pp. 445–65, quoted in J. Buzard, *The Beaten Track: European Tourism, Literature and the Ways to 'Culture', 1800–1918* (Oxford, 1993), p. 155.

explorer's gaze might depend on 'the Bodleian of his own breast' was not in fact confined to the culture of literary tourism: indeed, it was also reflected in the reputation of the most celebrated scientific travellers, including Humboldt and Darwin. Humboldt's commitment to a synthesis between scientific observation and scholarly learning was perhaps exceptional; the more general point, as Dorinda Outram has argued, is that voyages of exploration in the late eighteenth and early nineteenth centuries raised troubling questions about the relation between the knowledges of the field and those of the study or cabinet (as discussed above, chapter 1).[12] On the one hand, many explorers defined their projects in opposition to the theoretical speculations of 'armchair geographers': to them, there was no substitute for the knowledge gained by voyages into the unknown, and indeed it was associated precisely with challenging the authority of the sedentary philosopher. On the other, the value of adventurous exploration in itself was questioned by those advocating a more systematic approach to the development of geographical knowledge; thus for Colonel Jackson (secretary of the RGS between 1841 and 1847), the 'labours of the cabinet' were just as noble and as deserving of recognition as those of the field.[13] It is perhaps significant that Jackson was himself a victim of controversies over the running of the Society during the 1840s: while he championed the case for theoretical geography within the RGS, others regarded it as the preserve of a clique. In the words of one of Jackson's hostile critics,

> Poor travellers are now excluded from all opportunities favourable to the development of truth. The insulting sneer, or the cold exclusion of excessive civility, debar them from again troubling the officials with the results of their labours; and the Society is now very generally admitted to be a mere delusion and snare, where a few cunning map-makers and closet geographers combine to denounce discoveries opposed to their theories and vain speculations.[14]

Arguments over the relation between observation in the field and theorising in the study were to remain a chronic feature of the nineteenth-century culture of exploration.

According to astronomer John Herschel, the ideal scientific observer

12. See also C. Greppi, 'On the spot: L'artista-viaggiatore e l'inventario iconografico del mondo (1772–1859)', *Geotema*, 8 (1997), pp. 137–149.
13. On Jackson's plea for the recognition of the work of 'sedentary geographers', see his 'Note regarding the labours of the RGS' (1837) and 'On the adjudication of the medals of the RGS' (1840), Additional Papers, RGS Archives.
14. *Pictorial Times*, 12 September 1846, quoted in H. R. Mill, *The Record of the Royal Geographical Society* (London, 1930), p. 56.

was someone who did not merely accumulate facts, but also conducted experiments: indeed this was precisely the difference between 'passive' and 'active' observation.[15] Justifying the utility of science in terms which his readers would appreciate, Herschel cited the example of Captain Basil Hall's reliance on astronomical observations in a remarkably accurate navigation of an 8,000-mile voyage from the west coast of Mexico, round Cape Horn to Rio de Janeiro, during which land had not been sighted for three months. 'It is needless to remark', Herschel noted, 'how essentially the authority of a commanding officer over his crew may be strengthened by the occurrence of such incidents, indicative of a degree of knowledge and consequent power beyond their reach'.[16] The plotting of a trans-oceanic route was a kind of travelling experiment in which a hypothesis, based on both *in situ* lunar observations and mathematical calculations using astronomical tables, was tested against the experience of navigating in uncharted waters. If the ship itself was the principal instrument in this experiment,[17] its captain was represented by Herschel as the exemplary man of science, whose authority depended on the use of systematic scientific methods. Yet the problem of authority in the case of field observation was far more problematic than Herchel's exemplar could accommodate. The validity of a hypothesis about navigation could perhaps be demonstrated (or at least not refuted) by the safe arrival of a ship at a fixed destination; in many other circumstances, the manner and outcome of a field experiment could not so readily be established. Moreover, a naval captain's authority over his crew (represented here, significantly, as no more than passive spectators) was not equivalent to the reputation of a scientific observer among his peers: while the one (according to Herschel at least) could be secured by a simple demonstration, the other would depend on the negotiation of the observer's credibility.

The problem of credibility, vital to the development of experimental science in Europe, was particularly acute in the case of observation in the

15. J. Herschel, *Preliminary Discourse on the Study of Natural Philosophy* (London, 1851 edn), pp. 76–9. Herschel's tract (first published in 1830) was an influential statement of nineteenth-century scientific epistemology: indeed, one historian suggests that to be scientific in the Victorian era was to be 'as much like Herschel as possible'. See W. Cannon, 'John Herschel and the idea of science', *Journal of the History of Ideas*, 22 (1961), p. 219.
16. Herschel, *Preliminary Discourse*, p. 29. Soon after, Hall himself wrote of the 'magical influence' of an authoritative naval captain over his crew: 'The effects of being well commanded', *Fragments of Voyages and Travels* (London, 1852 edn), vol. i, pp. 56–62.
17. R. Sorrenson, 'The ship as a scientific instrument in the eighteenth century', in H. Kuklick and R. Kohler (eds), *Science in the Field* (Chicago, 1996), pp. 221–36.

field, where on-the-spot verification was so often impossible. However it was defined, the field was necessarily a more open and diffuse space than the study or the laboratory, and it was inhabited by a wide range of people practising different kinds of observation. How, then, were observations in the field to be trusted? The gender, class and ethnicity of the observer were important but not necessarily sufficient bases for the credibility of a traveller's observations within the scientific community: a British naval officer unfamiliar with the arts of lunar observation and astronomical calculation, for example, could not have provided Herschel with his paradigm. One answer to the problem of scientific credibility lay in the use of ever more sophisticated instruments and calculations designed to minimize the intrusion of subjectivity into the reporting of information: the extension, as it were, of the space of the laboratory into the field.[18] However, this strategy was more applicable to some kinds of observation than to others: while relatively precise and calibrated scientific instruments were essential to the recording of many forms of meteorological or magnetic data, for example, the identification of a new species, the interpretation of a geological formation or the description of manners and customs relied on different kinds of skill. Some explorers, indeed, attempted to validate their efforts in other ways entirely: when Winwood Reade finally arrived at the banks of the Niger in 1869, for example, the first thing he reached for was his copy of Herodotus. While Reade may be regarded as a literary traveller rather than a scientific observer in the strict sense, this example at least reminds us that the authority of the explorer was established principally through the writing of a travel narrative, either first- or second-hand.[19] Ironically, Herschel's exemplary man of science, Basil Hall, would become more familiar to the reading public during the 1830s as a writer of popular travel literature, including nine volumes of *Fragments of Voyages and Travels*. Moreover, even if we confine ourselves to scientific exploration narrowly defined, the use of sophisticated instruments did not in itself bypass the problem of trust: the instruments themselves could not turn belief into knowledge.[20]

18. M.-N. Bourguet and C. Licoppe, 'Voyages, mesures et instruments: une nouvelle expérience du monde au siècle des lumières', *Annales Histoire, Sciences Sociales*, 52 (1997), pp. 1115–51.
19. See chapter 5 below; also B. Greenfield, 'The problem of the discoverer's authority in Lewis and Clark's *History*', in J. Arac and H. Ritvo (eds), *Macropolitics of Nineteenth-century Literature: Nationalism, Exoticism, Imperialism* (Philadelphia, 1991), pp. 12–36.
20. S. Shapin, 'Placing the view from nowhere: historical and sociological problems in the location of science', *Transactions of the Institute of British Geographers*, 23 (1998), pp. 5–12; C. Withers, 'Voyages et crédibilité: vers une géographie de la confiance', *Géographie et Cultures*, 33 (2000), pp. 3–19.

Judgements about the credibility of travellers' observations continued to depend on a variety of assumptions, including the status of the observer, the means of observation, the manner in which observations were reported and the audience to which they were directed.[21] In this context, what Bruce Hevly calls 'the authority of adventurous observation' deserves special attention: it finds expression in a variety of settings, from African exploration to the science of glacial motion.[22]

While observation was the key term in the lexicon of empirical science, then, *how* and *what* to observe were far from self-evident. To see with the eyes of the ordinary traveller, or the crew of an ocean-going vessel, was one thing: to observe scientifically was another. The task of instruction manuals like *Hints to Travellers* was to direct the inquiries of the traveller in a manner useful to science: in a sense, to define his field of vision. In the case of geographical science, however, this project was to prove deeply problematic. *Hints to Travellers*, I shall argue, was an attempt to exert authority on a field of knowledge that was already too large and diverse to be mastered.

The Discipline of Observation: *Hints to Travellers*

The first edition of *Hints to Travellers* appeared in 1854, buried within the pages of the Royal Geographical Society's *Journal*. Its immediate origins lay in Francis Galton's suggestion that travellers required advice on the use of appropriate instruments in the field, which had been referred to the Society's expeditions committee in 1852. This gave rise to a report by two eminent naval surveyors, Robert Fitzroy and Henry Raper, which eventually appeared in the first part of *Hints to Travellers*.[23] It was accompanied by a series of appendices, including papers by Rear-Admiral W. H. Smyth (past president of both the RGS and the Astronomical Society),[24] Admiral F. W. Beechey (an Arctic explorer,

21. As indicated in the responses to Winwood Reade and Henry Morton Stanley (discussed in chapters 5 and 6). See also S. McCook, ' "It may be truth, but it is not evidence": Paul du Chaillu and the legitimation of evidence in the field sciences', in Kuklick and Kohler, *Science in the Field*, pp. 177–97.
22. B. Hevly, 'The heroic science of glacier motion', in Kuklick and Kohler, *Science in the Field*, pp. 66–86.
23. 'Hints to travellers', *Journal of the RGS*, xxiv (1854), pp. 328–58; RGS Expeditions Committee Minutes, November 1852 to February 1853 (RGS Archives). The membership of the expeditions committee at this time also included Murchison, Sabine and Arrowsmith.
24. On Smyth's reputation as an astronomer, see J. Dreyer and H. Turner (eds), *History of the Royal Astronomical Society, 1820–1920* (London, 1923), pp. 76, 142–3, 201–6.

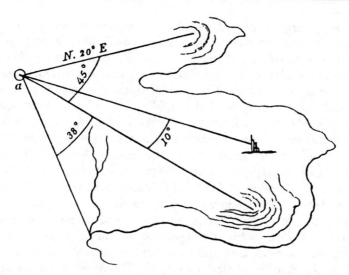

3.1 Illustration of map sketching, from *Hints to Travellers* (1854 edition).

hydrographer and future RGS president), Lieutenant-Colonel W. H. Sykes (a retired Indian officer, statistician and meteorologist)[25] and Francis Galton (the African traveller subsequently better known as a scientist of heredity). The contents of this first edition were largely taken up with instruments and measurements: prospective travellers were thus advised to equip themselves with a sextant, horizon, pocket-sextant, compass, micrometer, sympiesometer, two pocket chronometers, two thermometers, two barometers, two aneroids and two boiling thermometers, together with writing and drawing materials. There was also some advice on map-drawing, astronomical observations and the packaging of instruments. Several appendices included further advice on a variety of subjects, including topographical mapping, the taking of bearings and the use of thermometers to determine heights, some suggestions on 'outfit for an explorer', a list of headings in 'descriptive geography' and a series of 'hints for collecting geographical information' in the form of over a hundred questions relating to topography, hydrography, natural history and ethnography (figure 3.1).

Two features of the first and subsequent editions of *Hints to Travellers* emerge quite clearly: an insistence on the need to record observations

25. Sykes was an influential figure at the British Association, active in a number of sections, including the statistical, where he 'was known to be a strict disciplinarian who denounced speculations unsupported by facts': J. Morrell and A. Thackray, *Gentlemen of Science: Early Years of the British Association for the Advancement of Science* (Oxford, 1981), p. 296 n. 306.

in a standardized form and a repeated emphasis on the use of reliable scientific instruments. These features are evident in a range of other instruction manuals issued to travellers and explorers in the field during the middle decades of the nineteenth century. *Hints to Travellers* needs to be seen in the context of this wider discourse on field observation. This discourse encompassed the publications of government departments (notably the Hydrographic Office's guidelines on surveying),[26] military and naval officers (such as Belcher's *A Treatise on Nautical Surveying*, which itself included a chapter entitled 'hints to travellers'),[27] learned societies (such as the ethnological questionnaires produced by the British Association and the Ethnological Society)[28] and influential scientific entrepreneurs (such as the instruction manuals for zoological collectors published by William Swainson and others).[29] Perhaps the best-known of these publications was the *Manual of Scientific Enquiry*, intended for naval officers and 'travellers in general', which was published by the British Admiralty in 1849. The *Manual*, edited by John Herschel, contained essays by the most distinguished representatives of British science, including George Airy (on astronomy), Edward Sabine (on magnetism), William Whewell (on tides), Charles Darwin (on geology), Richard Owen (on zoology), William Hooker (on botany), James Prichard (on ethnology) and William Hamilton (on geography).

Read in this wider context, it would clearly be possible to interpret *Hints to Travellers* as the product of a more general impulse to discipline observation in the field, valorizing some kinds of observation as scientific and others as unscientific.[30] However, we need to pay closer attention to the nature of this impulse: how and what to observe were matters of contention. There were significant differences between these various instructional manuals in the kinds of information to be recorded, the means of observation and indeed the status of field observation. These differences may also be detected within a single work, such as *Hints to Travellers*: scratching the surface of the text, it is possible to discern a striking degree of ambivalence over its form and content. We can begin with the title: these were to be 'hints' rather than instructions, general points of guidance intended for the independent gentlemanly traveller rather than official commands to political or

26. A. Day, *The Admiralty Hydrographic Service, 1795–1919* (London, 1967); Luciana Martins, 'Mapping tropical waters', in D. Cosgrove (ed.), *Mappings* (London, 1999), pp. 148–68.
27. E. Belcher, *A Treatise on Nautical Surveying* (London, 1835), pp. 262–81.
28. Urry, *'Notes and Queries'*, pp. 45–6.
29. Larsen, *Not Since Noah*, chs 4–5.
30. Cf. A. Blunt, *Travel, Gender and Imperialism: Mary Kingsley and West Africa* (New York, 1994), pp. 65–71.

scientific functionaries.[31] The first edition of *Hints to Travellers* was effectively an amalgam of advice from various authorities rather than a systematic manual of instruction issued on behalf of the Society – a collection of individually authored papers accompanied by extracts from earlier works. The list of 'hints for collecting geographical information', for example, was simply reprinted from a circular intended for the use of missionaries and other travellers, published in 1837.[32] Likewise, the list of headings on 'descriptive geography' was derived, unacknowledged, from the contents of Colonel Jackson's *What to Observe* (1841). Jackson's book was itself an English version of his *Aide-mémoire du voyageur*, published in 1834, and it is significant in the present context that this earlier work had been criticised for its lack of attention to scientific instruments and the practice of astronomical, magnetic or geodesic observation.[33] *What to Observe* anticipated the emphasis of many contributors to *Hints to Travellers* on the need for precise, standardized observation. Yet in character and scope Jackson's book was closer to the Enlightenment spirit of philosophical travel than its successor, to Montesquieu rather than to Herschel.[34]

The manner in which *Hints to Travellers* first appeared is also revealing: instead of being published as a separate volume, it was printed in a somewhat fragmented form within the pages of the Royal Geographical Society's *Journal*. The Society's ambivalence about the very idea of such a publication was clear from the somewhat apologetic preface (written by Henry Raper) which preceded it:

31. The term would have been familiar to earlier generations of scientific explorers: the advice given by the Royal Society to Captain Cook prior to his *Endeavour* voyage also took the form of 'Hints'. See John Beaglehole (ed.), *The Journals of Captain James Cook on His Voyages of Discovery*, vol. 1 (London, Hakluyt Society, 1955), pp. 514–19.

32. *Hints for Collecting Geographical Information* (London, 1837); [W. H. Smyth], *The Royal Geographical Society and its Labours* (London, 1846), p. 17.

33. *Journal of the Royal Geographical Society*, 4 (1834), pp. 229–39; *Bulletin de la Société de Géographie*, 2nd series, 2 (1834), p. 289. In *What to Observe*, Jackson included an additional section on 'instruments and operations' and omitted the 'preliminary discourse' on travel and discovery which had appeared in his *Aide-mémoire*.

34. Amid its 'endless variety of questions', for example, we find the following suggested for the study of morals and manners:

Are the inhabitants generally an imaginative or a reflective people? Are they lively or phlegmatic? Are they distinguished by any virtues or vices, and what are these? Are they brave or cowardly; proud or modest; hospitable or inimical to strangers; cruel or humane; confiding or distrustful; witty or obtuse? Are they peaceable or warlike; patriotic or cosmopolite; industrious or idle; sober or debauched; frank or deceitful; religious or profane; liberal or parsimonious; honest or thievish, etc? (Jackson, *What to Observe*, p. 223)

A complete system of instructions adapted to general application would embrace every point which could present itself to the notice of the accomplished traveller, and such a work would be an encyclopaedia. On the other hand, a few general remarks of an elementary nature would be superfluous to an individual of moderate attainments, while it could not possibly impart the necessary qualifications to one who had no other knowledge or experience of the subject. Again, the nature of the observations which a traveller may make must depend on the character and quality of the instruments he carries. . . . But this is not all; differences prevail amongst experienced travellers themselves, not merely as to details of observations, the degree of accuracy which it is advisable to aim at, and other matters, but as to whether particular instruments should be carried or not.[35]

This statement deserves close attention. As well as acknowledging disagreement among geographers over the merits of different instruments, it highlights a difficulty faced by the authors of all such works: the extent to which the techniques of scientific observation could be practised by travellers in general. The Admiralty *Manual*, for example was, like *Hints to Travellers*, intended to be intelligible to the educated traveller; indeed, the Admiralty Lords had specifically stipulated that they did 'not consider it necessary that this Manual should be one of very deep and abstruse research', and that its instructions 'should not require the use of nice apparatus and instruments'.[36] Significantly, however, it is clear that in his capacity as editor, John Herschel had some difficulty with these instructions. He noted dryly in his preface that there were some sciences (such as magnetism and meteorology) in which 'no observation worth recording can be made without the aid of instruments and methods of observation and reduction decidedly both nice and delicate': indeed, in some circumstances, as Airy remarked in his chapter on astronomy, a bad observation was worse than no observation at all.[37]

The RGS Council's ambivalence about the publication of *Hints to Travellers* reflects a basic uncertainty over whether the provision of general advice to untrained explorers 'should be deemed within the province of the Royal Geographical Society' at all. This anxiety was expressed more directly in the unpublished version of the report of the expeditions sub-committee which led to the publication of *Hints*. In response to the suggestion that the RGS should publish such a volume,

---

35. 'Hints to travellers', *Journal of the RGS*, xxiv (1854), pp. 328–9; Expeditions Committee Minutes, 17 January 1853 (RGS Archives).
36. Herschel, *Manual of Scientific Enquiry*, p. iii.
37. Herschel, *Manual of Scientific Enquiry*, p. v.

Fitzroy and Raper warned that the circulation of 'a few general remarks of a merely elementary character' would be worthless, 'since the observations of a traveller whose qualifications were confined to such narrow limits could possess no value for geography except of the lowest order'. Nothing less than the Society's very 'credit and character' was at stake: 'it would be inconsistent with the character of the Society, especially in times of increasing precision in every department of scientific research, to countenance the hasty accumulation and publication of crude or valueless results, by persons who have not devoted the time and attention necessary to entitle their labours to consideration'.[38]

This ambivalence about the publication of advice to untrained observers, together with acknowledged differences over its contents, helps to account for the somewhat chaotic form in which *Hints to Travellers* first appeared – a miscellany of papers on instruments, measurements and outfit, together with a compilation of extracts from earlier works, such as *What to Observe* and 'Hints for collecting geographical information'. The fear that such a publication might be associated in the public mind with more popular guidebooks seems to have prevented a more coherent effort before the 1860s. The title 'hints to travellers' had already been anticipated or borrowed by the authors of more popular guidebooks for travellers within and beyond Europe, and the well-established genre of the tourist guidebook was fair game for the satirist (cf. figure 3.2).[39] Anxiety over the ownership of geographical knowledge may also shed some light on the hostile reception given to more avowedly popularizing works, such as Harriet Martineau's book *How to Observe – Morals and Manners*, published by Charles Knight in 1838 on behalf of the Society for the Diffusion of Useful Knowledge. In a vituperative review by J. W. Croker for the *Quarterly Review*, the mouth-piece of geographical conservatism, the book was ridiculed as 'the very foolishest and most unfeminine farrago we have ever met of apocryphal anecdotes, promiscuous facts, and jumbled ideas – picked at random (or at least which might be so) out of the Penny Magazine and such like repositories'.[40] What seems to have offended Croker, even more than Martineau's embrace of the idea of 'philosophical travel' and her emphasis on sympathy as a prerequisite for the understanding of cultural difference, was the idea that the methods of the enlightened observer were in principle available to all

38. Unpublished Sub-Committee Report on Hints to Travellers (RGS Archives, Journal MSS, Misc., 1854).
39. Buzard, *The Beaten Track*, pp. 155–72.
40. 'How to observe – morals and manners', *Quarterly Review*, 58 (1839), pp. 61–72 (p. 72); M. Brightfield, *John Wilson Croker* (London, 1940), pp. 422–3.

3.2 'I'm Monarch of all I Survey'. Illustration from F. C. Burnand, *Tracks for Tourists, or the Continental Companion ... A Sure Guard against All Tricks upon Travellers* (London: Bradbury & Evans, 1864). By permission of the British Library.

travellers, irrespective of their class, gender and education. (In this respect, a contrast was drawn between Martineau's book and its predecessor in the *How to Observe* series, a work on geology by Henry De la Beche: 'This author labours under the disadvantage of knowing a good deal of the matter he writes about, which makes his book rather perplexing to the uninformed, for whose use the society professes to publish.'[41])

While such views may shed some light on conservative resistance to the involvement of the RGS in more 'popular' works, they did not prevent others from recommending Martineau's work or being involved in the activities of organizations like the Society for the Diffusion of Useful Knowledge, though the emphasis was generally on the passive reception of knowledge rather than popular participation in making knowledge itself. Thus Francis Beaufort at the Admiralty was heavily involved in the production of cheap maps for the Society in the 1830s, and it has been estimated that 25,000 copies of his maps had been sold

41. 'How to Observe', p. 61.

by 1841.[42] By the 1860s, anxieties at the heart of the geographical establishment over the diffusion of geographical knowledge appear to have given way to a different strategy, heralded by the appearance of a second and free-standing edition of *Hints to Travellers*, explicitly addressed to the untrained gentlemanly traveller 'who, for the first time in his life, proposes to explore a wild country'.[43] These words were Francis Galton's, and it appears that he was to be the predominant influence on the next three editions. In 1855, Galton had himself published a more unreservedly 'popular' handbook on the *Art of Travel*, which he described simply as 'a manual to all those who may have to "rough it", whether they be travellers, missionaries, emigrants, or soldiers'.[44] (It is possible that this is what Galton had in mind when he approached the Society about the need to provide more assistance to travellers in 1852). *The Art of Travel* overflowed with practical advice on how to locate and purify water, make fire, set up camp, secure roads and build bridges, and suggestions for all manner of expedition equipment, including saddlery, wagons, guns, traps and medicine. (A brief section on scientific instruments, reprinted from *Hints to Travellers*, was included, almost as an afterthought.) For Galton, the art of conducting an expedition in unfamiliar territory was akin to mounting a military campaign; thus in 1855 (on the recommendation of Colonel Sir James Alexander, an early recipient of an RGS grant) he recycled his book in the form of a series of illustrated lectures to army officers at Aldershot on the 'arts of campaigning'.[45] *The Art of Travel* constructed the ideal traveller as a resourceful leader of men, equally capable of exploiting local knowledge ('To kindle a spark into a flame by blowing is quite an art, which few Europeans have learnt, but in which every savage is proficient') and maintaining the standards of civilized life in the bush ('A thick dressing-gown is of very great comfort'). Particular emphasis was placed on the need for discipline, with advice to expedition leaders on their relations with both their fellow-Europeans ('Discountenance cliques being formed among the men, and promote

42. A. Friendly, *Beaufort of the Admiralty* (London, 1997), pp. 240–1. Colonel Jackson had referred to Martineau's work approvingly in *What to Observe* (p. 223).
43. *Hints to Travellers*, 2nd edn (London, 1865), pp. 3–4.
44. F. Galton, *The Art of Travel: Or, Shifts and Contrivances Available in Wild Countries* (London, 1855), p. iii. This and subsequent quotes are from the second edition published in 1856.
45. F. Galton, *Arts of Campaigning: An Inaugural Lecture Delivered at Aldershot* (London, 1855); F. Galton, *Catalogue of Models Illustrative of Camp Life* (London, 1858). See also J. E. Alexander to Norton Shaw, 10 August 1856 (RGS Archives, Fellows' correspondence).

merriment, singing, fiddling, and so forth, with all your power') and 'natives' ('A frank, joking, but determined manner, joined with an air of showing more confidence to the savages than you really feel, is the best'). In sum, *The Art of Travel* was as much concerned with conduct in the field as with the collection of scientific information.[46]

Returning to *Hints to Travellers*, we find that the initial ambivalence concerning the manual's format and function was overcome in subsequent editions through what was effectively an awkward compromise. The editions of the 1860s onwards might best be interpreted as hybrid texts, grafting the pragmatic tone of Galton's *The Art of Travel* onto the scientific aspirations of Herschel's *Manual*. The contents of the seven editions of *Hints to Travellers* published between 1865 and 1901 were progressively revised and expanded. The 1865 edition, for example, included notes on 'Photography for travellers and tourists' by Dr Pole and 'Hints on the collection of objects of natural history' by the Amazonian explorer Henry Walter Bates, newly appointed assistant secretary at the RGS. The 1871 edition incorporated more information on artificial horizons, compasses, watches, barometers and theodolites. The 1878 edition (published in a smaller format 'for the convenience of travellers') included more astronomical tables, similar to those found in handbooks on navigation, intended to assist travellers in the calculation of latitudes from meridian observations of the stars and planets. The 1883 edition incorporated an enlarged section written by John Coles, the Society's newly appointed instructor in practical astronomy and surveying, and new sections on anthropology and medical hints for travellers. The expansion continued in 1889 and 1893, with the inclusion of further advice on anthropology[47] and a new section by John Scott Keltie on 'industry and commerce'. Finally, the eighth edition of *Hints* (published in 1901) was divided into two volumes, including over two hundred pages of astronomical tables.[48]

To what extent did the changing form and content of late-nineteenth-century editions of *Hints to Travellers* reflect a change in attitude towards the scientific training of explorers? In his presidential address of 1876, Rutherford Alcock drew attention to the changing nature of geographical exploration: 'The progress of science and exact knowledge in every direction creates new exigencies. Distinction to the future

---

46. Galton, *The Art of Travel*, pp. 27, 58, 82, 84.
47. In view of my emphasis on the heterogeneity of *Hints to Travellers*, it is worth emphasizing that the anthropological section of the 1889 edition included contributions written from rather different points of view by E. B. Tylor, A. W. Franks, J. G. Frazer, Harry Johnston and Francis Galton.
48. Further editions appeared in 1906, 1921 and 1935.

explorer can only be secured therefore by a certain scientific training. It can no longer be won by mere descriptive details'.[49] During this period, the RGS inaugurated a series of specialist scientific lectures and established training courses in surveying for prospective explorers. Yet such innovations had a relatively limited impact; indeed, as Stoddart notes, the representation of scientists on the RGS Council actually declined after 1870.[50] Francis Galton's schemes to promote the scientific training of travellers met with considerable resistance; equally contentious were Douglas Freshfield's attempts to raise the Society's profile in geographical education and training. For example, Clements Markham (who served as either secretary or president of the RGS for a total of 37 years after 1863) portrayed both Galton and Freshfield as 'doctrinaires' seeking to divert the RGS from its true mission in the field of geographical exploration and scholarship.[51] Such differences are more than simply signs of personal acrimony among leading fellows of the RGS; they mark a striking lack of consensus over the nature and boundaries of geographical knowledge itself. While the Society projected itself as a centre of an expanding archive of geographical knowledge, the RGS was always less a centre than an arena, a site where competing visions of geographical knowledge were debated and institutionalized. The troubled history of *Hints to Travellers* provides one example of this process at work.

While the emphasis on scientific measurement and instrumentation was retained and indeed expanded in successive editions of *Hints to Travellers*, the remit of the manual was progressively widened to incorporate an ever wider variety of advice on outfit, organization and techniques of observation. In an introductory essay to the 1889 and 1893 editions, addressed to the 'would-be explorer', Douglas Freshfield articulated a philosophy markedly different from that falteringly expressed in 1854. Noting that social and technological change had considerably expanded the opportunities for travel, he candidly acknowledged that 'professional' scientific explorers would form a minority of readers, the vast majority being untrained travellers or tourists. While he reiterated the need for careful field observation, Freshfield put a new gloss on the changing contents of *Hints to Travellers*: 'the old conception of geography which looked on it as pure topography, as equivalent to surveying and map-construction, is fast

---

49. *Proceedings of the Royal Geographical Society*, 21 (1876–7), p. 23. Thanks to Max Jones for this reference.
50. D. Stoddart, *On Geography* (Oxford, 1986), pp. 66–7.
51. C. Markham, *The Royal Geographical Society* (Ms, c.1900, RGS Archives), pp. 173–5, 449–57.

dying out, and travellers, as well as geographers, are becoming familiar with the idea that their business is to furnish a picture of the earth's surface as it is, and in relation to its inhabitants'. This call to 'picture the earth's surface as it is' required more than a specialist's eye; indeed, as Freshfield pointedly remarked, 'there is no one more in need of warning and advice than the specialist or "scientist" who confines himself to one branch of knowledge'.[52]

Fields of Knowledge

The interpretation of *Hints to Travellers* offered in this chapter has significant implications for our understanding of the role of the Royal Geographical Society in the production of geographical knowledge during the nineteenth century. Manuals for the would-be geographer, as for the anthropologist, botanist, geologist or zoologist, might be regarded as attempts to reconcile different forms of knowledge – the philosophical and the practical, the theoretical and the empirical, the global and the local, the study and the field. There are also connections to be made between the proliferation of instructional literature for travellers and the institutionalization of European science: scientific societies promoted particular ways of conducting observation in the field, and this disciplinary effort played a part in the institutional development of metropolitan science. The Royal Geographical Society's project to co-ordinate the collection of geographical knowledge on a more centralized basis, in part through the publication of *Hints to Travellers*, may thus be interpreted as an attempt to establish itself as a centre for the production of geographical knowledge, a continuation of the Banksian project by other means.

On my reading, however, *Hints* appears less a coherent assertion of a geographical way of seeing, than an unstable attempt to resolve some fundamental dilemmas about the means and status of observation in the field. That there was no consensus on such questions was evident from the unsettled form in which *Hints to Travellers* first appeared; and the shifting contents of successive editions could not finally resolve them. Continuing differences on what and how to observe can be detected within its pages; while beyond them, the very notion of the field observer as a mere collector of information was constantly under-

52. D. Freshfield, 'Preliminary hints', in *Hints to Travellers* (1889), p. 4 and p. 2. This essay was excluded from subsequent editions, probably on the orders of Clements Markham: for his criticisms of Freshfield's editions, see Markham, *The Royal Geographical Society*, pp. 167–71.

mined. Observation could not so easily be detached from self-reflection: indeed, according to such philosophical travellers as Darwin and Humboldt, the progress of science depended precisely on the relation between observing and reflecting. As Darwin had advised the prospective geologist in the Admiralty *Manual*, 'the best method of obtaining this power of observation, is to acquire the habit of always seeking an explanation of every geological point met with; for one mental query leads to another . . . With his increasing knowledge he will daily find his powers of observation, his very vision, become deeper and clearer.'[53] To the explorer in search of a reputation, meanwhile, the picture of the traveller as merely the fact-gathering functionary of metropolitan science was anathema. Explorers like Livingstone, Burton and Speke fashioned themselves as the proud makers of geographical science rather than as its humble employees: indeed, that goes some way to explain their often difficult relationship with institutions like the RGS. 'Modern "hinters to travellers" direct the explorer and the missionary to eschew theory and opinion', complained Burton in 1860.

> We are told somewhat peremptorily that it is our duty to gather actualities not inferences – to see and not to think, in fact, to confine ourselves to transmitting the rough material collected by us, that it may be worked into shape by the professionally learned at home. But why may not the observer be allowed a voice concerning his own observations, if at least his mind be sane and his stock of collateral knowledge be respectable?[54]

53. Darwin, 'Geology', pp. 164–5.
54. R. F. Burton, *The Lake Regions of Central Africa*, vol. i (London, 1860), p. viii.

Chapter 4

Missionary of Science: David Livingstone and the Exploration of Africa

On 15 April 1874, an autopsy was conducted at the offices of the Royal Geographical Society in Savile Row by Sir William Fergusson, with two other doctors, Robert Moffat and John Kirk, in attendance. The remains of Dr David Livingstone had arrived earlier that morning at the Southampton docks, after a long journey begun eleven months before at Chitambo's village, near Lake Bangweulu. Definitive proof of the identity of the body was eventually located: a fracture to the bone of the left arm, which Livingstone had suffered as a result of his mauling by a lion in 1844, an event famously recorded for posterity in an illustration to his *Missionary Travels*.[1] For the next two days, Livingstone's body lay in state, surrounded by palms and lilies in the map room of the RGS, while final preparations were made for the funeral in Westminster Abbey. On 18 April, his coffin was borne into the Abbey by several of his closest associates, included Henry Morton Stanley, whose encounter with Livingstone had so astonished the geographical establishment two years earlier, John Kirk, Consul General at Zanzibar, who had been botanist and medical officer on Livingstone's Zambezi expedition, Horace Waller, the Anglican clergyman who was soon to edit Livingstone's *Last Journals*, and the hunter-travellers, William Oswell and William Webb. Among these mourners was Jacob Wainwright, a black African whose passage to London had been paid for by the Church Missionary Society, his presence designed to affirm the bond between Livingstone and black Africa (figure 4.1). In life, Livingstone had been an unreliable and sometimes disappointing hero; in his death, he had become something infinitely more noble. Each of

1. F. Cartwright, 'The left arm of David Livingstone', *King's College Hospital Gazette* (1979), pp. 136–7.

4.1 Jacob Wainwright posed beside Livingstone's coffin, 1874. Yale Divinity School Library, Record Group no. 72, Horace Waller Papers; used by permission.

the pall-bearers on that day in April 1874 were staking a claim upon his name as well as his body. While the effort to memorialize him was subsequently to take many forms – Livingstone the missionary, Livingstone the geographer, Livingstone the imperial pioneer – their combined effect was to consecrate his reputation as the patron saint of African exploration.

Contemporary accounts of Livingstone's funeral celebrated the story of the transport of his body to the coast of Africa by his two African servants, Chuma and Susi; according to the *Illustrated London News*, this feat was 'a grander and more touching memento of the great missionary explorer than any tomb'.[2] A body that had endured the ravages of disease and the discomfort of life in the bush for so long was now translated – the term seems quite appropriate in this context – by his 'faithfuls' to the coast of Africa, and thence to its final resting place. During a lifetime of African travel, Livingstone had battled with bouts of malarial fever, pneumonia, chronic dysentery, leech bites, foot ulcers and haemorrhoids, not to mention depression and paranoia.[3] But the

2. *Illustrated London News*, 25 April 1874, p. 383, quoted in T. Barringer, 'Fabricating Africa: Livingstone and the visual image, 1850–1874', in *David Livingstone and the Victorian Encounter with Africa* (National Portrait Gallery, 1996), pp. 171–200 (quote from p. 194).
3. T. Jeal, *Livingstone* (London, 1973), pp. 139–40, 310–16, 326.

myth-makers transformed these ailments into something more than physical signs of frailty; and his legendary will-power and physical endurance in the field provided them with ample material. Horace Waller, for example, was to describe Livingstone as a kind of human plough, a 'hard unflinching instrument, who had gone through lands and tribes and tough problems, and had cut furrows in a wilderness of human life which no one had heard of or dreamed of'.[4] The image of Livingstone as a maker of ways through the African landscape was an enduring one. In *Livingstone the Pathfinder* (1912), Basil Mathews described Livingstone as a 'hero-scout', and his body as a tool of conquest: 'as one who "marched breast forward" for thousands of miles through marsh and forest, over mountain pass and across river swamps, in loneliness and hunger, often with bleeding feet . . . Livingstone is the Coeur-de-Lion of our Great Crusade'.[5]

Livingstone's body was integral to his reputation as an explorer. It was represented in the field as being in perpetual motion, warring with the elements, scarred by the battle with Africa, yet resilient to the last. 'The mere animal pleasure of travelling in a wild unexplored country is very great', he once noted in his journal: 'When on lands of a couple of thousand feet elevation, brisk exercise gives health, circulates the blood, and the mind works well; the eye is clear, the step is firm, and a day's exercise always makes the evening's repose thoroughly enjoyable'.[6] At home, the figure of Livingstone the explorer was described as a summation of the manly virtues of empire: selfless dedication, heroic valour and scientific mastery. The picture presented in *Livingstone the Pathfinder* was resolutely physical: 'He revelled in the sheer joy of walking, that toned his body to splendid trim and strengthened his muscles till they were cable-like in their tireless strength.'[7] Yet celebrations of Livingstone's physique (reflecting in this case Edwardian preoccupations with physical fitness) were rarely expressed quite so nakedly. Contemporary images more usually associated the body of the explorer with a particular style of dress and posture. Livingstone was often portrayed, in portraits and statuary, wearing his so-called 'consular cap', with its tarnished gold band, a striking visual symbol of his authority and determination. The cap features prominently in visual images of his famous encounter with a lion, an event which took place thirteen years

4. H. Waller, 'The Universities Mission to Central Africa', *Quarterly Review*, 168 (1889), pp. 229–48 (quote from pp. 229–30).
5. B. Mathews, *Livingstone the Pathfinder*, 2nd edn (London, 1913), p. 214.
6. H. Johnston, 'Livingstone as an explorer', *Geographical Journal*, 41 (1913), pp. 423–46 (p. 443).
7. Mathews, *Livingstone the Pathfinder*, p. 6.

4.2 'The missionary's escape from the lion' from David Livingstone's *Missionary Travels and Researches in South Africa* (1857).

before he was appointed a roving consul in central Africa (figure 4.2). While it had no direct connection with his consular appointment, Livingstone was particularly attached to his cap: as one of his admirers later recalled, 'it had the curious fascination for him that some articles of clothing seem to exercise on their owners, and grew to be part of his personality'.[8] Indeed, so much was it 'part of his personality' that the cap has since become something of a fetish, treasured by its possessors and displayed to the public as a relic of an age of heroic exploration.[9] In conjunction with his Bible and sextant, which also figure prominently in many portraits and statues, the cap became a veritable talisman for his followers. These objects served an iconic function, symbolizing that potent combination of politics, religion and science which composed the Livingstone myth.

The effort to keep the Livingstone myth alive was to prove remarkably successful. At a meeting of the RGS in March 1913 to celebrate the centenary of his birth, Harry Johnston described Livingstone as a 'martyr to that form of religion which we call science'.[10] (If this appears to anticipate Conrad's lament for the martyred explorer, it may also be

8.   A. Z. Fraser, *Livingstone and Newstead* (London, 1913), p. 89. One biographer suggests that its design followed that of caps worn by British naval officers: J. Macnair, *Livingstone the Liberator* (London, 1940), pp. 370–2.
9.   See F. Driver, 'Old hat, I presume? The history of a fetish', *History Workshop Journal*, 41 (1996), pp. 230–34.
10.   Johnston, 'Livingstone as an explorer', p. 445.

noted that the terms Geography Militant and Geography Triumphant were drawn from the idea of the Church Militant and the Church Triumphant, as in the Book of Common Prayer). Others made similar claims about many of Livingstone's predecessors in the field of African exploration, such as Mungo Park and Thomas Bowdich; indeed, in the year of Livingstone's funeral, the French geographer Henri Duveyrier published an extraordinary map of African necrology, littered with the names of Europeans who had died exploring the continent. But none was to hold as eminent a position in the rolls of African martyrology than Livingstone himself.[11] The figure of martyrdom required exploration to be conceived of as something more than worldly ambition: and its appropriation by agnostics such as Johnston is particularly telling, as it indicated that scientific labour could be described in the language of the sacred. Livingstone's burial in the Abbey in 1874 confirmed his place in the pantheon of national heroes: eight years later, he would be joined by Charles Darwin, whose interment in the Abbey has been interpreted as marking the final moment of the incorporation of a new scientific priesthood within the establishment.[12] On the day of Livingstone's own funeral, while the attention of the geographical community was focused on the proceedings inside the Abbey, a large section of the crowd outside moved on to the Embankment, a few hundred yards away, to witness another 'miracle of science': the confirmation of scientific predictions (made weeks earlier) that the Thames would rise to a great height. Late-Victorian free-thinkers proclaimed this as a vindication of the authority of science over superstition, a sign of the movement in public opinion towards a rational, secular view of the world.[13] Yet the events within the Abbey, and their legacy, stand as a reminder that science too had its martyrs and myths.

Harry Johnston's portrait of Livingstone as a 'martyr to that form of religion which we call science' was one of many attempts to appropriate the explorer's legacy. Just as his followers disagreed over the best way

11.   H. Duveyrier, 'L'Afrique nécrologique', *Bulletin de la Société de Géographie de Paris*, 6th series, 8 (1874), pp. 561–644 (thanks to Mike Heffernan for this reference). See also W. Reade, 'African martyrology', *Belgravia*, 1 (1867), 46–54.
12.   For a compelling account of the significance of Darwin's burial in the Abbey, see J. Moore, 'Charles Darwin lies in Westminster Abbey', *Biological Journal of the Linnean Society*, 17 (1982), 97–113.
13.   The story is told in Moncure Conway's memoirs, published thirty years later, although the date of Livingstone's funeral is wrongly identified: M. D. Conway, *Autobiography, Memoirs and Experiences*, vol. ii (London, 1904), p. 331. And 1874 was also the year of John Tyndall's famous 'Belfast Address' to the British Association, in which he attacked metaphysical dogma in the name of scientific materialism: see D. Livingstone, 'Darwinism and Calvinism: the Belfast-Princeton connection', *Isis*, 83 (1992), pp. 408–28.

to continue Livingstone's work, so too have historians continued to argue right up to the present day over whether Livingstone was really a missionary, really a geographer or really an imperial pioneer. The enduring power of the Livingstone myth surely lay precisely in the fact that it appealed simultaneously to all these different interests. If we are to understand what Livingstone's life and work meant to the Victorians, therefore, we need to consider more carefully the various contexts in which his African projects took shape. This requires a broader conception of the culture of exploration than that hitherto provided by historians of geography. In particular, we need to know more about the different networks of interest that sustained Livingstone both in his life and after his death.[14] Each of these networks was represented by one of the elements in the iconography of the Bible, the sextant and the 'consular cap': the missionary and anti-slavery lobby, the Royal Geographical Society and the organs of the imperial state.

Missionaries and Philanthropists

David Livingstone's name was and still is closely associated with the missionary effort in Africa. His portrait took pride of place in the London Missionary Society's Board Room in Westminster; and, according to its president (speaking in 1953) 'every Director of the Society on entering the room finds his eyes focused upon that portrait'.[15] Although Livingstone's formal relationship with the LMS came to an end in 1857, his name was subsequently to be associated with many other missionary organizations, most notably the Universities Mission to Central Africa (UMCA), whose foundation owed much to his inspiration. If Livingstone provided a symbol for pioneering missionary endeavour in Africa, this owed less to his own success in converting Africans than to his energy in promoting the idea of a moral mission for the British in Africa. In particular, his well-publicized assaults on the institution of slavery found ready support within the liberal intelligentsia.

14. For an invaluable account of the institutional and intellectual contexts in which African matters were debated during the second half of the nineteenth century, see D. Helly, '"Informed" opinion on Tropical Africa in Great Britain, 1860–1890', *African Affairs*, 68 (1969), pp. 195–217. See also P. Curtin, *The Image of Africa: British Ideas and Action, 1780–1850* (London, 1965); H. A. C. Cairns, *Prelude to Imperialism: British Reactions to Central African Society, 1840–1890* (London, 1965); R. Rotberg (ed.), *Africa and Its Explorers* (Cambridge, 1970); R. C. Bridges, 'Europeans and East Africans in the age of exploration', *Geographical Journal*, 139 (1973), pp. 220–32.
15. *Geographical Journal*, 120 (1954), p. 18.

Livingstone sometimes described geographical exploration as a means rather than an end in itself. As he famously remarked in the closing pages of his best-selling work, *Missionary Travels* (1857), 'I view the end of the geographical feat as the beginning of the missionary enterprise.' Such remarks may easily be misinterpreted if they are read out of context. Livingstone himself had a remarkably broad conception of the 'missionary enterprise', as becomes clear from the sentence which follows: 'I take the latter term in its most extended signification, and include every effort made for the amelioration of our race; the promotion of all those means by which God in His providence is working, and bringing all His dealings with man to a glorious consummation'.[16] In this sense, Livingstone argued, scientists, soldiers and merchants were active missionaries, working for the same end: the moral and spiritual elevation of mankind. In so far as they affected his work as an explorer, Livingstone's spiritual beliefs were in fact distinctly malleable. It was in fact the very plasticity of Livingstone's religious affiliations that enabled his work to be taken up by such a wide range of missionary and philanthropic organizations.

To understand the significance of Livingstone's reputation among missionaries and philanthropists, it is important to consider the character and extent of the networks through which they operated in the mid-Victorian period. The largely Congregationalist London Missionary Society, for example, had been founded in 1795, and by the time Livingstone joined (in 1838) it had a world-wide network of missions across the globe, including southern Africa. The UMCA was by contrast an Anglican organization, established in response to Livingstone's 1857 appeal to the young men of Cambridge.[17] Although the failure of its first attempt to found a mission at Magomero gave rise to considerable controversy at home, the Universities Mission was later to establish a network of stations in East Africa from its base in Zanzibar. The UMCA's house journal *Central Africa*, which was distributed to all its supporters, carried a map of East central Africa on its covers showing the 'field' of the Universities mission, as if it were an imperial possession. Similar journals were published by the much larger Church Missionary Society, which had long established missions in other parts of Africa.

Alongside the missionary societies, other influential philanthropic organizations gave Livingstone their vocal support. The origins of Livingstone's connection with the anti-slavery movement is usually

16. D. Livingstone, *Missionary Travels* (London, 1857), pp. 673–4.
17. P. Elston, 'Livingstone and the Anglican Church', in B. Pachai (ed.), *Livingstone, Man of Africa* (London, 1973), pp. 61–85.

traced by his biographers to his attendance, on 1 June 1840, at a particularly momentous anti-slavery meeting at Exeter Hall, in the Strand. Here the anti-slavery campaigner Thomas Fowell Buxton preached the gospel of commerce and Christianity as the only remedy for the extinction of the African slave trade. Buxton was closely associated with the Society for the Extinction of the Slave Trade and the African Civilisation Society, which promoted the ill-fated Niger Expedition of 1841–2.[18] Exeter Hall was a regular venue for some of the most influential philanthropic societies of the day, and their concerns made even those of the imperial government seem parochial. As one visitor put it, the voice of Exeter Hall was 'heard all over the earth': 'Exeter Hall has a fame. Since its erection, about 1831, no other place in the world has attracted such crowds of social renovators, moral philosophers, philanthropists and Christians. Of late years, almost every great measure for the amelioration of the condition of the human family has had there its inception, its progress and its triumph.'[19]

Of all the organizations associated with Exeter Hall, two took a particular interest in the exploration of Africa and its moral implications: the Aborigines Protection Society (founded in 1837) and the British and Foreign Anti-Slavery Society (founded in 1839). The interest of the former lay in protecting the welfare of indigenous peoples beyond Europe, while the latter campaigned against the evils of slavery. Both Societies built on more than a generation of campaigns against the slave trade, and both co-ordinated world-wide networks of information, their journals (the *Colonial Intelligencer and Aborigines' Friend* and the *Anti-Slavery Reporter*) regularly detailing the latest developments in every continent. (The high moral tone of such movements provided sceptics with ample ammunition. While Dickens's picture of 'telescopic philanthropy' in *Bleak House* is probably the most famous instance of satirical commentary, it was only an example of a much wider vein of criticism. In 1844, for example, a writer for *Punch* caustically noted that 'with many of the worthy people of Exeter Hall, distance is essential to love.')[20] Like Livingstone, these societies portrayed the values of liberty, humanity and justice as sacred gifts, to be bestowed by the British on the world at large. The Anti-Slavery Society represented its mission as an appeal to the fraternity of the human family; in

18. H. Temperley, *White Dreams, Black Africa: The Anti-Slavery Expedition to the River Niger, 1841–2* (New Haven, Conn., 1991).
19. W. McDonnell, *Exeter Hall: A Theological Romance*, 10th edn (Boston, 1885), p. 3. 'Exeter Hall' had both a physical and a symbolic existence; the term referred both to a meeting hall near the Strand and to a broader movement of philanthropic concern.
20. 'Exeter Hall Pets', *Punch*, 6 (1844), p. 240.

the words of its motto (placed in the mouth of the subjugated slave), 'Am I not a man and a brother?' The Aborigines Protection Society, meanwhile, extended the empire of paternalism still further: its founding aim was 'to assist in protecting the defenceless and promoting the advancement of uncivilised tribes'.[21]

The philanthropists of Exeter Hall could be remarkably critical of some aspects of European expansion, especially where slaves, guns and alcohol were concerned. They were to play a particularly prominent role in the criticisms of Henry Morton Stanley's methods of exploration in central Africa (see below, chapter 6). Yet their perspectives were inevitably bound by the preconceptions of the day. While the liberals of Exeter Hall insisted on the indivisibility of the 'human family' (in opposition to the more virulent strains of racial theory), they nevertheless drew on an established stock of racial stereotypes, often drawing unfavourable contrasts between the characters of the Negro, the Arab and the European. Moreover, the quest for the abolition of slavery was not entirely disinterested; indeed it was to offer one of the most important moral justifications for the late-nineteenth-century scramble for Africa. 'Among colonial nations', David Davis has argued, 'Britain led the way in assimilating anti-slavery to an imperial self-image, linking humanitarianism in the most subtle ways to strategic and commercial interests'.[22] Whether or not this charge can be laid at the door of the early Victorian philanthropists, it is clear that the slogan of 'legitimate commerce' popularized by Exeter Hall in the 1830s was to be plagiarised by the advocates of the new imperialism in the 1880s. There were some, even at the time, who were willing to expose this as sham philanthropy. The Scottish explorer Joseph Thomson once dismissed 'legitimate commerce' as 'magic words which give such an attractive glamour to whatever can creep under their shelter, [obscuring] the most shameful and criminal transactions'.[23] What had begun as a catch-all solution to the problem of the slave trade ended as a justification for colonial exploitation: free trade, but on European terms.

One of the most influential figures within late-Victorian missionary and anti-slavery circles was Horace Waller, a lay missionary for the

---

21. Aborigines Protection Society, *First Annual Report* (London, 1838), p. 3. See also H. Temperley, *British Anti-Slavery* (Columbia, 1972), pp. 65–6; A. M. and E. H. Kass, *Perfecting the World: The Life and Times of Dr Thomas Hodgkin, 1798–1866* (Orlando, 1988), pp. 270–1.
22. D. B. Davis, *Slavery and Human Progress* (Oxford, 1984), p. 285. See also D. Helly, *Livingstone's Legacy: Horace Waller and Victorian Myth-making* (Athens, Ohio, 1987), pp. 1–16, 45–8.
23. J. Thomson, 'The results of European intercourse with the African', *Contemporary Review* (March 1890), p. 345.

UMCA who first met Livingstone at the mouth of the Zambezi in 1861. Through his role in a number of organizations, notably the Anti-Slavery Society (whose committee he joined in 1870) and the Royal Geographical Society itself, Waller became an active participant in debates over British involvement in East and central Africa during the last third of the nineteenth century. Moreover, his close relationship with the Zanzibar Consul John Kirk gave him a crucial entrée into the heart of the political establishment. In his capacity as the editor of Livingstone's *Last Journals* for the publisher John Murray, Waller carefully composed a potent image of Livingstone as a saintly figure and a worthy emblem of British imperial enterprise in Africa. As Dorothy Helly has shown in a detailed study of the genesis of the *Last Journals*, Waller edited out those aspects of Livingstone's character which were increasingly evident in his journals and letters during his last years, including frustrated diatribes against institutions and individuals in England, and numerous complaints about his servants.[24] His portrait of the moment of Livingstone's death, in a kneeling posture represented as an act of prayer, was an extraordinarily powerful image, reproduced in countless biographies ever since.

Horace Waller's extensive network of contacts, as well as his remarkable enthusiasm for both writing and intrigue, tells us much about the wider context in which African exploration was promoted during the 1860s and 1870s. Where African affairs were concerned, geographical concerns melted into philanthropic ones; and anti-slavery campaigns could find their way into the very heart of Whitehall. Waller's personal diaries for the mid-1870s, when he was installed as Rector at Twywell, Northamptonshire, provides a glimpse of the close relations between scientific, philanthropic and political interests in Africa.[25] In January 1875 we find Waller making time within his normal round of pastoral duties to attend an anti-slavery meeting in the City of London, dine with Edmund Sturge, John Kirk and Bartle Frere, attend meetings at the Royal Geographical Society, correspond with General Gordon, visit the Zoological Gardens in Regent's Park, shoot pheasant with William Webb at Newstead Abbey, address the prestigious Society of Arts on progress in East Africa and mull over the first reviews of his edition of Livingstone's *Last Journals*. Such sources provide striking evidence of the intersections between scientific, political and philanthropic networks with an interest in African exploration.

24. Helly, *Livingstone's Legacy.*
25. Waller's diaries for 1875 and 1876 are held at the Yale University Divinity School, New Haven, USA.

Geographers

If Livingstone's fame as an African explorer was sustained by a constellation of missionary, scientific and political interests, there was one institution above all others which came to be associated with his travels – the Royal Geographical Society. The revival of the Society's fortunes during the 1850s and 1860s owed much to Roderick Murchison's skill in exploiting public interest in controversies over African exploration generally, and above all in the search for the sources of the Nile (see above, chapter 2). In this context, the Society's influence on the conduct of expeditions is perhaps less significant than its role in turning African exploration into something of a national obsession. Under Murchison's presidency, the RGS developed into one of the most fashionable scientific societies in London, known especially for its 'African nights'. Leading Fellows exercised considerable influence in the corridors of power, largely through informal channels; it was Murchison, for example, who was to secure David Livingstone's consular appointments in central Africa, as well as John Kirk's in Zanzibar (see below). Livingstone was awarded a prize by the RGS for his discovery of Lake Ngami in 1849, and in 1854 his journey across southern Africa was hailed by Murchison as nothing less than 'the greatest triumph in geographical research which has been effected in our times'.[26] In 1857, the relationship between the two men was marked by a public exchange of gifts: Livingstone received the Society's Gold Medal and, soon after, dedicated his best-selling *Missionary Travels* to Murchison. If Livingstone's reputation was in no small measure dependent on Murchison's influence, the investment paid ample dividends for the RGS. This bargain was not without its critics: in a pamphlet published in the year of Livingstone's funeral, William Cooley poured scorn on the official rhetoric of selfless philanthropy: 'He took the present gains derivable from public patronage; the RGS the steady income of popularity.'[27]

The RGS claimed a long-standing interest in the exploration of Africa; indeed, through its connection with the African Association, which it absorbed in 1831, this history was routinely traced by contemporary historians of geography back to the late eighteenth century. Whereas the most well-known expeditions before the 1840s had taken place in West and South Africa (as represented in the travels of Mungo Park and William Burchell, for example), the focus of attention during the next two decades was to be East and central Africa. The quest for

26. *The Times*, 8 August 1854, cited in Jeal, *Livingstone*, p. 158.
27. W. D. Cooley, *Dr Livingstone and the RGS* (London, 1874), p. 20.

the Nile sources preoccupied scholars and explorers alike, and the RGS showered honours upon those whose journeys threw new light on the question, including Charles Beke (1845), Richard Burton (1859), John Hanning Speke (1861), James Grant (1864) and Samuel Baker (1865). The claims of these explorers routinely exceeded the evidence they supplied. For example, having traversed the north-western fringes of Lake Victoria with Grant in 1860–3, Speke triumphantly cabled London from Khartoum to declare that 'The Nile is settled.'[28] The two men received a hero's welcome in London, and a year later they were pictured in Henry Wyndham Phillips's remarkable portrait exhibited in the Royal Academy (figure 1.5). Phillips's portrait was only one of many efforts to ennoble the art of African exploration, here presented as an endeavour involving a range of faculties – intellectual powers as well as physical strength, creative imagination as well as discipline. Yet such images ought not to be viewed simply as straightforward 'reflections' of contemporary (British) assumptions about African exploration.[29] Phillips's portrait, as I argued in chapter 1, needs to be seen in the context of contemporary disputes over Speke's claim to have settled the question of the Nile sources. The bitterness of such disputes provides some indication of the profound tensions which surrounded claims to authority in the field of exploration.

The grand meeting organized by the RGS at Burlington House to celebrate the return of Speke and Grant in 1863 provided one indication of the Society's investment in the business of African exploration. The rendering of this event in the *Illustrated London News* (figure 4.3) once more depicted the two explorers standing either side of an African youth, in determined yet impassive mood, their erect posture contrasting markedly with the rapture of the handerkerchief-waving crowd. Behind them, alongside the portraits of what appear to be military and royal figures, is part of a huge map of Africa. Such spectacular cartographic displays were a common feature of public meetings concerned with Africa, whether they were designed to promote missionary activity, to debate the location of rivers or lakes or to contemplate imperial expansion. Maps of the continent provided the backdrop for some of the most famous geographical gatherings during this period, including those at the British Association's annual meetings and at the Royal

28. A. Maitland, *Speke* (London, 1971), p. 177. For a discussion of Speke's writings, see T. Youngs, *Travellers in Africa: British Travelogues, 1850–1900* (Manchester, 1994), pp. 84–93.
29. On visual depictions of African exploration and travel, see especially Barringer, 'Fabricating Africa'; M. Stevenson (ed.), *Thomas Baines: An Artist in the Service of Science in Southern Africa* (exhibition catalogue, London, 1999).

4.3 Reception for Speke and Grant organized by the Royal Geographical Society at Burlington House, 22 June 1863 (*Illustrated London News*, 4 July 1863).

Geographical Society itself. Meanwhile popular exhibitions intended to celebrate British achievements in Africa were festooned with maps of all kinds, showing the progress of European knowledge of the continent and the extent of British influence (see chapter 7). The names of British explorers and their sponsors were inscribed on the map of Africa, marking the lakes, mountains and settlements which they located. Livingstone's own baptism of the Victoria Falls, which he first saw in November 1855, is perhaps the most obvious example; seven years later, Speke named the northerly outlet from Lake Victoria 'Ripon Falls', after the RGS President. (Roderick Murchison himself had five geographical features in Africa named after him, and no less than twenty-three world-wide.)[30] Each explorer into the African interior colonized a new bit of territory, opening it up for others to follow. The process was graphically illustrated in Winwood Reade's 'Map of African Literature' published in 1873, the year of Livingstone's death, which showed the white spaces of the continent being gradually colo-

30. R. Stafford, *Scientist of Empire: Sir Roderick Murchison, Scientific Exploration and Victorian Imperialism* (Cambridge, 1989), pp. 28–9.

nized by the names of innumerable European explorers, Livingstone's being the most prominent of all (see figure 5.3).[31]

Contemporary tributes to Livingstone's accomplishments as a geographer, especially on his return from Africa in 1856, were unrestrained: 'I say that what this man has done is unprecedented', claimed the Astronomer Royal. 'You could go to any point across the entire Continent along Livingstone's track and feel certain of your position'.[32] From the perspective of the twenty-first century, however, it is Livingstone's contribution to the popularization of an imaginative vision of Africa which attracts most attention. During the second half of the nineteenth century, images of the map of Africa found expression in a wide variety of objects and practices, from commodity advertising to the school room. As a young child in the 1860s, Augusta Fraser (whose family were close associates of Livingstone) found Sir Roderick Murchison's quizzes on the geography of Africa 'deliciously easy, a fringe of coast towns, and a few very sparsely scattered names throughout the vast interior, being at that time all that was required'. Fifty years later, however, she noted somewhat ruefully that the map had become much more 'crowded and complicated'.[33] African geography was lived as well as learned: the journeys of African explorers like Livingstone could be re-enacted at home, with the help of a little imagination. A year after his celebrated meeting with Livingstone in 1871, Henry Morton Stanley was taking a leading part in an African Exploring Expedition with the help of five children at Newstead Abbey, imagining the local woods to be African forest and the local inhabitants to be hostile tribes.[34] The power of such imagined geographies endured. Having devoted the rest of his adult life to African exploration, Stanley spent his last years busily re-creating his own imagined geography of the 'Dark Continent' in the garden of a mock-Tudor mansion at Furze Hill, in Surrey, where he retired in 1899. Here a small lake was transformed into 'Stanley Pool', the pine trees into the 'Ituri forest' and, somewhat incongruously, a mere stream into the 'Congo'.[35] Stanley's labours at Furze Hill, as we shall see in chapter 6, were the end-product of a long history of material and imaginative labour, as much at 'home' as in the 'field'.

31. W. Reade, *The African Sketch-Book* (London, 1873). The map bears a striking resemblance to Duveyrier's map of African necrology published a year later: see note 11 above.
32. Macnair, *Livingstone the Liberator*, p. 193.
33. Fraser, *Livingstone and Newstead*, p. 140.
34. Fraser, *Livingstone and Newstead*, p. 198.
35. D. Stanley (ed.), *The Autobiography of Henry M. Stanley* (London, 1909).

Many of the most celebrated African explorers of the second half of the nineteenth century portrayed geography as a manly science, dedicated to the mastery of the earth; the purpose of their expeditions into Africa was ultimately to establish order in place of chaos. In their hands, the map became as much an instrument of authority as the gun; and both the terrain and its inhabitants were reduced to obstacles to be overcome. As Samuel Baker put it on his return from his expedition to the Southern Sudan in 1873, 'All obstacles have been surmounted. All enemies have been subdued – and the slavers who had the audacity to attack the troops have been crushed. The slave trade of the White Nile has been suppressed – and the country annexed so that Egypt extends to the equator.'[36] While the methods of a Baker or a Stanley undoubtedly differed from those of Livingstone, they used his crusade against slavery to claim a degree of moral legitimacy for their quasi-military campaigns. Like many African explorers of his generation, Stanley consistently portrayed his work as putting into effect what Livingstone had only dreamed of: the European conquest of Africa by one means or another. Although Livingstone himself did not live to see the rapid territorial expansion of the British Empire in Africa, he did bequeath it a sense of mission, which was subsequently to be exploited for imperial ends. To make this point is not necessarily to argue that Livingstone or indeed African explorers as a whole actually brought imperial rule into being; rather, their writings helped to produce an image of Africa as a field for European endeavour, and the myths which surrounded them – above all the image of Livingstone as a humanitarian pioneer – provided a potent means of justifying subsequent imperial adventures.[37]

It is in this sense that the mid-Victorian explorers can be seen as the pioneers and (in Livingstone's case) the spiritual forefathers of the new imperialism in Africa. The fact that explorers like Livingstone, Burton and Baker received financial support and official authority from the British government or its surrogates provides only one measure of their significance in the history of empire-making; more significant, perhaps, is their role in the dissemination of myths and fantasies about the exploration of Africa. The rhetoric of 'darkest Africa' was put in place well before the late nineteenth century; Stanley's *In Darkest Africa* (1890) marked its high-point, not its origin. As Brantlinger puts it,

---

36. R. O. Collins, 'Samuel White Baker', in Rotberg, *Africa and Its Explorers*, pp. 141–173 [p. 170].
37. R. Bridges, 'The historical role of British explorers in East Africa', *Terrae Incognitae*, 14 (1982), pp. 1–21; Bridges, 'Europeans and East Africans'.

'Africa grew "dark" as Victorian explorers, missionaries and scientists flooded it with light.'[38] Explorers differed over the extent to which the darkness could be lifted; the writings of Richard Burton, for example, provide a marked contrast with those like Livingstone or Speke, who expressed optimism about the prospects for the regeneration of Africa. But for Livingstone himself, central and East Africa was a landscape above all to be cultivated. And others were ready to follow him into the field.

Politicians

On the face of George Gilbert Scott's new buildings for the Colonial Office in Whitehall, completed in 1875, a year after Livingstone's funeral, there are a number of small busts and figures designed by the sculptors Armstead and Philip. On the ground floor, five allegorical figures represent the continents of Europe, Asia, Africa, America and Australasia, while on the first floor, in the window soffits just visible from the street, there are a number of small busts, including Captain Cook, Sir John Franklin, William Wilberforce and David Livingstone.[39] That these images were deemed suitable adornments for such an august office of state tells us much about late-Victorian efforts to promote the humanitarian face of empire-building. Livingstone in many ways embodied the virtues of the other figures; he was the scientific explorer, heroic adventurer and anti-slavery campaigner combined. It is true that his relationship with government departments was never particularly close, and he relied heavily on intermediaries, such as Roderick Murchison and John Kirk, to make his case in the corridors of power. None the less, his name and what it represented came to be closely linked with British imperial designs in Africa.

The history of government policy towards British involvement in Africa – and the character of the 'official mind' that was responsible for directing it – has long been the subject of debate among historians.[40] The role of explorers in relation to this history has been somewhat obscured by the fairly narrow definition of the 'official mind' employed

---

38. P. Brantlinger, 'Victorians and Africans: the genealogy of the myth of the Dark Continent', *Critical Inquiry*, 12 (1985), p. 166.
39. M. H. Port, *Imperial London: Civil Government Building in London, 1851–1915* (New Haven, Conn., 1995), pp. 258–9.
40. The classic work is R. Robinson and J. Gallagher, *Africa and the Victorians: The Official Mind of Imperialism* (London, 1961).

in the most influential work on the subject. The 'imperial mind' was in fact composed of many compartments, including not only the Foreign and Colonial Offices, but also the India Office and other branches of the imperial state. Furthermore, as Roy Bridges has pointed out, it is also necessary to consider a still broader constellation of interests, which constituted what Bridges calls the 'unofficial mind' of imperialism.[41] In this context, the composition of the RGS, and its informal networks of patronage, is of particular relevance: many of its leading Fellows belonged to the growing service class, and took a direct interest in the management of British overseas interests. For them, as much as for the Foreign Office, the formal acquisition of territory was only one way through which British interests in Africa could be secured; indeed it was frequently a last resort, designed to thwart the ambitions of other European powers or crush some immediate military or political threat. As long as traditional means of influence were sufficient to secure British interests abroad, a policy summed up in a famous phrase as 'the imperialism of free trade', the formal establishment of colonies was frequently deemed unnecessary. The power of the mid-Victorian empire cannot therefore be judged merely by the amount of land placed under formal colonial rule; this would be, in an equally famous phrase, 'rather like judging the size and character of icebergs solely from the parts above the water-line'.[42]

Broadly speaking, it was gentlemanly capitalism that set the dominant tone of British expansionism during the middle decades of the nineteenth century. The Victorian re-invention of the culture of the gentleman was visible in the changing character of its leading institutions – Parliament, the City of London and the public schools – as well as in more popular texts devoted to the cult of respectability. Expansion overseas, it has recently been suggested, was 'the export version of the gentlemanly order'.[43] The huge growth in international trade and the vital contribution of the City of London to British wealth, and the service sector more generally, provided direction to British policy abroad, leading to selective expansion where conditions for trade were promising. While Livingstone's dreams for central and East Africa found comparatively little commercial support during his lifetime, the Foreign Office was quick to identify commercial and stra-

41. Bridges, 'The historical role of British explorers in East Africa', pp. 18–21. See also Helly, '"Informed" opinion on Tropical Africa'.
42. J. Gallagher and R. Robinson, 'The imperialism of free trade', *Economic History Review*, 6 (1953), p. 1.
43. P. J. Cain and A. G. Hopkins, *British Imperialism: Innovation and Expansion, 1688–1914* (London, 1993), p. 34.

tegic advantages in having a political presence in Zanzibar, imposing an anti-slave trade treaty in 1845 and using military force to shore up its regime in 1859. The appointment of John Kirk as Vice-Consul there in 1866, and Consul-General in 1873, marked a new phase in the expansion of British interests in the region. Kirk's close relationship with Livingstone dated from his appointment as 'economic botanist' to the Zambezi expedition in 1858. He was subsequently to be a key point of contact for all those missionaries, explorers, traders and administrators who saw themselves as following in Livingstone's footsteps in East Africa.

It was through his connections at the Royal Geographical Society that Livingstone first came to the attention of the Foreign Office. Roderick Murchison was Livingstone's prime advocate, publicizing his expeditions, securing a publisher for his *Missionary Travels* (John Murray, also responsible for the *Journal* of the RGS) and promoting his cause in Whitehall. Well before his triumphal return to Britain from his trans-African expedition in December 1856, Livingstone had entered into negotiations with Murchison concerning a further African expedition. Ever ready to exploit the publicity that had already been generated by Livingstone's discoveries, Murchison is said to have interrupted his Christmas holiday with Palmerston to promote Livingstone's cause. He approached Lord Clarendon, the Foreign Secretary, pressing the case for official support, waxing lyrical about the 'paradise of wealth' (both mineral and agricultural) waiting to be exploited on the Upper Zambezi, and going so far as to suggest that the British might seek to acquire the territory from the Portuguese. Livingstone himself encouraged these clandestine moves, in the hope that a government appointment would free him from financial dependence on the LMS. (There were recent precedents for such official support; in 1856, Burton and Speke had begun their famous expedition to the lakes of East Africa, sponsored by both the RGS and the Foreign Office.) By May 1857 the deal brokered by Murchison had taken shape: Livingstone was to be appointed, at an annual salary of £500, as a 'roving consul' in an area which included Mozambique and a large expanse of territory to the west. On 11 December 1857 the House of Commons were told of Livingstone's plans to lead a government-sponsored expedition to the Zambezi; the following day Livingstone was Palmerston's guest of honour at 10 Downing Street.

Murchison's lobbying secured the full co-operation of the Foreign Office and the Admiralty in preparations for the Zambezi expedition, which set sail from Birkenhead in March 1858. Livingstone's instructions to his officers give a clear indication of his hopes for the future role of the British in the whole of central and East Africa. The opening paragraph is worth quoting at length, for it encapsulates the spirit of so many contemporary expeditions to Africa:

> The main object of the Expedition . . . is to extend the knowledge already attained of the geography and mineral and agricultural resources of Eastern and Central Africa, to improve our acquaintance with the inhabitants, and to engage them to apply their energies to industrial pursuits and to the cultivation of their lands with a view to the production of raw material to be exported to England in return for British manufactures; and it may be hoped that by encouraging the natives to occupy themselves in the development of the resources of their country a considerable advance may be made towards the extinction of the slave trade, and the natives will not be long in discovering that the former will eventually become a more certain source of profit than the latter.[44]

Information, resources, cultivation and commerce: these were the watchwords of Livingstone's mission, and they won official sanction at the highest level. While the Foreign Office remained wary of more ambitious schemes involving the colonization of land by British settlers, much to Livingstone's disappointment,[45] it found nothing exceptionable in his moralizing language. Habits of industry were to be cultivated, free labour was to replace slavery, the ethos of private property was to be promoted, and the 'moral influence' of 'a well regulated and orderly household of Europeans' was to be encouraged. 'We come among them', Livingstone told his colleagues, 'as members of a superior race and servants of a Government that desires to elevate the more degraded portions of the human family.' Such a formula, symptomatic of the mid-Victorian accommodation between racism and humanitarianism, speaks volumes about the confidence and ambition of the civilizing mission. It was not (yet) a strictly imperial mission; but the time for empire-building was not far off.

Memorializing Livingstone

Few of Livingstone's biographers have resisted the temptation to present Livingstone as a martyr, though they have differed over the cause he died for, some opting for the civilizing mission, others for 'com-

---

44.   R. Coupland, *Kirk on the Zambesi: A Chapter of African History* (Oxford, 1928), p. 103.
45.   On official attitudes towards Livingstone's subsequent and final expedition, see R. Bridges, 'The sponsorship and financing of Livingstone's last journey', *African Historical Studies*, 1 (1968), pp. 79–104.

merce and Christianity', and still others for what Harry Johnston referred to as 'that form of religion which we call science'.[46] The image we are usually given of Livingstone in his last years is that of a lone wanderer seeking after truth and justice, his ambitious plans for the colonization of Central Africa officially spurned, his arduous search for the sources of the Nile constantly frustrated. In the course of the next three decades, however, the British colonization of large parts of Africa was to become a reality. In this respect, it is tempting to regard Livingstone's meeting with Stanley at Ujiji in 1871 as a significant moment of transition. For many of his critics, as we shall see in chapter 6, Stanley symbolized the coming of a new era of 'exploration by warfare'. Where Livingstone had brought light, they argued, Stanley brought corruption; as the *Anti-Slavery Reporter* put it, 'he, in fact, will act as a dark shadow to throw up the brightness of Livingstone's fame'.[47] The prediction was not wide of the mark. Livingstone's posthumous reputation was to remain virtually untarnished by the controversies surrounding Stanley's own empire-making expeditions; indeed, if anything, it was enhanced by them. It was as though the cruel realities of empire could be redeemed simply, and only, by an image: the martyrdom of the explorer.

On 23 October 1953, one hundred years after the commencement of Livingstone's most celebrated African journey, a small group of dignitaries gathered to unveil a statue dedicated to his memory in London (figure 4.4). Perhaps inevitably, the site chosen was the Royal Geographical Society's modern headquarters at 1 Kensington Gore, a few yards from the Royal Albert Hall. The guest of honour was Oliver Lyttelton, Churchill's controversial Colonial Secretary; he was joined by Livingstone's grandson (representing the Livingstone Memorial Trust at Blantyre), the General Secretary of the London Missionary Society and the President of the RGS. Reading the report of this event published in the *Geographical Journal*, one gets a distinct sense of *déjà vu*.[48] It is as though fifty years of Livingstone memorials – marking anniversaries of his birth, his first missionary journey, his writings and his death – have been sculpted into one moment, incorporating all the various aspects of his heroic reputation as a geographer, a missionary and a pioneer of empire. Yet in some ways 1953 was a singularly ill-chosen moment to memorialize the man who, in the words of the Colonial Secretary, had 'unlocked the door of the African continent and opened a new page in its history'. For, just as Lyttelton was recalling Lord

46. Johnston, 'Livingstone as an explorer', p. 445.
47. *Anti-Slavery Reporter*, November 1878, p. 118.
48. *Geographical Journal*, 120 (1954), pp. 15–20.

4.4 Unveiling of the Livingstone Memorial at the Royal Geographical Society, 23 October 1953 (*Geographical Journal*, 120, 1954). By permission of the RGS-IBG.

Curzon's rousing tribute to Livingstone's heroic virtues forty years earlier, Britain's African empire was beginning to crumble. On 16 December 1953, Lyttelton found himself the subject of an unprecedented censure motion from the Labour Party front bench for his handling of African affairs, including the proposed federation in Central

Africa and the Mau Mau rebellion in Kenya.[49] (Lyttelton's views about Africans were not really so distant from Curzon's: as he remarked in the House of Commons, 'So far, the continent of Africa has made little contribution to the civilisation, art, letters or enlightenment of mankind.')[50] The wind of change was gathering; and in only a matter of years, it was to sweep across the continent with a force that no Colonial Secretary could contain. By 1966 the African empire was history; but the statue remained, obstinate and aloof, seemingly untouched by the turbulence of the world which it still inhabits.

49. D. Goldsworthy, *Colonial Issues in British Politics, 1945–1961* (Oxford, 1971), pp. 24–9, 205–53. More generally, see R. Rotberg, *The Rise of Nationalism in Central Africa* (Cambridge, Mass., 1966).
50. Hansard, vol. 522 (1953–4), col. 409.

Chapter 5

Becoming an Explorer: The Martyrdom of Winwood Reade

In November 1866, an essay on 'African martyrology' appeared in the first issue of *Belgravia*, a minor literary magazine. The subject was the history of European exploration of the River Niger from the late eighteenth century to the mid-nineteenth, and the author was Winwood Reade, nephew of the novelist Charles Reade and an aspiring explorer. His essay took the form of a romance, in which lone explorers like Mungo Park played the part of martyrs to a noble cause – the same cause which Conrad was later to characterize as 'Geography Militant'.

The tale begins not in Africa, but on the quayside in Southampton, where Reade is working as a medical assistant in a temporary cholera hospital. The epidemic has taken its victims, we are told, but these are assuredly not martyrs; and the conquest of the disease by medicine has brought to an end any prospect of a larger purpose in the struggle. From this site of anonymous death in the cholera wards, Reade turns towards Southampton water, which in his eyes is transformed into the swamps of Sierra Leone:

> Who has not been tempted at least once in life to give up our rapid but monotonous railway-life for the excitements of savage solitude? As a nation we are the slaves of civilisation, with its groove-life of fixed habits, single purposes, and domestic ties; but we have inherited the nomade instinct from our ancestors. . . . When a great traveller enters a London drawing-room there are more rustling of flowers, and whispering behind fans, than welcome the novelist or even the poet.[1]

---

1. W. Reade, 'African martyrology', *Belgravia*, 1 (1867), pp. 46–54, quote from p. 47 (originally published November 1866).

But the explorer's search for a reputation, Reade warns, has its 'dark side': the rolls of 'African martyrology' measure the price of militant geography.

In order for death of the explorer to be represented as a martyrdom, as we have seen in the case of David Livingstone, the mundane experience of travel had to be ennobled: exploration was rendered less as a journey across territory than as a quest for truth, the explorer transfigured into the bearer of larger values of religion, science or culture. The imaginative work involved was not confined to the pages of travel narratives or heroic biographies: it also helped to fashion the identity of explorers themselves. The figure of martydom haunted Winwood Reade throughout his life, and followed him to his grave. After his death in April 1875, he was buried in a small churchyard near his ancestral home at Ipsden, Oxfordshire. A huge cross, now leaning precariously over the grave, was marked with the following inscription:

> William Winwood, eldest son of William Barrington and Elizabeth Reade of this Parish. Born December 26 1838, died April 24 1875. Possessed of great abilities and indomitable energy he shortened his days by repeated journeys of exploration in West Africa and by excessive literary labors at home. He was the first white man who visited the cannibal tribe of Fans and the first to ascertain the source of the Niger. In the Ashantee campaign he was always in the front. He shared in the defence of 'Abrakrampa', fought in the ranks of the 42nd Highlanders at the great battle of 'Amoaful' and was the only civilian present at the capture of Comassie.

Adding yet another name to the rolls of African martyrology, this epitaph might have been written by Reade himself. Yet there are signs of other stories on these stones: the references to 'repeated journeys' abroad and 'excessive literary labors' at home, together with the clumsy quotation marks around the African place-names, strike a more ambivalent note. The very site of the inscription was presumably intended to erase a still more troubling memory for Reade's immediate family: his declaration of war against Christianity in *The Martyrdom of Man*, a book which has been described as a 'substitute bible for secularists'.[2] Winwood Reade's journey from aspiring explorer to free-thinking rebel is the subject of this chapter.

Winwood Reade was a far from eminent Victorian. His credentials as an African explorer rested on three journeys to West Africa: the first (in 1861–2) as an independent traveller, the second (1868–70) with the support of the Royal Geographical Society, and the third as the reporter

2. W. S. Smith, *The London Heretics* (London, 1967), p. 5.

for *The Times* on the Ashanti War (1873–4). While he is all but forgotten today, Reade's search for a reputation during his brief adult life provides a telling case-study in the construction of the identity of the explorer. His idiosyncratic contribution to the literature of African travel, represented by works such as *Savage Africa* (1863) and *The African Sketch-Book* (1873), has been virtually ignored by historians,[3] partly because his writing is difficult to place in a single category, meandering as it does between travel narrative and imaginative fiction. Moreover, as an explorer Reade made little in the way of an original contribution to the scientific knowledge of West Africa. Although he was associated with various scientific institutions during the 1860s, he was always a marginal figure; indeed, his sense of marginality is painfully evident throughout much of his writing. Yet it was the peculiar skill of the Victorians to turn failure into a kind of martyrdom; and in this sense, Reade's achievement was exemplary. His search for an identity as a writer and explorer eventually led him to cast his own martyrdom on a much larger stage: the struggle for authority between science and religion. *The Martyrdom of Man*, a quasi-Darwinian world history published in 1872, subsequently gained a wide readership among intellectuals: indeed, it was hailed as a master-work by figures as diverse as H. G. Wells, Cecil Rhodes and W. E. B. Du Bois.

Late-Victorian free-thinkers portrayed Reade's death, weeks after completing his last novel (*The Outcast*), as yet another kind of martyrdom. Visitors to his London lodgings in the spring of 1875 found him estranged from his family, 'rapidly dying of starvation and depression', and shortly before his death his friend Humphry Sandwith moved him to his country house at Wimbledon.[4] Moncure Conway later recalled his last days there as a final vindication of the free-thinker's belief in science, truth and beauty: 'There he had all the alleviations that medical science could bring; there, embowered with trees, the invalid, seated on the veranda, looked forth on the golden gorse of the common, listened to the merry laughter of children, and was soothed by songs of nightingale and skylark.'[5] The serenity of Reade's last days were disturbed, however, by an evangelist who somehow got into the house and exhorted him to repent before it was too late. As one historian

---

3. For a notable exception, see J. D. Hargreaves, 'Winwood Reade and the discovery of Africa', *African Affairs*, 56 (1957), 306–16.
4. Humphry Sandwith to Frederick Maxse, 15 April 1875 (Maxse Papers 200, West Sussex Record Office). Maxse provides a touching account of Reade's last days in a letter to Sandwith's biographer, T. H. Ward, dated 23 October 1884 (Maxse Papers 200).
5. M. Conway, *Autobiography, Memoirs and Experiences*, vol. ii (London, 1904), p. 152.

justly remarks, 'for melodrama and irony it is an image of mental torture which cannot be matched in the most florid novels of the age'.[6] Nevertheless, Reade is said by his free-thinking friends to have remained unrepentant to the last. Sandwith reported his last words in a final note to Darwin, with whom Reade had corresponded in the last years of his life: 'I die a philosopher. I have no fear of the future, mark that.'[7]

Becoming an Explorer: From *Flâneur* to Man of Science

Why did Winwood Reade, aspiring novelist and heir to an estate, seek to become an explorer? Readers of his writings would have been left in little doubt that the primary reason was his search for a reputation: becoming an explorer was his route to fame, in the manner of a Park or a Speke. His first journey, in 1861, seems to have been inspired by Paul Du Chaillu's sensational claims about African gorillas and cannibals, which were widely publicized in the London press.[8] Yet by the time he published his most famous work, *The Martyrdom of Man* in 1872, Reade was presenting African exploration as a means to a larger aim: the development of a secular vision of world history, unencumbered by the superstitions of the past. Beyond the pages of his published works, moreover, yet another motive comes into view. From what can be gathered of his experiences as a young man, it appears that Reade's journeys were as much an escape as a quest: a flight not only from the bonds of family, but also from the world of civilization and commerce in which he so often cast himself as a victim – the wayward heir, the novelist bruised by his critics, the free-thinker rebelling against the orthodoxies of his time. As historians, we do not have to choose between these different motivations for travel: at different times, each helped to shape Reade's vision of himself as an explorer in the making.

Reade's travel narratives are explicitly centred on his own quest for identity: the account of his second and most significant journey,

6. Smith, *The London Heretics*, p. 25. The story of this event is probably derived from an 1883 sermon by the free-thinker Moncure Conway, who describes it as 'the last martyrdom of Winwood Reade': see M. Conway, 'The martyrdom of man', in Conway, *Addresses and Reprints, 1850–1907* (Boston, Mass., 1909), p. 274.
7. Humphry Sandwith to Charles Darwin, 25 April 1875 (Darwin Papers, vol. 177, f. 30, Cambridge University Library).
8. S. McCook, ' "It may be truth, but it is not evidence": Paul Du Chaillu and the legitimation of evidence in the field sciences', in H. Kuklick and R. Kohler (eds), *Science in the Field* (Chicago, 1996), pp. 177–97.

published in the *African Sketch-Book* (1873), is thus entitled 'The adventures of an author in search of a reputation':

> In 1861, I was wild, youthful and ambitious, with a mind burning in my body, and money burning in my pocket. I had heard some curious stories of the Coast, thought I had discovered a short cut to glory, travelled more than a twelvemonth in the country, and came back with body and pocket none the better for the trip, and glory as far off as before. . . .
>
> However, my mind in cooling had expanded, and was drawn out from the narrow circle in which it had hitherto been confined. . . . I read books of science, which excited me more than romances, for they discoursed on subjects mysterious and sublime. . . . I took up the study of medicine, and as the time passed on, began to hunger after Africa again . . . I became frantic to come out here again; the idea possessed me like a spirit; I could think of nothing else.[9]

Here we have an author who places his own history at the heart of his text, casting it as a movement from youthful ambition to mature reason. Even before his first visit to West Africa, at the age of twenty-two, Reade had written three books, none of them successful. His early attempts at novel-writing had been greeted with appalling reviews, and an unoriginal work on the mysteries of the druids (*The Veil of Isis*) had been ridiculed by scholars. In the face of such setbacks, Reade constructed himself as an outcast and a rebel, not least from his family, whom he described in a letter to fellow-novelist Rosina Bulwer-Lytton as 'small ignorant people who have lived in a rural groove all their lives, and who think that a young man to have the independence to think and do differently from themselves must be a monster hardened in iniquity'.[10] Determined to 'achieve something worth achieving', Reade set out to re-invent himself as an heroic explorer. The moment of self-realization, according to his own narrative, came when he finally arrived on the banks of the Niger in 1869 (figure 5.1):

> Henceforth no one can say I am only a writer; for I have proved myself a man of action as well as a man of thought. When in the morning I have taken my coffee, which sets my brain in a tremble and a glow, I walk

9.   Reade, *The African Sketch-Book*, vol. ii (London, 1873), pp. 351–2.
10.   Winwood Reade to Rosina Bulwer-Lytton, 17 May 1860 (Lytton Papers, Ms Eng. letters.e.7, Bodleian Library, Oxford). Reade seems to have regarded Rosina, the estranged wife of the novelist Edward Bulwer-Lytton, as a natural ally. Her treatment by her husband was a *cause célèbre*: See V. Blain, 'Rosina Bulwer-Lytton and the rage of the unheard', *Huntington Library Quarterly*, 53 (1990), 211–36.

5.1 Frontispiece to Winwood Reade's *The African Sketch-book* (1873), vol. ii.

along the red path, and as the country unfolds itself before me I say,
'This is mine; here no European has been; it is Reade's land'.[11]

Reade's account of his passage from youth to maturity was written
with an eye to his earlier book *Savage Africa* (1863), in which he had
described himself as more a dilettante than an explorer: 'If I have any
merit, it is that of having been the first young man about town to make
a *bona fide* tour in Western Africa; to travel in that agreeable and
salubrious country with no special object, and at his own expense; to
flaner in the virgin forest; to flirt with pretty savages; and to smoke his
cigar among cannibals.'[12] Once an aimless *flâneur*, Reade now claimed
for himself the title of dedicated explorer. Yet travel writing for him
was still a consuming passion. His narrative took the form of a series
of letters addressed not to the gentlemanly scientist but to the 'woman
of the world', while Africa itself became 'this land of my Love'. The
story of scientific exploration, Reade insisted, was no less captivating
than that of romantic tourism, and was in some ways more so; the
history of 'African martyrology' did not end with Mungo Park.

Reade first entered the metropolitan world of the scientific literati in
the spring of 1863, having returned from his first African journey to
rekindle the controversy over Paul Du Chaillu's travels that had erupted

11. Reade, *The African Sketch-Book*, vol. ii, page 476.
12. W. Reade, *Savage Africa* (London, 1863), preface.

two years earlier.[13] He read papers at the Geographical, Zoological and Anthropological Societies, and attached himself to a sequence of hero-figures, including Murchison, Burton, Huxley and, eventually, Darwin. Like many other aspiring explorers, he soon found an ally in Henry Walter Bates, assistant secretary at the Royal Geographical Society from 1864.[14] 'Though scientific men are not the most agreeable company always', Reade confided to Rosina Bulwer-Lytton, 'they are at all events instructive. . . . Hovering round the circles of science and literature are usually some fine intellects. . . . These are the men to know.'[15] All Reade's heroes had made their reputations as scientific explorers, and all were involved in debates over evolutionary thinking during the 1860s. It is important to emphasize here that these controversies were not confined to men of science. The period between the publication of *Essays and Reviews* in 1860 and Darwin's *Descent of Man* in 1871 was one of immense ferment, in which politicians, churchmen, scientists and novelists did battle over the meaning of new conceptions of race, natural selection and evolution. These battles were far from merely intellectual exercises: they were also struggles for authority.

Nowhere was this more clear than in the proceedings of the Anthropological Society, whose council Reade had joined soon after it was established in 1863.[16] Its founder, James Hunt, promoted the Society as a vehicle for a new kind of racial science, underpinning the study of all aspects of human culture and society: a 'science of man' in both the broadest and the most literal senses. Hunt rejected the monogenetic account of human evolution associated with the older Ethnological Society, and was far more pessimistic about the prospects for the

---

13. McCook, 'It may be truth', pp. 193–4. Although McCook suggests that Reade was regarded by the scientific community as a more reliable witness than du Chaillu, the parallels between the two are striking.
14. 'Every traveller, both English and foreign, who landed on our shores made his way to Bates': E. Clodd, *Memories* (London, 1916), p. 68.
15. Winwood Reade to Rosina Bulwer-Lytton, 10 May 1863 (Lytton Papers). In the following week, Reade had an appointment with T. H. Huxley, who advised him to undergo a medical and scientific training: Winwood Reade to Rosina Bulwer-Lytton, 17 May 1863 (Lytton Papers); Huxley Diary, 15 May 1863 (Huxley Papers, no. 70[6], Imperial College London).
16. Reade read a paper on the 'Bush tribes of Central Africa', and subsequently represented the Society during his travels in America in 1866–7. He was offered, but declined, the title of 'Visiting Secretary to West Africa' before his second expedition in 1868: 'On the bush tribes of Equatorial Africa' *Anthropological Review*, 1 (1863), pp. xix–xxiii; Anthropological Society of London, Council Minutes, 9 June 1863, 20 November 1866, 14 April 1868 (Royal Anthropological Institute Archive); Winwood Reade to Thomas Huxley, 2 June 1868 (Huxley Papers 25, ff. 41–2).

improvement of 'savage races'.[17] The differences between the leadership of the two rival Societies emerged particularly starkly during the controversy over Governor Eyre's suppression of the Jamaican rebellion, which divided the British intelligentsia from top to bottom.[18] Hunt's frustration at the refusal of the British Association to make room for a new section on anthropology only intensified his growing alienation from the scientific establishment.[19] Richard Burton, another leading figure in the Society, gave voice to this sense of marginality by describing it as a 'Refuge for Destitute Truth', an arena for the discussion of questions of race and sex which elsewhere were either suppressed or addressed circuitously.[20] In the eyes of its critics, however, the 'Refuge for Destitute Truth' attracted men whose scientific credentials were less than pure: Joseph Hooker, for example, described the Anthropological Society as 'a sort of Haymarket to which the demi-monde of science gravitated on its establishment'.[21]

The anthropologists' call to speak the unspeakable was in part an appeal to extend the frontiers of science; in the controversy which followed Huxley's celebrated encounter with Wilberforce at the British Association in Oxford in 1860, there was no doubt where the anthropologists stood. Yet the 'ethnologicals' were hardly scientifically conservative; amongst their number were Huxley, Darwin and Lubbock. What distinguished the 'anthropologicals', therefore, was not simply a call to extend the dominion of science to man himself, but to do so on the basis of a particular style of racial and sexual politics. The anthropologicals were far more enthusiastic about embracing the idea of racial difference; they were relativists in more than one sense, never ceasing to emphasize the essential differences between the physical and moral characters of societies across the globe. They regarded the refusal of their critics to concede the innate character of the differences between races as not only unscientific but unmanly. In this context, the exclusion

17. G. Stocking, 'What's in a name? The origins of the Royal Anthropological Institute', *Man*, 6 (1971), 369–90; R. Rainger, 'Race, politics and science: the Anthropological Society of London', *Victorian Studies*, (1978), 51–70.
18. B. Semmel, *The Governor Eyre Controversy* (London, 1962); C. Hall, 'Competing masculinities: Thomas Carlyle, John Stuart Mill and the case of Governor Eyre', in her *White, Male and Middle Class* (Cambridge, 1992), pp. 255–95.
19. 'Anthropology at the British Association' *Anthropological Review*, 3 (1865), pp. 354–71; 'President's Address', *Journal of the Anthropological Society*, 3 (1865), pp. lxxxv–cxii.
20. R. Burton, 'Notes on certain matters connected with the Dahoman', *Memoirs of the Anthropological Society of London*, 1 (1863–4), p. 308; W. Reade, 'English scientific societies', *The Galaxy*, 3 (1867), pp. 733–41.
21. D. Lorimer, *Colour, Class and the Victorians* (Leicester, 1978), pp. 156–7; G. Stocking, *Victorian Anthropology* (New York, 1987), pp. 248–54.

of women from their meetings was of critical importance.[22] The new 'science of man' was, they argued, the preserve of men; open enquiry demanded closed rooms.[23]

Winwood Reade's involvement in the Anthropological Society during the 1860s was related to his growing sense of marginality as a writer: in both his romantic novels and his sensational travel narratives, he courted notoriety by representing himself as a bohemian.[24] For Reade, the main attraction of the new anthropology was its apparently fearless rejection of convention in matters of race and sexuality. As he put it in a letter to Rosina Bulwer-Lytton in May 1863:

> There is a new Society springing up (the Anthropological) for the study of man – the highest form of creation has certainly received less attention from science than flowers and stones. Possibly you think that the latter merit most. I should imagine that the life of a botanist or geologist must be delightful for a man who is tired of the world's troubles, and who can look at a beautiful woman or converse with a charming one without feeling palpitations of the heart. I suppose there are natures which attain to [sic] that degree of stoicism.[25]

The notion that the new science might provide a channel for the articulation of erotic desire was far from exceptional. Burton's fascination with sexual esoterica was shared by many of his circle, including the poet Algernon Swinburne, whose enthusiasm for de Sade scandalized even his friends, Thomas Bendyshe, the Cambridge scholar and translator of the *Mahabharata*, and Lord Houghton, the dilettante socialite.[26] Topics discussed at meetings of the Anthropological Society included cannibalism, polygamy, phallic worship, circumcision and infibulation. The infamous Cannibal Club, a coterie within the Society, revelled in its reputation as a subversive fraternity. Its dinners were held at Bartolini's Hotel, in Leicester Square, in the company of a mace

22. Anthropological Society of London, Council Minutes, 5 August 1863.
23. On the significance of the exclusion of women from scientific meetings, see E. Richards, 'Huxley and woman's place in science: the "woman question" and the control of Victorian anthropology', in J. R. Moore (ed.), *History, Humanity and Evolution* (Cambridge, 1989), pp. 253–84.
24. Winwood Reade to Rosina Bulwer-Lytton, 14 May 1860, 8 June 1860 (Lytton Papers). For a contemporary attack on the immorality of 'sensation novels' (including Reade's *Liberty Hall*) see the *Quarterly Review*, 113 (1863), pp. 482–514.
25. Winwood Reade to Rosina Bulwer-Lytton, 21 May 1863 (Lytton Papers).
26. D. Thomas, *Swinburne: The Poet in His World* (London, 1979), pp. 61–5, 95–6; F. Brodie, *The Devil Drives: A Life of Sir Richard Burton* (London, 1967), pp. 195–9; J. Pope-Hennessy, *Monckton-Milnes* (London, 1951), pp. 122–6; Algernon Swinburne to Houghton, 5 January [1869] (Houghton Papers, 24/84, Trinity College Cambridge).

representing the ebony head of an African gnawing at an ivory human thigh-bone. The 'Cannibal catechism', a blasphemous parody of Christian prayer and teaching composed for one of these dinners, is commonly attributed to Swinburne.[27]

The appeal of the new anthropology to Reade and his associates also needs to be seen in the wider context of contemporary challenges (the work of Darwin included) to the authority of natural theology, and especially the idea that human beings were special creations. Huxley's essays on *Man's Place in Nature* (1863) placed humanity at 'one with the brutes', at least in terms of shared processes of species development. Hunt's paper on the 'Negro's place in nature' (1864) argued for a polygenetic account of human origins, concluding that 'the analogies are far more numerous between the negro and the ape, than between the European and the ape'.[28] While Huxley loudly disputed Hunt's conclusion and his politics, he shared his faith in the authority of science over scripture as far as the question of origins was concerned. The contents of the *Anthropological Review* left readers in no doubt of the challenge that was being mounted in the name of science. The volume for 1865, for example, contained reviews of Büchner's *Force and Matter*, an influential argument for materialism and atheism, and Lecky's *History of Rationalism*. 'Few things are more observable in the scientific world than the change of tone which has taken place within the last few years on the subject of authority', it was claimed; 'Everywhere the supremacy of facts is now recognized.'[29]

In view of Reade's subsequent reputation as a martyr to the cause of free thought, it is interesting to note that early members of the Anthropological Society also included Charles Bradlaugh and Moncure Conway, though neither played an active part in its proceedings. The relationship between the Society and evangelical Christianity was increasingly fraught; on one occasion in 1866, the Christian Union Institution (the Society's neighbour in St Martin's Place) objected to the view of a skeleton standing in a window of the Society's museum.[30] Leading anthropologists, including Burton and Hunt, were openly contemptuous of the 'sentimental' views on race and slavery attributed to Exeter Hall. Reade's own view of black Africans was certainly racist, though it differed from Hunt's in one important respect: he argued that

27. E. Gosse, 'A poet among the cannibals', in *Books on the Table* (London, 1921), pp. 63–6; *The Cannibal Catechism* (privately printed, London, 1913).
28. J. Hunt, 'On the negro's place in nature', *Memoirs of the Anthropological Society of London*, 1 (1863–4), 1–64 (p. 52).
29. 'The plurality of the human race', *Anthropological Review*, 3 (1865), pp. 120–32 (p. 120).
30. Anthropological Society of London, Council Minutes, 20 March 1866.

the moral character of the West African was the result of degeneration, and that a degree of 'civilization' could be restored. None the less, he was convinced of the futility of Christian missionary work, and his outspoken paper on this subject provoked a storm of controversy in 1865. Reade argued that the effort devoted to Christian missionary work in black Africa was both ineffective and counter-productive, partly because of the institution of polygamy (which he argued served a sound purpose in Africa) and partly because Christian dogma was simply unintelligible to 'savages'. Taking his cue from Richard Burton, he concluded that Islam (characterized as 'Oriental Christianity') was much better suited to the task of civilizing black Africa.[31] The paper attracted a variety of responses, including one from the liberal Bishop Colenso of Natal (whom Reade praised as 'the Martin Luther of a new reformation').[32] Colenso's reservations about Reade's paper were mild in comparison with others who described it as an 'unequivocal attack on Christianity'; his views on polygamy were ridiculed as the 'savage' prejudices of an impressionable 'literary lounger', even to the extent of questioning his own sexual conduct as a traveller in Africa.[33] In response, Reade challenged the missionary campaign against fetish worship, drawing a pointed comparison to the use of mistletoe in English houses at Christmas.[34] In the eyes of many missionaries, including David Livingstone himself, the controversy exposed the innately atheistical tendencies of the anthropologists.[35]

This very public controversy resulted in the resignation of several members from the Council of the Anthropological Society, including Winwood Reade.[36] Having enrolled, probably on Huxley's advice, as a student at St Mary's Hospital medical school (where he may have been

31. W. Reade, 'Efforts of missionaries among savages', *Journal of the Anthropological Society*, 3 (1865), pp. clxiii–clxviii.
32. J. W. Colenso, 'On the efforts of missionaries among savages', *Journal of the Anthropological Society*, 3 (1865), pp. ccxlviii–cclxxxii.
33. H. Burnard Owen, 'Missionary successes and negro converts', *Journal of the Anthropological Society*, 3 (1865) pp. clxxxiv–cciv, pp. ccxliv–ccxlvi; J. Reddie, *loc cit*, pp. ccxxii–ccxxxiv.
34. Letters from W. Reade, *Journal of the Anthropological Society*, 3 (1865), pp. ccxiv–ccxv, and pp. ccxcii–ccxciv. The symbolic significance of mistletoe was a theme Reade had explored in *The Veil of Isis* (London 1861) and would return to in *The Martyrdom of Man*. It was also to form the central motif of Frazer's *The Golden Bough*.
35. D. Livingstone to J. Kirk, 11 May 1865 (Universities Mission to Central Africa Archives, Miscellaneous Letters, ff. 182–3, Rhodes House, Oxford).
36. Anthropological Society of London, Council Minutes, 6 June 1865, 2 August 1865.

THE MARTYRDOM OF WINWOOD READE 101

lectured by St George Mivart),[37] Reade spent the summer of 1866
working in a cholera hospital in Southampton.[38] Shortly afterwards, he
visited the United States, where he moved in the literary and scientific
circles of Boston and New York, exploiting the connections of his uncle
Charles (who disapproved of his 'roving propensities').[39] He kept in
contact with his acquaintances in Britain, writing for example to
Swinburne to tell him of the sensation that the American edition of
Poems and Ballads had created,[40] and to Huxley on American scientific
controversies over Darwinism.[41] In the absence of direct evidence, it is
difficult to assess the impact of Reade's American experience on his
views on race, religion and politics, though it is clear that his encounter
with men such as Gray and Agassiz encouraged his growing interest in
debates over the moral implications of evolutionary thought. Perhaps,
too, his experience in America led him to re-evaluate his views on race
and slavery. The account of the history of the anti-slavery movement in
Britain and America presented in *The Martyrdom of Man* (1872) was,
as we shall see, quite different from what we should expect from an
associate of Hunt and Burton during the 1860s, as indeed was the
whole tenor of the work.[42]

37.   Reade enrolled as a perpetual student on 1 January 1864 (thanks to Kevin
Brown, the archivist at St Mary's, for this information). St George Mivart was
Professor of Comparative Anatomy at St Mary's and was a close associate of
Huxley during the mid-1860s: in *On the Genesis of Species* (London, 1871), Mivart
was to raise objections to the idea of natural selection.
38.   During the cholera outbreak in Southampton in 1866, Anspach House on
West Quay was used as a temporary hospital: Winwood Reade was appointed for
two months as a house surgeon (*Quarterly Report of the Officer of Health, August
to November 1866*, Southampton City Archives). While he was in Southampton,
Reade attended a banquet in support of Governor Edward Eyre (*Hampshire
Advertiser*, 25 August 1866).
39.   Charles Reade to James T. Fields, 23 July 1867 (Fields Papers FI 3627,
Huntington Library, San Marino). I am grateful to Alice Clareson for giving me
access to Thomas Clareson's unpublished biography of Charles Reade, which
includes this reference. For examples of Winwood Reade's journalism at this time,
see 'The London clubs', 'The British stage' and 'English scientific societies', *The
Galaxy*, 3 (1867), pp. 191–5, 271–9, 733–41; 'African romance', *The Nation*, 9
May 1867; 'Heroes of central Africa', *Atlantic Monthly*, 19 (1867), pp. 625–35.
40.   The letter is addressed to 'Algernon Swinburne, Pagan, suffering persecution
from the Christians': C. Watts-Dunton, *The Home Life of Swinburne* (London,
1922), p. 19. There is very little evidence on the extent of their association, although
it was through Swinburne that Reade met the artist and spiritualist Seymour Kirkup
in Italy: C. Y. Lang, *The Swinburne Letters*, vol. i (New Haven, 1959), pp. 102–3.
41.   Winwood Reade to Thomas Huxley, 24 March 1867 (Huxley Papers, vol. 25,
f. 40).
42.   The poetic style of *The Martyrdom of Man* would surely not have appealed
to Hunt: compare, for example, 'Race in history', *Anthropological Review*, 3

Disappointed by his experiences in London and America, Reade spent some time casting around for an opportunity to return to Africa. An application to serve as the special correspondent for *The Times* in the Abyssinian war was unsuccessful.[43] Eventually, through Henry Bates at the RGS, he found a sponsor, the West African trader, Andrew Swanzy.[44] Once more, he was obsessed with the need to make his name; as he explained to Swanzy before his departure in 1868, 'it is not my desire to return to England till I have *done something* which is not likely to be for some years'.[45] Reade had become convinced that achievement in African travel meant something more than mere tourism; the romantic adventurers of a former age were now to be succeeded by trained men, 'disciples of Darwin, Huxley and Lyell, [searching] in strange latitudes for those secrets of nature which men of science wish to know'.[46] This language of 'discipleship' is surely significant: Reade, like so many aspiring explorers, was keenly aware of the need to attach himself to the leading men of the day. 'It is extremely difficult to establish a footing in London scientific society', Joseph Hooker once advised Henry Bates; 'it is all along of the struggle for life!'[47] In his own struggle for a reputation, Reade now reinvented himself as a missionary of science.

Reade's second expedition was thus conceived, at least in part, as a scientific venture. He was equipped by the Royal Geographical Society, and consulted leading authorities in entomology before his departure. With Bates's encouragement, he attempted to collect insects; he sent botanical specimens to Joseph Hooker at Kew; he promised to collect ethnological data for Huxley; and he corresponded with Darwin, sending him answers to his questions on the domestication of animals,

---

(1865), pp. 233–48. This essay (very probably written by Hunt) is particularly critical of Buckle, a 'mere scholar', and makes a strong distinction between 'literary' and 'scientific' accounts of human development.

43. Mowbray Morris to Winwood Reade, 30 August 1867 (Times Archives, News International, London). Reade later unsuccessfully applied to join the Livingstone Relief Expedition, and served as the *Times* correspondent during the Ashanti war: see W. Reade, *The Story of the Ashantee Campaign* (London, 1874), p. 132.

44. Reade, *The African Sketch-Book*, vol. ii, pp. 352–3. On Swanzy, see G. Shepperson, 'A West African partnership: Winwood Reade and Andrew Swanzy', *Progress: The Unilever Quarterly*, 51 (1965), pp. 41–7; H. Swanzy, 'A trading family in the nineteenth century Gold Coast', *Transactions, Historical Society of Ghana*, 2 (1956), pp. 87–120; D. Helly, ' "Informed" opinion on tropical Africa in Great Britain, 1860–1890', *African Affairs*, 68 (1969), pp. 195–217.

45. Winwood Reade to Andrew Swanzy, 10 March 1868 (United Africa Company (UAC) archives, Unilever House), emphasis in the original.

46. Reade, 'African martyrology', p. 54.

47. E. Clodd, 'Memoir', in H. W. Bates (ed.), *The Naturalist on the River Amazons* (London, 1892), p. lxvi.

sexual selection and human expression. Frequently, however, Reade's lack of training got the better of him; he mishandled his specimens, confessed his ignorance of zoology, entomology and botany, and quickly tired of the labour of insect collecting.[48] Commenting on his travel narratives (forwarded by Swanzy to the RGS), Francis Galton observed drily that 'the net geographical results of Mr Reade's four very lengthy and diffuse letters appear to be exceedingly small'; while Reade's subsequent report of his journey to the Upper Niger was considered more worthy of attention, it was said to have been 'written with a political not a geographical purpose'.[49]

Reade was set more on making a daring journey than on discovering a new species or an uncharted lake; in particular, he pinned his hopes on reaching the source of the Niger. In his published travel narrative, this appears less a voyage of exploration than a quest for fame, in which the author himself is always at the centre of attention (figure 5.2). Reade's initial task of opening a route to the Ashanti capital of Kumasi from Assinie on the Ivory Coast (which would have benefited Swanzy's trade) was soon frustrated. A second journey inland from Sierra Leone resulted in a delay for three months at Falaba in what Reade later described as 'circumstances of physical but especially mental misery'.[50] This episode features prominently in Reade's account of the expedition in *The African Sketch-Book*, where it is presented as a trial of his courage and determination; indeed, of his masculinity.[51] A third journey into the interior finally enabled Reade to reach the Niger, though not quite its source, and this was his moment of triumph: 'I am satisfied I

48. Winwood Reade to Charles Darwin, 19 May 1868 and 1870 (Darwin Papers 176 f. 33 and f. 36); Winwood Reade to Joseph Hooker, 14 January and 3 December 1869 (Hooker Correspondence, vol. 184, ff. 184–5, Royal Botanic Gardens, Kew); Winwood Reade to Thomas Huxley, 2 June 1868 and 17 January 1869 (Huxley Papers 25, ff. 41–3); Reade, *The African Sketch-Book*, vol. ii, pp. 37–44.
49. Francis Galton, reports on Winwood Reade, 'Letters from the Coast of Guinea' (1869) and 'Journey to the Upper Waters of the Niger from Sierra Leone' (1870), Journal MSS, RGS Archives. Summaries were published in *Proceedings of the RGS*, 13 (1868–9), pp. 353–9; 14 (1869–70), pp. 185–8.
50. Winwood Reade to Andrew Swanzy, 27 June 1869 (UAC archives).
51. According to Reade, his insistence on returning to Falaba, against the advice of the Governor at Freetown, won the approval of his African servant:

> When the official interview was over, Fila said to the Governor that he wanted to say one more word. Then his face lighted up, his manner became excited, and pointing at me, he exclaimed: That is a Man! I believe that I almost blushed, and certainly never in my life have I had such a compliment, or felt so proud. The gold medal of the Geographical Society would not have given me more pleasure. (*The African Sketch-Book*, vol. ii, p. 456)

5.2 'Very suggestive', from Winwood Reade, *The African Sketch-book* (1873), vol. ii, p. 121.

have made a genuine and original exploration' he wrote to Swanzy in December 1869. 'Nobody will be able to call me a mere writing traveller, which people are prone to do when a book of travels displays literary skill.'[52]

For Reade, the exploration of Africa was as much a literary as a geographical challenge. The 'Map of African Literature' which he included with the *African Sketch Book* (figure 5.3) was thus more than a convenient contrivance: it expressed his faith in the power of the written word to make sense of the continent. On his travels in West Africa he continued to read and write extensively, asking Swanzy to send him editions of the works of Goethe, Schiller and Ruskin (the last of which he described as 'a useful aid in the art of observation and description').[53] Self-evidently, Reade depended on far more than books during his African travels: he relied heavily on the assistance of European missionaries, traders and officials, as well as many unnamed African servants and porters. But few of them receive much attention in his writings, in contrast with his collection of books, 'brought out not as furniture, but as friends'.[54] When he finally reached the banks

52. Winwood Reade to Andrew Swanzy, 26 December 1869 (UAC archives).
53. Winwood Reade to Andrew Swanzy, 27 June 1869 and 26 December 1869 (UAC archives).
54. Reade, *The African Sketch-Book*, vol. i, p. 11.

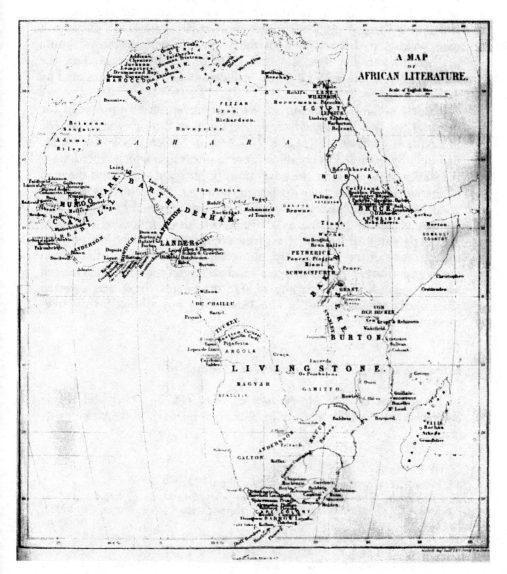

5.3 'Map of African Literature', from Winwood Reade, *The African Sketchbook* (1873), vol. ii.

of the Niger, in 1869, he reached not for the sextant or artificial horizon borrowed from the Royal Geographical Society (which he had in fact left behind on the coast) but for his copy of Herodotus.[55] If Reade's literary preoccupations seem curiously out of place in a man seeking to become one of the scientific *avant-garde*, it should perhaps be recalled that the first issue of *Nature* appeared in the same year, opening with Goethe's 'Aphorisms on Nature' translated by T. H. Huxley.[56]

Reade's second expedition to West Africa eventually provided the material for two works, which appear to have little in common: *The Martyrdom of Man* (1872) and *The African Sketch Book* (1873). He had initially intended to combine these in one book, which would 'have the stamp of the scholar, the adventurer (in its good sense) and the man of the world'.[57] Soon after his return, however, he decided to separate what he called the 'historical work' from the 'personal narrative'. The former, originally planned as a history of Africa modelled on James Tennent's study of Ceylon,[58] evolved eventually into *The Martyrdom*; the narrative of travel ended up, along with various works of fiction in the *Sketch Book*.[59] Reade justified his decision on the basis of gendered assumptions about his reading public: the *Sketch-Book* was directed particularly at women, while *The Martyrdom* was a book for the free-thinking man.

Darwin's Disciple: *The Martyrdom of Man*

In his preface to *The Martyrdom of Man* (1872), Winwood Reade described the book as a study in 'universal history', with Africa at its centre:

55. Reade, *The African Sketch-Book*, vol. ii, pp. 377, 474–6.
56. D. Roos, 'The "aims and intentions" of *Nature*', in J. Paradis and T. Postlewait (eds), *Victorian Science and Victorian Values* (New Brunswick, 1985), pp. 159–180 (p. 168).
57. Winwood Reade to Andrew Swanzy, 6 June 1870 (UAC archives).
58. Winwood Reade to Andrew Swanzy, 8 January 1871 (UAC archives). Tennent's *Ceylon* (London, 1859) was a panoramic survey, covering many aspects of geography, climate, zoology, economy, culture, language and politics.
59. The book included an extraordinary short story entitled 'Hollowayphobia', discussed below in chapter 9. Reade's decision to include such tales in *The African Sketch-Book* reflected his conviction that even the best travel narrative had a limited shelf life: 'I have observed that books of travel do not live unless there is something in them besides travels' (Winwood Reade to Charles Darwin, 9 November 1870, Darwin Papers 85, f. 89).

I began it intending to prove that 'Negroland' or Inner Africa is not cut off from the main-stream of events, as writers of philosophical history have always maintained, but connected by means of Islam with the lands of the East; and also that it has, by means of the slave-trade, powerfully influenced the moral history of Europe and the political history of the United States. But I was gradually led from writing the history of Africa into writing the history of the world.[60]

The book provided a lyrical portrait of the flow of human history, divided into four parts headed 'War', 'Religion', 'Liberty' and 'Intellect': the rise and fall of the ancient Egyptians, Persians, Greeks and Romans; the origins and development of Judaism, Christianity and Islam; the history of modern Europe and America, especially in relation to the Enlightenment, slavery and the anti-slavery movement; and the prospects for the future evolution of the human race in the light of a scientific understanding of the cosmic process. Reade did not offer a scholarly account of world history, as in Buckle, or a scientific exposition of human descent, as in Darwin. Instead, he wove a vast poetic tapestry, whose multiple threads connected past and present, humanity and nature. The drama of history was treated as a natural process of growth, in which innate instincts of self-preservation and reproduction inevitably gave rise to development. While war, slavery and religion had once been necessary, Reade argued, they would not always be so;[61] in the future only science could guarantee human progress. For humanity to achieve its vocation, nature had to be understood without reference to a supernatural being: 'We can conquer Nature only by obeying her laws, and in order to obey her laws we must first learn what they are. When we have ascertained, by means of science, the method of Nature's operations, we shall be able to take her place and to perform them for ourselves.'[62]

Although it made little immediate impact, *The Martyrdom of Man* was widely read by late-Victorian and Edwardian intellectuals and writers. In an early Conan Doyle novel, published in 1890, that great explorer Sherlock Holmes recommended its 'daring speculations' to Dr Watson; at about the same time, Sidney Webb was quoting it in his

60. Winwood Reade, *The Martyrdom of Man* (London, 1943), p. xxi (subsequent references are to this edition). Hegel was the main target of Reade's complaint: see also *The African Sketch-Book*, vol. ii, p. 318.
61. Reade, *The Martyrdom of Man*, pp. 403–6.
62. Reade, *The Martyrdom of Man*, p. 412. Reade famously anticipated a number of scientific innovations, including the discovery of a new motive force to replace steam, the invention of air transport and the manufacture of artificial foodstuffs.

love letters to Beatrice Potter.[63] Cecil Rhodes had read the book as an Oxford undergraduate soon after its publication: he later declared that 'it made me what I am'.[64] It was subsequently acclaimed by Harry Johnston as 'the first rational exposition of the relations of mankind to the mystery which shrouds the how and wherefore of man's existence',[65] by H. G. Wells, as 'an extraordinarily inspiring presentation of human history as one consistent process', the work of a 'great and penetrating genius' and a prime inspiration for his *Outline of History*,[66] by V. S. Pritchett as 'the one, the outstanding, dramatic, imaginative, historical picture of life, to be inspired by Victorian science',[67] and by the African-American sociologist W. E. B. Du Bois as a seminal work in an African-centred world history.[68] The distinctiveness of *The Martyrdom of Man* lay less in its contents than in its idiosyncratic style, an amalgam of romanticised *naturphilosophie*,[69] universal history and scientific rationalism. And what made the book so 'daring', even to a Sherlock Holmes, was its attempt to present a Darwinian view of humanity, coupled with a forthright assault on Christianity.

Describing himself as a 'disciple' of Darwin, Reade claimed inspiration from his reading of both *The Origin of Species* and *The Descent*

---

63. Watson was too preoccupied with the case (in *The Sign of Four*) to read Reade's book; Beatrice Potter, however, later recalled it as a 'classic'. See B. Potter, *My Apprenticeship*, 2nd edn (London, 1945), p. 113; N. Mackenzie (ed.), *The Letters of Sidney and Beatrice Webb, vol. 1: Apprenticeships, 1873–1892* (Cambridge, 1978), p. 168; P. Morton, *The Vital Science: Biology and the Literary Imagination* (London, 1984).
64. R. Rotberg, *The Founder: Cecil Rhodes and the Pursuit of Power* (Oxford, 1988), p. 100.
65. H. Johnston, *Liberia* (London, 1906), vol. i, p. 257.
66. H. G. Wells, *The Outline of History* (London, 1920), p. vi; H. G. Wells, *'42 to '44* (London, 1944), p. 167. For recent discussions of the influence of *The Martyrdom of Man* on Wells, see L. Stover, 'Applied natural history: Wells versus Huxley', in P. Parrinder and C. Rolfe (eds), *H. G. Wells under Revision* (London, 1990), pp. 125–33; P. Parrinder, *Shadows of the Future: H. G. Wells, Science Fiction and Prophecy* (Liverpool, 1995), pp. 129–30.
67. V. S. Pritchett, 'Books in general', *New Statesman and Nation*, 25 (1943), p. 323.
68. 'One always turns back to Winwood Reade's *Martyrdom of Man* for renewal of faith': W. E. B. Du Bois, *The World and Africa: An Inquiry into the Part which Africa Has Played in World History* (New York, 1947), p. x. Reade had at one point considered entitling the book 'Africa's Place in History': Winwood Reade to Charles Darwin, 21 February 1871 (Darwin Papers 89, ff. 172–4).
69. Cf. N. Jardine, 'Naturphilosophie and the kingdoms of nature', in N. Jardine, J. Secord and E. Spary (eds), *Cultures of Natural History* (Cambridge, 1996); A. Cunningham and N. Jardine (eds), *Romanticism and the Sciences* (Cambridge, 1990).

of Man, published in 1871.[70] With Bates' encouragement, he had begun corresponding with Darwin shortly before his departure for West Africa in 1868, offering his services in the collection of 'philosophical' information on the habits of its animal and human populations.[71] While his ability to answer Darwin's queries on human expression was limited, he reported faithfully on the domestication of animals, the relations between the sexes, and native ideas of beauty. Much to Reade's pleasure, Darwin drew liberally on this information in *The Descent of Man*. In turn, Reade sought Darwin's advice on the passages about the origin of language which he intended to publish in *The Martyrdom of Man*, pointing out what Darwin was only too aware of: 'I make no apology for asking your advice because if I say anything ridiculous you will suffer for it. My views will be called Darwinian; the master is usually held responsible though of course unjustly for the opinions of his pupils'.[72] Darwin responded by sending Reade the latest works on evolution and urging him to tone down some of his remarks on extinction and on religion. On the eve of publication, Reade expressed his debt to Darwin in an effusive letter: 'My obligations to you, in respect of this book, are greater than they are to any other writer, dead or alive.'[73] Soon after, the two men met (as they had met at Down House in 1871), and Reade sent Darwin a proof copy of his Preface.

While Reade saw his task as popularizing Darwinism, in many respects he was a poor Darwinian. Indeed, he says as much in his letters to Darwin, in which he describes natural selection as a 'secondary law which superintends and arranges all details', while the 'primary law' is the 'law of growth'.[74] This view, which owes more to Comte and Spencer than to Darwin, saw a purposefulness in evolution rather than a universe subject to blind chance.[75] Furthermore, the poetic temper of

---

70. 'Your book – The Origin – has had considerable influence on my mind. If I had read it earlier in life it might have completely changed the course of it': Winwood Reade to Charles Darwin, 31 January 1871 (Darwin Papers 176, f. 44). For Reade's reaction to *The Descent*, see Reade to Darwin, 21 February 1871 (Darwin Papers 89, ff. 172–4).
71. Winwood Reade to Charles Darwin, 19 May 1868 (Darwin Papers 176, f. 33).
72. Winwood Reade to Charles Darwin, 12 September 1871 (Darwin Papers 176, f. 47).
73. Winwood Reade to Charles Darwin, 12 March 1872 (Darwin Papers 176 f. 55).
74. Winwood Reade to Charles Darwin, 18 September 1871 (Darwin Papers 176, f. 49). See also *The Martyrdom of Man*, p. 330.
75. On the differences between a developmental and a strictly Darwinian view of history, see P. Bowler, *The Invention of Progress: The Victorians and the Past* (Oxford, 1989), pp. 12–13.

Reade's writing was far from Darwin's ideal of patient scientific description; while the 'master' kept his prose under control, even in moments of rapture at the sublimity of nature,[76] his 'pupil' showed no such restraint. As a novelist turned explorer, Reade was neither competent to judge nor especially interested in the finer points of detail in arguments between scientists; as he admitted to Darwin concerning his disagreement with Mivart, 'it is useless for any to enter this controversy unless they are thoroughly acquainted with zoology'.[77] Finally, in his treatment of Christianity Reade was far more outspoken than Darwin, whose canonization as an exemplary Victorian depended on a far more accommodating relationship with established religion.[78] What Reade took from Darwin was a conception of human life as an integral part of nature; and what he found in Darwinism was a rallying-point against orthodox theology.

Reade himself identified the 'Darwinian' section of The Martyrdom of Man as the fourth and final section, which provided an overview of human evolution, concluding with an outspoken denunciation of Christian theology. Soon after publication, he wrote to Darwin telling him of the torrent of criticism the book had received, and expressing some regrets about its somewhat convoluted form. But of his views on religion he was unrepentant: 'I mean to devote my life to war on Christianity.'[79] While recent historians have questioned the utility of military metaphors in historical accounts of the impact of Darwinism on religious thought, we should not underestimate the symbolic and emotional significance of such forthright declarations.[80] What was exceptional here was not so much Reade's lack of faith (which was common among many of his peers, including Bates at the RGS)[81] as his

76. On what has been called Darwin's 'duality of vision', see D. Stoddart, 'Grandeur in this view of life', in his On Geography (Oxford, 1986), pp. 219–229; D. Stoddart, 'Darwin and the seeing eye: iconography and meaning in the Beagle years', Earth Sciences History, 14 (1995), pp. 3–22; J. Paradis, 'Darwin and landscape', in J. Paradis and T. Postlewait (eds), Victorian Science and Victorian Values (New Brunswick, 1985), pp. 85–110.
77. Winwood Reade to Charles Darwin, 18 February 1872 (Darwin Papers 88, ff. 74–5). On Mivart, see note 37 above.
78. J. R. Moore, 'Freethought, secularism, agnosticism: the case of Charles Darwin', in G. Parsons (ed.), Religion in Victorian Britain, vol. 1: Traditions (Manchester, 1988), pp. 274–319; J. R. Moore, 'Darwin lies in Westminster Abbey', Biological Journal of the Linnean Society, 17 (1982), 97–113.
79. Winwood Reade to Charles Darwin, 20 May 1872 (Darwin Papers 176, f. 61).
80. J. R. Moore, The Post-Darwinian Controversies (Cambridge, 1979), p. 13.
81. Clodd, 'Memoir', pp. lxxxv–lxxxvii; H. P. Moon, Henry Walter Bates, 1825–1892 (Leicester, 1976), pp. 59, 67. Edward Clodd, the late-Victorian popularizer of free thought, was Bates's close friend and executor.

desire to express his views publicly, and in terms which alternated so dramatically between the militant and the poetic. The final section of *The Martyrdom of Man* attracted more attention than anything else that Reade had written. Not content with his attempt to historicize Jesus, he concluded the work with an outspoken attack on Christian dogma: 'Supernatural Christianity is false. God-worship is idolatry. Prayer is useless. The soul is not immortal. There are no rewards and there are no punishments in a future state.'[82] Such bald statements led one reviewer in *The Athenaeum* to describe *The Martyrdom of Man* as a 'thoroughly worthless book, needlessly profane and indecent into the bargain', and another in the *Saturday Review* to characterize it as 'wild, mischievous, and ... blasphemous'.[83] In an address in Liverpool in December 1872 the Prime Minister, William Gladstone, denounced it as one of a fresh crop of irreligious works (also including books by Comte, Spencer and Strauss).[84] In the Preface to *The Martyrdom of Man*, Reade tells us that his views on Christianity were expressed 'in opposition to the advice and wishes of several literary friends, and of the publisher'. Indeed, the publishers, Nicholas Trübner, (who had also been responsible for the *Anthropological Review*), seem to have taken legal advice before proceeding with the book.[85]

A question arises here about the wider context in which *The Martyrdom of Man* was written and read. Lambasted by a few reviewers, but ignored by most, the book was far from an immediate success. Its sales were slow at first, though they grew exponentially, the cumulative print run reaching 10,000 in the mid-1890s and over 20,000 by 1912; its sales in the Rationalist Press edition published between 1924 and 1948 alone amounted to 130,000.[86] As these figures suggest, *The Martyrdom of Man* achieved a much wider fame in the twentieth century than it did in the nineteenth. While a few late-Victorian

82. Reade, *The Martyrdom of Man*, p. 420.
83. *The Athenaeum*, 11 May 1872, pp. 587–8; *Saturday Review*, 12 October 1872, pp. 474–5.
84. J. M. Robertson, *A History of Freethought in the Nineteenth Century*, vol. ii (London, 1929), pp. 396–8. See also J. Stasny, 'W. Winwood Reade's *The Martyrdom of Man*: a Darwinian history', *Philological Papers*, 13 (1961), 37–49.
85. Nicholas Trübner & Co., Publication Book: item 102, p. 135 (Routledge Archive, University College London). Trubner had also published Charles Reade's best-selling novel, *The Cloister and the Hearth*: see M. Elwin, *Charles Reade: A Biography* (London, 1931), pp. 107–10.
86. Sales figures for the period 1872–1912 are derived from the Publication, Account and Print and Paper books of Trübner & Co. (Routledge Archive). These are confirmed by the figure given by Legge in his introduction to the eighteenth edition in 1910. The 1968 edition (with an introduction by Michael Foot) gives a figure of 130,000 sales for the period between 1924 and 1948.

free-thinkers acknowledge its influence in their memoirs, Reade himself is usually a marginal presence, if he is mentioned at all. He seems, for example, to have had no contact with Charles Bradlaugh and the secularist movement. Although he is fondly remembered by Moncure Conway, the freethinking Unitarian minister active in London during this period, it is as a somewhat isolated figure, a prophet rather than an activist.[87]

Similarly, there is little evidence that Reade moved in the kind of free-thinking circles associated with the liberal *Fortnightly Review* (although he once submitted a paper to the journal, and, like the positivist Frederic Harrison, also wrote for the *Pall Mall Gazette* in the early 1870s). This is perhaps surprising in view of the intellectual ferment which coincided with the publication of *The Martyrdom of Man*. Bagehot's essays on *Physics and Politics* and Leslie Stephen's on *Freethinking and Plainspeaking* appeared in book form in 1872 and 1873 respectively; the former was an attempt to apply the fruits of evolutionary anthropology to the understanding of political history, the latter an enthusiastic endorsement of the case for what Huxley had begun to call agnosticism. 'You cannot combine the mythology which is the spontaneous growth of one stage of intellectual development, with the scientific knowledge characteristic of another' wrote Stephen in an essay first published in 1872; 'We must be content to abandon much that is beautiful and that once was excellent.'[88] This was also Reade's conclusion in *The Martyrdom of Man*, though he expressed it more poetically: 'The soul must be sacrificed; the hope in immortality must die. A sweet and charming illusion must be taken from the human race, as youth and beauty vanish never to return.'[89] This sense of a fundamental transition, symbolized but certainly not inaugurated by what Stephen called the conflict between Darwinism and Divinity,[90] also found expression in the world of literature. Novels such as Bulwer-Lytton's *The Coming Race* (1871) and Butler's *Erewhon* (1872), the latter also published by Trübner, were the fruits of such speculation on the moral implications of Darwinism.

Reade's relative isolation from the liberal and free-thinking movements of his age reflects both his personality and his class formation.

87. M. Conway, *Autobiography, Memoirs and Experiences*, vol. ii (London, 1904), pp. 151–3. See also Smith, *The London Heretics*, pp. 24–5. On the secularist movement more generally, see E. Royle, *Radicals, Secularists and Republicans: Popular Freethought in Britain, 1866–1915* (Manchester, 1980).
88. L. Stephen, *Essays on Freethinking and Plainspeaking* (London, 1873), pp. 62, 71.
89. Reade, *The Martyrdom of Man*, p. 437.
90. See Moore, 'Freethought, secularism, agnosticism'.

To pronounce himself a heretic in a private letter to Darwin was one thing; to associate with the Bradlaughs of London was altogether another. Throughout the 1860s, Reade had been a member of the Conservative Club, and the journey from belief to atheism was in some respects easier than the transition from conservatism to liberalism, although, as I have noted, his changing views on anti-slavery may well have reflected his experiences in America. Nevertheless, his friends during the early 1870s included a number of wealthy liberals, including Andrew Swanzy (the patron of his second expedition), retired naval captain Frederick Maxse (an aristocratic radical) and Humphry Sandwith (a radical doctor), all three of whom stood for Parliament as advanced liberals during this period.[91]

The Martyrdom of Winwood Reade

It is impossible to understand a writer thoroughly till one has read his books by the light of his biography. It is necessary to know something of his disposition, of his tastes, and, above all, of the circumstances which have influenced his life.[92]

To read Winwood Reade's writings 'by the light of his biography' is to situate them within a number of contexts, intellectual, social, cultural and personal. But as a guide to what I have done in this chapter, this formula is insufficient. For, especially with so self-referential an author, we must also interpret Reade's life by the light of his writings. If his biography coloured his writings, his writings shaped his life – and, we might even say, the manner of his death. Throughout his career as an author and as an explorer, Reade was drawn to the figure of martyrdom: the martyrdom of the aspiring novelist bruised by reviewers and fleeced by publishers, the would-be anthropologist condemned, he thought, for speaking the truth, the explorer seeking in vain to penetrate the mysteries of the Dark Continent and, not least, the lone free-thinker

---

91.   Sandwith in 1868, Maxse in both 1868 and 1874, and Swanzy in 1874: T. H. Ward, *Humphry Sandwith: A Memoir* (London, 1884), p. 203; J. Hutcheson, *Leopold Maxse and the National Review* (New York, 1989), pp. 5–15; F. Pedler, *The Lion and the Unicorn in Africa: A History of the Origins of the United Africa Company, 1787–1931* (London, 1974), pp. 41–9. Maxse and Sandwith were advocates of land reform and Maxse was also a supporter of Charles Bradlaugh. See also F. Maxse, *The Causes of Social Revolt* (London, 1872); H. Sandwith, *The Land and Landlordism* (London, 1873).
92.   W. Reade, 'Mr. Swinburne: a sketch', *The Galaxy*, 3 (1867), pp. 682–4.

5.4 Portrait of Winwood Reade, from an album of Richard and Isabel Burton. By permission of the Wiltshire Record Office.

painfully described in *The Outcast*, a 'little freethinking book' written shortly before his death.

Winwood Reade himself described *The Outcast*, which he had printed at his own expense, as '*very* bold'.[93] The novel narrates the life of a parson whose faith in the biblical account of creation is shattered

93. Winwood Reade to Frederick Maxse, 3 March 1875 (Maxse Papers 203), emphasis in the original.

by an encounter with Lyell's *Principles of Geology*.[94] Rejected by his stern Calvinist father as an infidel, he is supported by the local parish doctor, in whose house also live three amateur scholars, an astronomer, a geologist and a comparative anatomist. He finds his way to lodgings near the British Museum, where he takes up menial work for a small publisher of dictionaries and encyclopaedias. But he is ruined by the gambling debts of his wife's brother, and overwork and ill-health eventually reduce him to poverty in Whitechapel, where his wife dies of exhaustion. However, unlike one of his friends (who dubs Malthus' *Essay on Population* 'the book of doubt' and Darwin's *Origin of Species* 'the book of despair'), the outcast-hero rejects suicide: 'God, you shall not conquer me; I will fight out my life to its natural end.'[95] He eventually recovers from his grief and ill-health, re-establishes his career as a writer and ends up inheriting his father's estate. Convinced of the injustice of his wife's death, he finally realizes the futility of the doctrine of future rewards and punishments. 'If I were a young man endowed with literary powers, and about to begin my career', the narrator concludes, 'I should adopt as the work of my life the Diffusion of Doubt.' His new 'religion of unselfishness' leaves him at peace: 'It has made me content. It has taught me to value and enjoy life, yet not to dread annihilation.'[96]

The Outcast is a minor classic of that late-Victorian genre of 'loss of faith' novels still celebrated by secularists: today it is even available on the world-wide web, courtesy of an American organization calling itself the Internet Infidels. If it is tempting to read the novel as a fictional representation of Reade's own experience, this is partly because the same has been said of much better-known works, especially Samuel Butler's *The Way of All Flesh* and Edmund Gosse's *Father and Son*. Both these books represented the loss of faith as an uncompromising struggle between the generations; and, in both, the scientific challenge to orthodox Christianity culminating in the work of Darwin was, in different ways, a central theme. Butler and Gosse must also have rubbed shoulders with Winwood Reade in the British Museum during the early 1870s.[97] The comparison is the more compelling because these authors

94. Lyell's *Principles of Geology* was a key text for evolutionary theorists: it had a major impact on the young Darwin, who took the first volume with him on the *Beagle*, picking up the second at Montevideo and the third at Valparaiso.
95. W. Reade, *The Outcast* (London, 1875), p. 213.
96. Reade, *The Outcast*, pp. 254, 257.
97. Butler lived in London from 1864 and often worked in the British Museum; he started writing *The Way of All Flesh* in 1873. Gosse began working in the cataloguing department of the British Museum in 1867. Neither of their books was published until the twentieth century.

are so ready to treat the experience of doubt not merely as an intellectual exercise but as the expression of a crisis which is at once personal, familial and social. Of course we do not have to read these novels literally to read them 'by the light of' their authors' biographies; they do not reproduce but re-present the transition to unbelief in a literary form. True, the hero of *The Outcast* is, like Reade himself, heir to a considerable country estate; furthermore, the breakdown of his relationship with his father, his encounter with the world of gentlemanly science and his search for a new vocation in London all mimic the author's own experience. Yet Reade's own rebellion against his family in fact preceded his public disavowal of Christianity, and there is no evidence that he had plans to enter the Church, though many of his family did so.[98] If we are to read his last novel by the light of his biography, then we must see it less as a reflection of his life than as a reworking, the projection of a new meaning onto his own experience by means of a fiction.

Reade's reputation as a martyr to the cause of free thought among his friends and admirers was sealed not merely by the publication of *The Outcast*, but also by the manner of his death. Visitors to his gloomy Marylebone lodgings during the spring of 1875 included the liberal doctor Humphry Sandwith, who found him 'rapidly dying of starvation and depression',[99] and the devout catholic Isabel Burton (what distressed her most, however, was his refusal to repent).[100] Writing to a friend in March 1875, having just signed the contract for *The Outcast*, Reade made light of his mortal illness: 'After all my African fevers and dysenteries safely got over I am to die of consumption like the heroine in a novel.'[101] As a writer and as an explorer, Reade perpetually described his life as a romance, with himself as the would-be hero; no wonder, then, that he was so ready to fictionalize his own death.

---

98. Of Winwood Reade's many younger brothers and sisters, one trained for the ministry, one served as a catechist in Australia, one joined the Catholic Church, one was a writer for the Christian Knowledge Society and one married a chaplain. His uncle Charles may have provided a model, though he had hardly rebelled in the manner of *The Outcast*: raised in a strict Calvinist atmosphere, he resisted his parents' wish that he enter the Church. See C. Reade, *A Record of the Redes of Barton Court, Berks* (Hereford, 1899), ch. 7; C. L. Reade and C. Reade, *Charles Reade: A Memoir* (London, 1887).
99. Humphry Sandwith to Frederick Maxse, 15 April 1875 (Maxse Papers 200).
100. I. Burton, *The Life of Captain Sir Richard Burton*, vol. ii (London, 1893), pp. 43–4.
101. Winwood Reade to Frederick Maxse, 3 March 1875 (Maxse Papers 203).

Chapter 6

Exploration by Warfare: Henry Morton Stanley and His Critics

The study of Geography ought to lead to something higher than collecting maps and books of travel and afterwards shelving them as of no further use. I would like to see maps in men's hands to be studied as generals study them before planning campaigns. I would like to see the manufacturer or merchant study them with the view of planning commercial campaigns, the man of capital pondering over them like men constructing a railroad across a country, or a military engineer designing defensive works.[1]

Henry Morton Stanley finds his place in conventional accounts of African exploration as the man who finally settled the long-running dispute over the sources of the Nile, synthesizing the fragments of knowledge gathered by his predecessors.[2] At the height of his fame, in January 1890, the *Contemporary Review* published an article by John Scott Keltie, Librarian at the RGS, entitled 'What Stanley has done for the map of Africa'. It contained two maps representing what was described as 'Central Africa, before Stanley' and 'Central Africa, after Stanley' (figure 6.1). The first showed the map as it was known about 1870. In the East were the sketchy outlines of the great lakes; in the West were the lower reaches of the River Congo. Between lay what Keltie described as 'the great blank', where 'the map was almost white,

---

1. H. M. Stanley, 'Central Africa and the Congo basin: or, the importance of the scientific study of geography', *Journal of the Manchester Geographical Society*, 1 (1885), pp. 6–25 (quote from p. 25).
2. W. Garstin, 'Fifty years of Nile exploration', *Geographical Journal*, 33 (1909), p. 117; J. N. L. Baker, *A History of Geographical Discovery and Exploration*, 2nd edn (London, 1937), pp. 325–43.

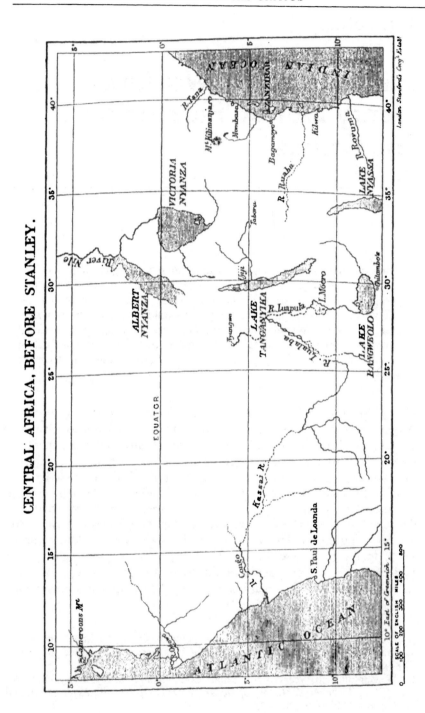

CENTRAL AFRICA, BEFORE STANLEY.

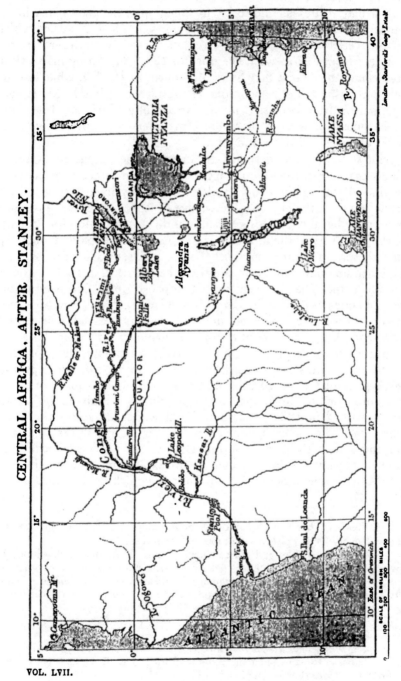

6.1 Central Africa, 'Before' and 'After' Stanley (from J. S. Keltie, 'What Stanley has done for the map of Africa' (1890), pp. 128–9.

with here and there the conjectural course of a river or two'. Stanley's great achievement was said to be the filling up of the great blank in the course of four momentous journeys: the first in 1871–2, during which he 'discovered' Livingstone; the second in 1874–7, when he crossed the continent from east to west; the third in 1879–84, during his work in establishing the Congo Free State; the fourth in 1887–9, while leading the Emin Pasha Relief Expedition. The result, according to Keltie, was a permanent transformation in the cartography of Africa: 'The blank has become a network of dark lines, the interspaces covered with the names of tribes and rivers and lakes.'[3]

Keltie's maps were designed to measure the extent of Stanley's achievement. Their titles alone suggested a fundamental divide, between the time of the 'great blank' and the time of knowledge; that is, a turning point in the effective knowledge of Africa by Europeans. Such tropes were hardly new; Joseph Banks and the Association for Promoting the Discovery of the Interior Parts of Africa had exploited much the same rhetoric a century earlier.[4] The blanks served a purpose, and Keltie had no doubt what it would be; as he remarked in 1890, 'Africa's time has come. The continent must be opened up to European enterprise. No one has done more than Mr Stanley to call this enterprise into activity.'[5] Yet Keltie's maps did not, and could not, tell all. For central Africa had long been a site of European imaginings; it was in this sense less a great blank than a reservoir of myth and fantasy, for explorers, novelists and anti-slavery campaigners alike. In his own writings and speeches, Stanley pictured central Africa as a primeval place of darkness, untouched by history yet full of possibility; his mission (as it had been described in 1884) was to strike 'a white line across the Dark Continent'.[6] The maps themselves, with their meagre traces of a lake here and a river there, provide few clues to the wider significance of Stanley's expeditions for the cultures of exploration and empire. As Keltie himself noted, Stanley's final journey (which he described as 'in

3. J. S. Keltie, 'What Stanley has done for the map of Africa', *Contemporary Review*, January 1890, pp. 126–40 (quotes from pp. 126, 130).
4. D. Middleton, 'Banks and African exploration', in R. Banks, B. Elliott, J. Hawkes, D. King-Hele and G. Lucas (eds), *Sir Joseph Banks: A Global Perspective* (London, 1994), pp. 171–6. On the significance of empty spaces in European maps more generally, see B. Harley, 'Silences and secrecy: the hidden agenda of cartography in early modern Europe', *Imago Mundi*, 40 (1988), pp. 57–76.
5. J. S. Keltie, 'Mr Stanley's expedition: its conduct and results', *Fortnightly Review*, 48 (1890), pp. 66–81 (p. 81).
6. Anon, *A White Line Across the Dark Continent* (London, 1884), cited in W. Louis, 'The Berlin Congo Conference', in P. Gifford and W. R. Louis (eds), *France and Britain in Africa* (London, 1971), p. 183.

some respects, the most remarkable expedition that ever entered Africa') resulted in comparatively little new geographical knowledge; indeed, it was 'not an exploring expedition in the strict sense of the term'.[7] Instead, Keltie portrayed it as half way between a military campaign and a heroic adventure. The Emin Pasha Relief Expedition had done something more than fill in the 'great blank': it had placed Stanley himself at the centre of attention. Reports of Stanley's exploits in Africa turned him into a public sensation: in Keltie's words, 'a Stanley telegram during these three years caused more excitement than the threat of a European war; the newsboys gave it preference to the winners of the last race'.[8]

The name Henry Morton Stanley was closely associated with the coming of a new age of sensational exploration. His 'discovery' of Livingstone at Ujiji on Lake Tanganyika in 1871 secured him a place in the popular mythology of exploration, and provided ready material for relentless parody on stage and street; his image, immortalized in Madame Tussaud's, was reproduced in countless advertisements selling everything from soap to Bovril. The helmet which he had raised to greet Livingstone became as famous as the doctor's so-called 'consular cap', thanks to the numerous photographs which were produced on his return to England. In much later portraits, he was pictured in less romantic terms, as if to mark the transition from youthful adventurer to commander-in-chief. Just as Stanley's expeditions were planned as military campaigns, so too were his books; as one obituarist noted in 1904, 'his pen moved over the paper like an army across the battle field'.[9] Stanley had an unrivalled gift for self-publicity; his experience as a journalist for the *New York Herald* accounts, in part, for the style of his best-known books, *How I Found Livingstone* (1872), *Through the Dark Continent* (1878) and *In Darkest Africa* (1890). The sheer volume of his writings, both public and private, suggests that Stanley was as much a man of words as a man of action; indeed, he represented the process of exploration in ways which have had a lasting impact on the modern world.

In this chapter, I am concerned with contemporary responses to Stanley's reputation as an explorer. These responses were in fact far more varied than Keltie's economical maps and well-chosen words suggest. Indeed, what we know of the popular response to Stanley seems as much designed to deflate his reputation as to enhance it. His portentous greeting to Livingstone in 1872 became a constant source of

7. Keltie, 'What Stanley has done', p. 130; 'Mr Stanley's expedition', p. 67.
8. Keltie, 'Mr Stanley's expedition', p. 66.
9. *The Times*, 25 May 1904.

embarrassment to him thereafter, inviting popular ridicule as much as reverence; following his election to the House of Commons in 1895, even the doorkeeper could not resist just one more 'Mr Stanley, I presume?'[10] And what had been intended as the crowning moment of his career as an explorer, the publication of *In Darkest Africa* in 1890 – was greeted as much with scepticism as with praise. In *A New Light Thrown Across Darkest Africa*, F. C. Burnand (the editor of *Punch*) lampooned Stanley's philanthropic pretensions, portraying the Emin Pasha Relief Expedition as nothing more than a publicity stunt staged for commercial gain (figure 6.2).[11] In comparing Stanley's self-promotional style to that of the showman, and associating it with the feminized glamour of the stage, Burnand was exploiting a long-running anxiety about the explorer's 'sensationalism', a theme we shall return to in chapter 8. It is important to note here that the burlesque response to Stanley both unsettled and reaffirmed the cult of the explorer, focusing attention on the question of his identity. As a satirical strategy, there was much to recommend it. The truth of Stanley's own identity was a constant source of intense public speculation throughout his life.[12] Stanley's own narration of himself in *How I Found Livingstone* (in which he unashamedly acknowledged that '*Ego* is first and foremost in this book') provided further ammunition.[13] In another Burnand burlesque, entitled *How I Found Stanley*, the narrator speculates on the possibility of yet another expedition, following the logic of Stanley's quests to an absurd conclusion: 'Suppose Stanley should have the misfortune to lose himself? I saw my road at once. *I would go and find Stanley.* And then somebody else could come out to find me. Then some one to find *him*, and so on. In the course of time, one-half of the world would be finding out the other half. This is the law of progress' (figure 6.3).[14]

10. F. McLynn, *Stanley: Sorcerer's Apprentice* (London, 1991), p. 375; I. Anstruther, *I Presume: Stanley's Triumph and Disaster* (London, 1956), p. 147.
11. F. C. Burnand, *A New Light Thrown Across the Keep it Quite Darkest Africa*, 6th edn (London, 1891), pp. 73–4.
12. Stanley was born in 1841 as John Rowlands, the illegitimate son of a Welsh pauper. He adopted the name Henry Stanley following his emigration to America in 1858, and throughout his life tried to suppress public knowledge of his original identity. See L. Jones and I. Jones (eds), *H. M. Stanley and Wales* (St Asaph, 1972); R. Hall, *Stanley: An Adventurer Explored* (London, 1974); F. McLynn, *Stanley: The Making of an African Explorer* (London, 1989).
13. H. M. Stanley, *How I Found Livingstone* (London, 1872), p. 69. See also T. Youngs, ' "My footsteps on these pages": the inscription of self and "race" in H. M. Stanley's *How I Found Livingstone*' *Prose Studies*, 13 (1990), pp. 230–49.
14. F. C. Burnand, 'Across the Keep-it Dark Continent, or How I Found Stanley', in F. C. Burnand (ed.), *Some Old Friends* (London, 1892), pp. 348–9. The same thought occurred to Thomas Stevens, who set out to East Africa in search of

6.2 'He Crosses the Equator', from F. C. Burnand, *A New Light Thrown Across the Keep it Quite Darkest Africa*, 6th edn (1891), p. 111.

The satirical reaction to Stanley's fame as an explorer was part of a spectrum of responses, which ranged from adulation to condemnation. While Stanley was hailed by the propagandists of empire as a heroic man of action, his motives and methods as an explorer attracted considerable criticism throughout his career. It is significant here that Stanley was regarded not just as an extraordinary individual, but also as the embodiment of a new phenomenon such as 'sensational geography' or 'exploration by warfare'. To consider the sources and

Stanley in 1889: T. Stevens, *Scouting for Stanley in East Africa* (London, 1890), p. 5.

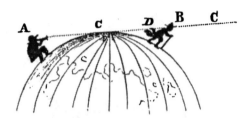

6.3 'In Search of Stanley', from F. C. Burnand, 'Across the Keep-it-Dark Continent, or How I Found Stanley' (1892), p. 398. (There was an accompanying key: 'A: myself, B: Stanley walking against the wind, C: Line of sight, D: Stanley's coat-tail blown by the wind'.)

character of these responses, it is necessary to adopt a contextual rather than a biographical approach, for I am concerned here less with the meaning of such controversies for Stanley, than with the meaning of Stanley for his critics. In this chapter, I focus principally upon two influential sources of criticism: the geographical establishment (represented by the RGS) and the philanthropic community (represented by Exeter Hall). Seen in this perspective, the cultural history of exploration appears much more heterogeneous than it might otherwise seem; a field of conflict and controversy, rather than a narrative of progress.

Geography Militant

Keltie's assessment of Stanley's achievements was shared by many of his admirers: in 1904, Sidney Low claimed that 'The map of Africa is a monument to Stanley.'[15] It was not merely that Stanley's expeditions had mapped the lakes and rivers of central Africa in more detail than ever before; nor even that his own, adopted, name had been inscribed on the surface of the map (as at Stanley Falls and Stanley Pool). For Stanley was also said to have played a leading role in the 'scramble for Africa', which left the territory of the continent, as Sidney Low put it, 'neatly divided off, and most of it tinted with appropriate national colours; the British, red; the French, purple; the German, brown; the Portuguese, green'. Stanley's work on the Congo was singled out as his pre-eminent achievement, precisely because it was here that exploration and empire were so closely linked. On the one hand, he was the first European to have followed the course of the river across central Africa: 'no single individual has revolutionized so large a tract of the earth's surface, with only a handful of armed men and a slender column of

15. D. Stanley (ed.), *The Autobiography of Henry M. Stanley* (London, 1909), p. 392.

camp-followers and attenders'. On the other, he had played a pivotal role in establishing the Congo Free State: according to Low, 'in the short space of five years the work was done! The Congo was policed, surveyed, placed under control. A chain of stations was drawn along its banks; systematic relations had been established with the more powerful native potentates; an elaborate political and commercial organisation had been established'.[16]

While few historians today would credit a single explorer with such a degree of influence on the political map of Africa, it is undoubtedly the case that Stanley played a more active role in the field of imperial politics than most other explorers. He was closely involved in the development of the Belgian King Leopold's African empire, and was simultaneously a vocal advocate of the extension of British influence in East Africa. And the motives behind the Emin Pasha Relief Expedition certainly cannot be understood without some appreciation of the wider commercial and political interests involved.[17] To describe Stanley as the 'Napoleon of African travellers'[18] thus seems particularly appropriate in view of the scale of his ambitions and the lengths he was prepared to go to realize them. His career as an explorer provides a bridge between what is sometimes regarded the golden age of African exploration (c.1851–78) and the era of the scramble (c.1884–91). Seen from the perspective of events in Africa rather than of the conference table in Europe, however, the two eras seem more difficult to distinguish. In the words of one historian, 'From the time of the Egyptian invasion of 1875–6 onwards, a multitude of Europeans – explorers, scientists, traders, financiers, missionaries – were scrambling everywhere, at the Sultan's palace in Zanzibar or far inland by the Great Lakes, scrambling for new knowledge, for a reputation, for markets, for concessions, for pagan souls.'[19] If the 1870s were indeed a critical turning-point in the history of European involvement in Africa, then Stanley might well be regarded as a key figure in the transition to new forms of imperialism in the closing decades of the nineteenth century.

Stanley's approach to geographical exploration in many ways embodied the cultural style of the new imperialism – bold, brash and uncompromising. In *How I Found Livingstone*, Stanley writes as the 'travelling correspondent of the New York Herald', less the scientific geographer

16. Stanley, *Autobiography of Henry M. Stanley*, pp. 393, 397, 400.
17. I. Smith, *The Emin Pasha Relief Expedition, 1886–1890* (Oxford, 1972); T. Youngs, *Travellers in Africa: British Travelogues, 1850–1900* (Manchester, 1994).
18. 'Henry Morton Stanley', *Scottish Geographical Magazine*, 20 (1904), p. 284.
19. R. Coupland, *The Exploitation of East Africa* (London, 1939), p. 319. See also R. Bridges, 'Europeans and East Africans in the age of exploration', *Geographical Journal*, 139 (1973), pp. 220–32.

than the narrator of an adventure. In his search for a scoop, he presents himself as a thoroughly modern figure, an interloper among 'gentlemen geographers'. More generally, he declares his faith in the possibility of progress in Africa: 'It is simply a question of money, which is the sinew of all enterprises. With a sufficient supply of it all Africa can be explored easily. Not only explored, but conquered and civilized. Not only civilized, but intersected by railroads from one end to the other, through and through.'[20] Stanley's second expedition was financed jointly by the *Daily Telegraph* and the *New York Herald*. Soon after his return in 1878, he began the first of many lectures to geographical societies and chambers of commerce on the economic opportunities created by the work of exploration. At the inaugural meeting of the Manchester Geographical Society in 1885, for example, he portrayed the world as a huge market place, its ports just 'so many stalls', its people 'so many vendors and buyers'.[21]

Stanley's geography was a science of action, dedicated to the subjugation of wild nature; its books and maps were weapons of conquest rather than objects of contemplation. One of the prime functions of geographical knowledge, he insisted, was to clear the path for capitalist enterprise. Exploration would be followed by the navigation of rivers and the establishment of trading stations, above all by modern forms of communication. As Stanley put it in 1891, 'Africa is being fettered to civilisation by rigid bars of metal which form the all-conquering railway.'[22] Nowhere was this vision more clearly displayed than in Stanley's account of his work for King Leopold, published in *The Congo and the Founding of Its Free State*, which, significantly, is sub-titled 'A story of work and exploration'. Here Stanley glories in the name *Bula Matari*, the 'breaker of rocks', narrating the establishment of a series of stations on the River Congo as a quest for mastery of the earth. The 'rugged' landscape around Vivi, we are told, 'breathed a grim defiance that was undeniable. Yet our task was to temper this obstinacy, to make the position scaleable, even accessible; to quicken this cold lifelessness; to reduce that grim defiance to submission'.[23] Stanley maintained that many European men were too weak, too sensitive, too intemperate or too cultured to meet this challenge: what was required was 'pure manliness', not 'vain fancies'.[24]

20. Stanley, *How I Found Livingstone*, pp. 681–2.
21. Stanley, 'Central Africa and the Congo basin', p. 8.
22. *The Times*, 2 May 1891, p. 13.
23. H. M. Stanley, *The Congo and the Founding of Its Free State*, 2 vols (London, 1885), vol. 1, p. 140.
24. Stanley, *The Congo*, vol. 2, pp. 266, 230.

Whenever Stanley addressed the themes of geography or exploration in general terms, in his writings or in his lectures, he portrayed himself as a protagonist in a battle. Stanley's geography was an instrument of war, and its targets were not merely to be found in central Africa. To understand the terms of the battle in which Stanley was engaged, we need to consider more carefully the controversies which surrounded him on the home front.[25] Stanley defined his own approach to exploration in opposition to two kinds of adversary. First, there were the 'armchair geographers', unsettled by what they regarded as his sensationalism: Stanley never missed an opportunity to contrast their gentlemanly theoretical speculations with his own first-hand experience as an explorer in the field. Second, there were the philanthropists who interpreted his methods as 'exploration by warfare': Stanley angrily dismissed their concerns about the welfare of indigenous peoples as 'soft, sentimental, sugar-and-honey, milk-and-water kind of talk'.[26] In both cases, the debates between Stanley and his critics raised far-reaching questions: about the purposes of geographical knowledge, the meanings of gentlemanly conduct, and the changing relationship between exploration and empire.

Sensational Geography

The controversy over Stanley's 'sensationalism' had its origins in the reception he received in 1872 on his return from having 'discovered' Livingstone. Such was the astonishment at the news that Stanley, a mere reporter for the notorious *New York Herald*, had succeeded where the Royal Geographical Society had failed, that the President, Sir Henry Rawlinson, cuttingly remarked that it must have been Livingstone who had discovered Stanley, and not the other way round.[27] When it became apparent that Stanley had achieved what he claimed, and had been entrusted with Livingstone's private journals and letters, the leading RGS Fellows were forced to accept what they had previously regarded

25. While this chapter focuses on arguments about Stanley's methods of exploration, it should also be remembered that his claims about the prospects of European settlement in central Africa were also contested: see, for example, J. Pope Hennessy and E. Dicey, 'Is central Africa worth having?', *Nineteenth Century*, 28 (1890), pp. 478–500.
26. 'Mr Stanley's recent explorations and discoveries in central Africa', *Proceedings of the Royal Geographical Society*, 22 (1877–8), pp. 144–65 (quote from p. 145).
27. *Proceedings of the Royal Geographical Society*, 16 (1872), p. 241; Livingstone Expedition Journal, 1 August 1872 (Stanley Papers, British Library).

as inconceivable. Hoping to make the best out of a bad situation, they invited Stanley to address the Geographical Section at the annual meeting of the British Association, held at Brighton in August 1872.

Stanley's appearance at the British Association attracted a crowd of around three thousand people to the Geographical Section. His lecture ('Discoveries at the North end of Lake Tanganyika') began in typical style: 'I consider myself in the light of a troubadour, to relate to you the tale of an old man who is tramping onward to discover the source of the Nile.'[28] Speaking in front of the obligatory map of Africa, Stanley proceeded to defend Livingstone's increasingly discredited theories about the river systems of central Africa. He dismissed all attempts to debate Livingstone's contention that the Lualaba River fed into the Nile as merely the speculations of armchair geographers; 'this was not a question of theory', he insisted, 'but of fact'. Stanley was clearly taken aback at the cool reception he received from the geographers. The Chairman, Francis Galton, only increased his discomfort by airing rumours about his true identity, which had been circulating in the press. (Stanley claimed to be an American, and had made every attempt to hide the truth of his upbringing as a workhouse child in North Wales.) In his concluding observations, Galton added insult to injury, with a distinctly sour remark about the shortcomings of 'sensational geography'.[29]

The Brighton meeting served to widen a growing rift between Stanley and the geographical establishment. Galton and others took exception to Stanley's journalistic ways, while Stanley was furious at what he took to be their attempt to humiliate him. In a letter to the *Daily Telegraph*, published on 28 August 1872, Stanley hit out at 'all statements that I am not what I claim to be – an American; all gratuitous remarks such as "sensationalism" as directed at me by that suave gentleman, Mr Francis Galton', and dismissed Rawlinson's comments on Livingstone's theories as 'wild, absurd and childish, to use the mildest terms'. At a dinner held a few days later, he continued the assault against those he was now calling 'the enemies of Livingstone', singling out for particular criticism 'Mr Francis Galton, FRS, FRGS, and God knows how many more letters to his name'.[30] In public, his adversaries were more circumspect; but in private, their contempt for Stanley was plain. Clements Markham, a future president, described him as a scoundrel and a blackguard, while Horace Waller (who was

28. *The Times*, 17 August 1872.
29. *Glasgow Herald*, 17 August 1872.
30. *Daily Telegraph*, 28 August 1872; *Manchester Examiner*, 2 September 1872. See also Stanley, *How I Found Livingstone*, pp. 468–70, 683–90.

later to edit Livingstone's *Last Journals*) dismissed Stanley as 'utterly unworthy of credence'.[31]

The controversies of 1872 turned on issues of social standing, scientific merit and moral legitimacy. As an outsider, Stanley quite simply lacked the credentials of either the gentleman or the scientist, and his assumed national identity (American) in combination with his profession (reporter) provided ample grounds for the testy reception he was accorded by the 'high priests of geographical orthodoxy'.[32] Galton later noted that 'Mr Stanley had other interests than geography. He was essentially a journalist aiming at producing sensational articles'.[33] The constant references to Stanley's 'sensationalism' were intended to highlight the distance between the sober proceedings of the geographers and Stanley's vulgar commercialism. Such responses resemble the reaction of the literary establishment to the 'sensation novels' of the same period; the use of the term in both contexts had an 'aura of patronizing disapproval', and reflected a similar anxiety about the relation between the craft of the specialist (novelist or geographer) and more popular traditions (melodrama or reportage).[34] As Markham privately declared in 1872, 'Damn public estimation. The fellow has done no geography!'[35] But the attempt to discredit Stanley met with limited success, not least because the RGS itself under Murchison had not been slow to exploit the 'sensationalism' surrounding African exploration in the 1860s (see chapter 4).[36]

Unable to disprove his claim to have 'discovered' Livingstone, Stanley's critics turned their attention to the man himself. From the evidence that survives in the form of private correspondence, it seems that

31.   C. Markham to F. Galton, 29 August and 7 September 1872 (Galton Papers, University College London); H. Waller to H. W. Bates, 9 October 1872 (Fellows Correspondence, RGS Archives).

32.   [S. Low], 'Henry Morton Stanley', *DNB Supplement* (London, 1912), p. 387.

33.   F. Galton, *Memories of My Life*, 3rd edn (London, 1909), p. 207. Another critic remarked that 'Mr Stanley may rest assured that he will win laurels as an explorer just in the degree in which he can forget he is a correspondent': L. Oliphant, 'African explorers', *North American Review*, 124 (1877), p. 391.

34.   W. Hughes, *The Maniac in the Cellar: Sensation Novels of the 1860s* (Princeton, 1980), p. 166.

35.   C. Markham, *Royal Geographical Society* (unpublished manuscript, RGS Archives), p. 399.

36.   Winwood Reade defended Stanley in precisely these terms, alluding to the publicity surrounding Paul Du Chaillu's expeditions to West Africa: 'The charge of sensationalism is unjust and is ludicrous when applied by a leading member of that Society which exhibited stuffed gorillas in its rooms, and promulgated stories about their thumping their breasts and scooping out negro skulls': *Pall Mall Gazette*, 26 August 1872.

Galton, together with the eminent physiologist William Carpenter (President of the British Association in 1872 and a well-established figure in the scientific community),[37] attempted to use rumours about Stanley's birthplace and parentage to discredit him. Such moves acquire added significance in the context of Galton's growing interest in the science of heredity: in *Hereditary Genius* (1869), he had argued that intellectual ability was principally a function of inheritance, a hypothesis he was to develop further in a study of *English Men of Science* (1874). Significantly, however, Galton selected for his studies only those who satisfied the conventional test of eminence: admitting the difficulty of defining a 'man of science', for example, he simply based his sample on the 'verdict of the scientific world' as reflected in the membership of scientific societies and the award of titles.[38] The idea that Stanley could simply talk his way into the same company clearly incensed the representatives of the new scientific elite, of whom Galton and Carpenter were notable representatives. Spurred on by Stanley's repeated attempts to obscure the truth of his origins, William Carpenter attempted to use his connections to prevent Stanley from meeting the Queen, fearing that this would firmly establish him in 'the public mind'.[39] But this private campaign proved unsuccessful, and Stanley's audience with the Queen had precisely the effect his critics had feared. With the support of influential sections of the press, notably *The Times*, Stanley made it clear that nothing short of an RGS medal would make amends for the way he had been treated. Much against the wishes of many Fellows (including Markham and Waller), the RGS eventually awarded Stanley its Gold Medal, in what seems primarily to have been a face-saving gesture.[40]

Style and status were not the only things at issue in 1872; what made the dispute so bitter was Stanley's claim to represent Livingstone. Even before he had set foot in London, Stanley was claiming that Livingstone had been virtually abandoned by his official sponsors. The débâcle of the RGS Livingstone Relief Expedition, which arrived in Zanzibar at precisely the moment when the world was learning of Stanley's success,

37.   A. Winter, 'The construction of orthodoxies and heterodoxies in the early Victorian life sciences', in B. Lightman (ed.), *Victorian Science in Context* (Chicago, 1997), pp. 24–50.
38.   F. Galton, *English Men of Science* (London, 1874), pp. 2–3.
39.   W. B. Carpenter to F. Galton, 2, 8 and 12 September 1872 (Galton Papers).
40.   C. Markham, *Royal Geographical Society*, p. 399; H. Waller to H. Bates, 25 October 1872 (RGS Archives); D. W. Forrest, *Francis Galton* (London, 1974), pp. 117–19. An editorial in *The Times* condemned the geographers in no uncertain terms: 'We cannot think without shame and indignation of the conduct of the RGS in this matter' (15 November 1872).

provided him with further ammunition. Some of his fiercest attacks were directed at John Kirk, the botanist turned vice-consul at Zanzibar, who had accompanied Livingstone on his Zambesi expedition in 1858–63. Kirk, an influential figure among both the geographers and the anti-slavery lobby in London,[41] was accused of failing to ensure the safety of supplies sent into the interior, and of using slaves to transport the goods.[42] He strongly denied these allegations, and the Foreign Office had no hesitation in giving him their support; as one official put it, 'I cannot help thinking that Mr Stanley the American may for his own purposes have prejudiced Livingstone against Dr Kirk and others who did their best to serve him at Zanzibar.'[43] This view was shared by Horace Waller, Kirk's brother-in-law: on hearing of Stanley's allegations, he wrote several letters to Livingstone imploring him to clear Kirk's name.[44]

The controversies of 1872 left a permanent mark on Stanley himself. 'All the actions of my life, and I may say all my thoughts, since 1872', he wrote long afterwards, 'have been strongly coloured by the storm of abuse and the wholly unjustifiable reports circulated about me then. So numerous were my enemies that my friends remained dumb.'[45] His critics too, most notably Waller and Kirk, continued to resent his attempts to appropriate Livingstone's reputation. If, as Dorothy Helly has argued,[46] Livingstone's most important legacy lay in the establishment of a myth to fit a new pattern of British influence in Africa, it is none the less clear that the myth-making process was fraught with conflict. On his death, Livingstone became almost a saint; small wonder, then, that the struggle to represent him was so fierce.

Exploration by Warfare

The geographical establishment became embroiled in a second round of controversy over Stanley's methods as an explorer in the wake of

41. Kirk later served as Vice-President of the RGS. See Coupland, *Exploitation of East Africa*, pp. 38–61, 134–224; Markham, *Royal Geographical Society*.
42. These charges were also made by Livingstone. See D. Livingstone to A. Livingstone, 18 November 1871, British Library Add. MS. 50,184, ff. 174–5; Stanley, *How I Found Livingstone*, pp. 16, 675–6.
43. Memorandum for Lord Granville, 29 July 1872: FO 84/1357 (Public Records Office).
44. H. Waller to D. Livingstone, 12 August and 25 November 1872 (Waller Papers, Rhodes House, Oxford).
45. Stanley, *The Autobiography of H. M. Stanley*, p. 289.
46. D. Helly, *Livingstone's Legacy: Horace Waller and Victorian Myth-making* (Athens, Ohio, 1987), pp. 26–7.

reports about his transcontinental African expedition, sponsored jointly by the *Daily Telegraph* and the *New York Herald*, in 1874–7. The origins of this controversy lay in Stanley's own account of a violent incident at Bumbire Island on Lake Victoria in August 1875, which reached the newspapers a year later.[47] What most concerned Stanley's critics was not simply the fact that he had used force; it was rather that, following a violent confrontation on the lake, he had planned an act of cold-blooded revenge, and appeared to revel in the violence which ensued. The result of the initial confrontation, he reported, was 'fourteen dead and wounded with ball and buck-shot, which, although I should consider to be very dear payment for the robbery of eight ash oars and a drum, was barely equivalent in fair estimation to the intended massacre of ourselves'. Stanley planned a punishment even more bloody; two hundred and eighty men, armed with muskets and spears, approached the island in eighteen canoes, under the American and British flags. Having enticed their opponents onto the shore, they slaughtered at least forty-two, injured many more, suffering only a few bruises themselves.[48] To his critics, Stanley's methods amounted to nothing less than 'exploration by warfare'. In the words of the *Saturday Review*, 'He has no concern with justice, no right to administer it. He comes with no sanction, no authority, no jurisdiction – nothing but explosive bullets and a copy of the *Daily Telegraph*.'[49]

The controversy over Stanley's conduct as an explorer reached well beyond the geographical establishment. Among the most outspoken critics of Stanley on this occasion were the representatives of two philanthropic societies associated with Exeter Hall, the Anti-Slavery Society and the Aborigines Protection Society.[50] The attitudes of these societies towards overseas exploration may be characterized as ambivalent. On the one hand, there was frequent condemnation of the effects of European contact in the Americas, Australasia, the Far East and Africa, where 'British enterprise and British valour have unhappily proved the means of scattering misery and devastation over many a fair portion of the globe'.[51] On the other, however, there was a lasting conviction that Britain could reclaim her moral virtue by espousing the values of 'legitimate commerce' in place of exploitation, civilization instead of barbarism. That the exploration of central Africa carried

47. McLynn, *Stanley: Sorcerer's Apprentice*, pp. 10–15.
48. *Daily Telegraph*, 7 and 10 August 1876; H. M. Stanley, *Through the Dark Continent*, 2nd edn, 2 vols (London, 1899), vol. 1, pp. 178–86, 228–9; Coupland, *Exploitation of East Africa*, pp. 324–9.
49. *Saturday Review*, 16 February 1878.
50. See chapter 4 above.
51. Aborigines Protection Society, *First Annual Report* (London, 1838), p. 8.

with it dangers as well as opportunities was clear from the *Anti-Slavery Reporter*'s criticisms of Sir Samuel Baker. Baker's low estimation of the indigenous population of central Africa ('a hopeless race of savages') was matched by a ruthless approach to 'civilization', which portrayed 'the musket and the bayonet' as 'precursors of permanent trade in savage countries'.[52] After one particularly violent confrontation during Baker's expedition to equatorial Africa in 1872, the *Reporter* had remarked: 'No doubt vengeance has been inflicted, at whatever cost, upon the provoking enemies of geographical exploration; but it may be questioned whether the way of violence is the most effectual one, even to that end'.[53]

Exeter Hall was the source of some of the fiercest criticism of Stanley's conduct during his second African expedition. After news of Stanley's violence on Lake Victoria had reached London in 1876, a joint committee representing the Anti-Slavery and Aborigines Protection Societies urged the Foreign Office that 'the murderous acts of retaliation he committed were unworthy of a man who went to Africa professedly as a pioneer of civilisation'.[54] The response of the British Government was unusually swift; the Foreign Secretary sent instructions to Stanley (via his old adversary John Kirk, now a full Consul at Zanzibar), that the British Flag was not to be used on his expedition.[55] A year later, the Anti-Slavery Society received further reports concerning Stanley's expedition from missionaries in East Africa, and these too found their way to the Foreign Office. Stanley was charged with excessive violence, wanton destruction, the selling of labourers into slavery, the sexual exploitation of native women and the plundering of villages for ivory and canoes. Kirk's unpublished report on these allegations held nothing back: 'if the story of this expedition were known it would stand in the annals of African discovery unequalled for the reckless use of power that modern weapons placed in his hands over natives who never before heard a gun fired'.[56]

Exeter Hall renewed its attack on Stanley's return to Europe in 1878, when he was the guest of honour at a formal reception organized by the RGS. In an article headed 'Geography and massacre', the *Anti-Slavery Reporter* complained that fundamental principles of justice and morality had been sacrificed for a 'reckless passion for geographical

---

52. H. A. C. Cairns, *Prelude to Imperialism: British Reactions to Central African Society, 1840–1890* (London, 1965), pp. 204–6.
53. *Anti-Slavery Reporter*, 1 April 1873, p. 130.
54. *Colonial Intelligencer*, 1 (1874–8), January 1877, p. 357.
55. J. Kirk to H. M. Stanley, 11 December 1876: FO 84/1454 (PRO).
56. J. Kirk to Derby, 1 May 1878, FO 84/1514 (PRO); J. Farler to A. Buzacott, 28 December 1877, Rhodes House MS, G2.

discovery'.[57] Such criticisms of the RGS were not unprecedented. In 1867, Exeter Hall and leading representatives of the RGS (including its President Sir Roderick Murchison) had found themselves on opposite sides in the controversy over Governor Eyre's suppression of the Jamaican insurrection; and in 1875, the *Reporter* had taken particular exception to an article by Clements Markham in the *Geographical Magazine*, which had painted a rosy picture of the condition of Chinese labourers in Peru.[58] Nevertheless, the geographical and philanthropic communities were not always at odds. As the exploitation of Livingstone's reputation suggests, the anti-slavery cause was represented within the RGS: probably the most active intermediary between the two communities during the 1870s and 1880s was the inveterate letter-writer Horace Waller. The smaller Aborigines Protection Society also had a constituency within the RGS, though its influence was less than it had been during Thomas Hodgkin's lifetime.[59] In a letter to the RGS Secretary in 1878, Robert Fowler (a treasurer of the Aborigines Protection Society and a Conservative MP) insisted that Stanley's 'heartless butchery of unfortunate natives has brought dishonour on the British flag and must have rendered the course of future travellers more perilous and difficult'.[60]

The representatives of the Royal Geographical Society found themselves in a delicate position in 1878; if they too disowned Stanley as merely the representative of the *Daily Telegraph* and the *New York Herald*, they would risk excluding the RGS from any association with his achievements. Although Markham's *Geographical Magazine* had already declared that 'knowledge is dearly bought at the cost of piratical proceedings of this nature',[61] it was becoming clear that Stanley's expedition would finally resolve the long-running dispute over the sources of the Nile. Indeed, James Grant had already described Stanley's exploration of Lake Victoria as 'one of the most important and brilliant that has ever been made in central Africa, or indeed in any other country'.[62] There were, however, two Fellows, unconnected with Exeter

57. *Anti-Slavery Reporter*, February 1878, p. 7.
58. Semmel, *The Governor Eyre Controversy* (London, 1962), pp. 116–17; *Anti-Slavery Reporter*, 1 September 1875, pp. 183–5; C. Markham, 'From China to Peru', *Geographical Magazine*, 1 (1874), pp. 367–70.
59. On Hodgkin, see pp. 45–6 above.
60. R. N. Fowler to F. Chesson, 5 February 1878, and R. N. Fowler to H. W. Bates, 29 January 1878, Rhodes House MS. C134/88 and C153/194 respectively; J. Flynn, *Sir Robert N. Fowler: A Memoir* (London, 1893), pp. 73–6.
61. 'Mr Stanley's proceedings in the Lake Region of Central Africa', *Geographical Magazine*, 3 (1876), p. 247.
62. J. A. Grant, 'On Mr H. M. Stanley's exploration of Lake Victoria Nyanza', *Geographical Magazine*, 3 (1876), p. 25.

Hall, who were prepared to criticize Stanley quite openly at meetings of the Society: H. M. Hyndman and Sir Henry Yule. Hyndman at that time was working as a journalist at the *Pall Mall Gazette*, though he later became better known for his prominent political role within the Social Democratic Federation.[63] Yule was a retired Indian officer turned scholar, then at the height of his career as an historical geographer of central Asia, having recently published his acclaimed translation of the works of Marco Polo.[64] While Hyndman was responsible for the initial attack on Stanley (and the publicity it attracted in the *Gazette* and elsewhere), Yule's support gave it credibility in the eyes of many Fellows, since he was both a medallist and a member of the RGS Council. Yule himself urged the RGS not to associate itself with Stanley's expeditions by showering him with awards and ovations. The word 'ovation' he pointed out 'was etymologically connected with *ovis*, a sheep; and when people got upon lines of excessive glorification, they were very apt to follow one another like a flock of sheep, and not see all the puddles they came across'.[65]

In response to these protests by a vocal minority of its Fellows, the Council of the RGS denied any responsibility for Stanley's actions. Little could be done, argued Sir Henry Rawlinson, since Stanley was neither a Fellow nor 'even an Englishman'; in any case, the Society 'was not established for the discussion of such subjects, which did not involve any principles of practical geography'. The President, Sir Rutherford Alcock, acknowledged the strength of feeling on Stanley's 'apparently ruthless slaughter and violence' on Lake Victoria; at the same time he insisted that 'the Society had no right collectively to censure him' on the basis of 'the hurried and sensational letters which had reached England'.[66] This response was hardly a satisfactory one, since the RGS

63.   While Hyndman's involvement with the RGS was short-lived, he later became acquainted with the anarchist geographer Kropotkin. He may well have been involved in the publication of David Nicoll's anti-Stanley pamphlet in 1890 (see below). See H. M. Hyndman, *The Record of an Adventurous Life* (London, 1911); C. Tsuzuki, *H. M. Hyndman and British Socialism* (Oxford, 1961).
64.   Yule later became president of both the Hakluyt and the Royal Asiatic Societies, and a vice-president of the RGS. He is mainly remembered today for his co-authorship of *Hobson-Jobson*. See A. Yule, 'Memoir of Sir Henry Yule', in H. Yule (ed.), *The Book of Ser Marco Polo*, 2 vols, 3rd edn (London, 1903), vol. 1, pp. xxvii–lxxxii; R. J. Bingle, 'Henry Yule: India and Cathay', in R. Bridges and P. Hair (eds), *Compassing the Vaste Globe of the Earth: Studies in the History of the Hakluyt Society* (London, 1996), pp. 143–63.
65.   H. Yule and H. Hyndman, *Mr Henry M. Stanley and the Royal Geographical Society* (London, 1878), p. 20.
66.   Yule and Hyndman, *Stanley and the Royal Geographical Society*, pp. 21, 24;

was not slow to issue collective congratulations to explorers in other circumstances. As one critic put it, 'It is impossible to contend that the Society can take credit only for the scientific achievements of its medallist . . . without passing some judgement upon the moral bearing of the acts.'[67] Yet this was the position which the Society's leading figures had apparently adopted. Their motives are not hard to discern; it is clear that they dreaded another unseemly public squabble, particularly at an ordinary meeting of the Society. Rawlinson had no time for such discussions; in a letter to Alcock, he dismissed Hyndman as 'one of the irrepressible genus of question mongers, or monomaniacs, who will insist on ventilating a crotchet'.[68]

Despite these attempts to suppress the issue, the controversy over the events on Lake Victoria resurfaced on Stanley's return to Britain in 1878. Several Fellows took exception (as the Anti-Slavery Society had done) to the message of congratulations which the Society sent to Stanley, as well as to the Council's early promise of a public meeting in his honour at St James Hall (attended by the Prince of Wales), followed by a grand dinner at Willis' Rooms. Still insisting that Stanley had yet to justify his actions, Henry Yule resigned from the Council in protest.[69] However, other senior Fellows remained silent. The African explorer Sir Samuel Baker wrote privately to Edwin Arnold, the influential editor of the *Daily Telegraph*, assuring him that Stanley could count on the support of the most prominent Fellows. Baker uncharitably dismissed the campaign against Stanley as the work of 'envious, stay-at-home do nothings': 'The fact is that the RGS is now so enormous (containing upwards of *three thousand* members) that it is no longer an angelic body – there is an undercurrent of malice exhibited prominently by at least one member, which under the cloak of philanthropy would stab a great reputation.'[70] Stanley himself used the Society's grand dinner to present a lengthy defence of his actions: 'What I have done at Bambireh [*sic*] and other places on the Victoria Nyanza and on the Kwango-Lualaba has been done to satisfy justice. Where I have failed to make peace Livingstone would have failed, and where I have made friendships with natives I made firmer and more lasting friendships than even

R. Alcock to H. W. Bates, 26 October 1876 (Fellows Correspondence, RGS Archives).
67.   J. E. Ritchie, *The Life and Discoveries of David Livingstone*, 2 vols (London, 1877), vol. 2, p. 203.
68.   H. Rawlinson to R. Alcock, 14 November 1876 (Fellows Correspondence, RGS Archives).
69.   H. Yule to F. Galton, 27 January 1878 (Galton Papers).
70.   S. Baker to E. Arnold, 20 January 1878 (Stanley Papers, British Library, RP 2435 ii) (emphasis in the original).

Livingstone himself could have made.'[71] In the wake of this resolute defence, the Council of the RGS effectively suspended further criticism. Meanwhile, the *Geographical Magazine* published a retraction of its earlier comments, declaring in March 1878 that it had done an 'injustice to Mr Stanley'.[72]

The debate over 'exploration by warfare' had far-reaching implications. It was argued by Stanley's critics that his excessive violence would jeopardize the lives of future explorers and missionaries; as Yule put it, 'How would the next Speke or Livingstone . . . fare upon the Lake?'[73] A similar line was taken by the Zanzibar Consul, John Kirk, who was quick to interpret subsequent hostility towards missionaries on Lake Victoria as the direct consequence of Stanley's actions.[74] In this respect, comparisons were later made with the more peaceful methods of other explorers, notably Joseph Thomson, who prided himself on having travelled to Lake Victoria through Masai territory without the loss of a single life.[75] Yet there was more at stake than practical considerations: whenever the conduct of explorers was debated, the figure of the 'gentleman' almost invariably made an appearance. Thomson's methods as an explorer, for example, were often described in the language of chivalry: in 1880 he himself remarked, with one eye on the controversies over Stanley, that 'a gentle word was more potent than gunpowder'.[76] Similarly, when Verney Cameron was asked how to avoid violence in the exploration of Africa (in 1876) he replied that 'the proper way to get on with the natives was to behave like a gentleman'.[77] Stanley's own position was clear: gentlemanly conduct had no meaning in Africa, where 'the savage only respects force, power, boldness and decision'.[78] Others went still further; the German explorer Carl Peters complained that Thomson's attempts at peaceful co-existence with the Masai, 'judged by a European standard', were actually ungentlemanly. Such an approach would be interpreted as weakness: 'I have found, after all, that the one thing which would make an impression on these wild sons

71. Yule and Hyndman, *Henry M. Stanley*, pp. 38–9.
72. 'Mr Stanley', *Geographical Magazine*, 5 (1878), p. 53.
73. Yule and Hyndman, *Henry M. Stanley*, pp. 20–1.
74. J. Kirk to Derby, 19 February 1878, FO 84/1514 (PRO). On this occasion, however, Kirk's allegations were described by one Foreign Office official as 'mere gossip, unsupported by any evidence'.
75. J. Thomson, 'Through the Masai country to Victoria Nyanza', *Proceedings of the Royal Geographical Society*, 6 (1884), pp. 690–710.
76. R. Rotberg, *Joseph Thomson and the Exploration of Africa* (London, 1971), p. 110.
77. *Geographical Magazine*, 3 (1876), p. 284.
78. Stanley, *Through the Dark Continent*, vol. 1, p. 216.

of the steppe was a bullet from the repeater or the double-barrelled rifle, and then only when employed in emphatic relation to their own bodies.'[79]

These debates reveal a degree of difference over conceptions of 'gentlemanly' conduct which extends well beyond the sphere of exploration. Mixed into the debate over Stanley's methods were further uncertainties about the authority of the explorer and the rights of indigenous peoples. Francis Galton, writing anonymously on Stanley's expedition in the *Edinburgh Review*, questioned 'how far a private individual, travelling as a newspaper correspondent, has a right to assume such a warlike attitude, and to force his way through native tribes regardless of their rights, whatever those may be'. Yet Galton failed to develop these remarks, as if these were not matters for scientific geographers. Stanley, he continued, had 'dissected and laid bare the very heart of the great continent of Africa'; beside this achievement, 'the death of a few hundred barbarians, ever ready to fight and kill, and many of whom are professed cannibals, will perhaps be regarded as a small matter'.[80] Whether or not irony is intended,[81] Galton's remarks broached a moral issue which was to provide the central point of reference in a still larger controversy over the 'Congo atrocities' which erupted in 1890, following Stanley's return from his last major expedition.

The 'Congo Atrocities'

Throughout the controversy over the events on Lake Victoria in 1875, Stanley's critics had exploited the gulf between his claims to high moral purpose and the 'policy of terrorism and revenge' he had apparently adopted; as one critic put it, 'The blunderbuss may be an admirable weapon, and the Bible is a noble element in civilisation. But when the two are combined, the effect is a little incongruous.'[82] Stanley himself responded in kind; in 1878 he was reported to have challenged the 'Exeter Hall Party' to mount a trans-African expedition armed with 'seven tons of Bibles, four tons of Prayer-books, any number of sur-

79.   C. Peters, *New Light on Dark Africa* (London, 1891), p. 222.
80.   [F. Galton], 'Stanley's discoveries and the future of Africa', *Edinburgh Review*, 147 (1878), pp. 167, 171; D. W. Forrest, *Francis Galton* (London, 1974), p. 120.
81.   A humanitarian critique would certainly have been out of character, given Galton's consistently negative observations on the indigenous peoples of southern Africa: see p. 45 above.
82.   Ritchie, *David Livingstone*, vol. 2, pp. 191, 197.

plices, and a church organ into the bargain'.[83] Yet he continued to claim the moral credentials of a follower of Livingstone, the saint of the British anti-slavery movement. In 1884 and 1885 he appeared at large anti-slavery meetings in Manchester and London, sharing platforms with leading figures from Exeter Hall.[84] Stanley's involvement in the anti-slavery movement at this time must be seen in the context of deliberations at the Berlin Conference, which resulted in the establishment of the Congo Free State under King Leopold's authority. For both Stanley and the Anti-Slavery Society associated themselves with the principle of legitimate commerce; and, more specifically, both opposed the extension of Portuguese sovereignty in the area of the Congo. Given the lofty philanthropic tone which surrounded Leopold's State during the 1880s, it is unsurprising that the *Anti-Slavery Reporter* should welcome Stanley's account of its foundation, published in 1885.[85]

Leading figures in the Anti-Slavery Society were quite willing to be associated with Stanley's last expedition (1887–90), whose ostensible purpose was the relief of Emin Pasha, following the collapse of Egyptian authority in the Sudan. On his return to London in 1890, Stanley was given a hero's welcome. Scientists, politicians, monarchs and philanthropists showered congratulations upon him at countless banquets and receptions, including those of the RGS (held in the Albert Hall) and the London Chamber of Commerce. A committee of Americans resident in Britain, organized by Henry Wellcome, presented Stanley with a trophy depicting the African continent superimposed on an American flag.[86] However, this triumphalism was not to last: at the very moment of Stanley's return, influential figures in the Anti-Slavery Society were expressing concern at reports of the transportation of unfree labourers from Zanzibar to the Congo. Horace Waller, Stanley's old enemy, had no doubts that this was nothing less than 'winked-at slavery'; as he declared in January 1890, 'The raw slave life is dragged from Nyassaland, worked upon in the Zanzibar mill and exported in British steamers to the Congo, there to be used up as Stanley used it up.'[87] It was as a result of Waller's pressure that Alfred Pease (a sympathetic MP) was asked to raise the issue in the House of Commons. Stanley's reaction

83. *Colonial Intelligencer*, 1 (1874–8), January 1878, p. 455.
84. *Anti-Slavery Reporter*, 5 November 1884, pp. 203–21, and July–August 1885, pp. 417–35.
85. Stanley, *The Congo*; *Anti-Slavery Reporter*, 20 June 1885, pp. 401–6. See also D. B. Davis, *Slavery and Human Progress* (Oxford, 1984), pp. 305–6.
86. *Daily Graphic*, 2 June 1890; H. Wellcome to W. Curtis, 20 March 1890, Wellcome Archives, Letter Book 2 (Wellcome Foundation, London).
87. H. Waller to C. H. Allen, 21 January 1890, Rhodes House MS. C69. Cf. H. Waller, *Ivory, Apes and Peacocks: An African Contemplation* (London, 1891).

was typical, and once more drew a connection between philanthropy and effeminacy; stung by the criticism, he launched a violent counter-attack on 'Quakerism, Peace Societies . . . and namby-pamby journalism'. This had the effect of widening the growing gulf between Stanley and the anti-slavery campaigners; the *Reporter* began to publish more critical pieces on labour in the Congo, largely at the instigation of Waller.[88]

In the course of 1890, further revelations about the Emin Pasha expedition irreparably damaged Stanley's reputation at Exeter Hall. Following the publication of Stanley's *In Darkest Africa*, several conflicting accounts of the expedition appeared, questioning the integrity and judgement of its leader: one member of the expedition, for example, complained that Stanley 'has no more philanthropy than my boot'.[89] Particular attention was paid to the experiences of the rear column, whose men were left to starve at Yambuya. The Anti-Slavery Society, meanwhile, attributed many of the failures of the expedition to Stanley's co-operation with Hamid Ibn Muhammad, the slave-trader known to Europe as Tippu Tib, who had been asked to supply the rear column on the Lower Congo.[90] The Aborigines Protection Society, free from any involvement in the expedition from the start, broadened the attack with fresh allegations concerning the use of virtual slaves as soldiers, the floggings inflicted on the journey up the Congo, the slaughter of natives and the burning of their villages.[91] A well-attended meeting at the Westminster Palace Hotel in December 1890 gave further publicity to the campaign over the 'Congo atrocities', as they were now being called. The meeting, chaired by Sir Robert Fowler (a critic of Stanley in 1878) heard loud condemnations of what was widely described as a military expedition rather than a journey of exploration. Henry Wellcome spoke in Stanley's defence, arguing that the employment of slaves and the flogging of miscreants was unexceptional among African explorers, including Livingstone himself: 'Stanley never killed natives if he could buy peace . . . Far

88. *Anti-Slavery Reporter*, May–June 1890, pp. 81–8; Anti-Slavery Society Minute Book, 2 May, 6 June, 4 July 1890, Rhodes House MS.
89. J. Bierman, *Dark Safari: The Life Behind the Legend of Henry Morton Stanley* (London, 1991), p. 325. For a careful reading of the various narratives associated with the expedition, see Youngs, *Travellers in Africa*, chs 4, 5.
90. *Anti-Slavery Reporter*, January–February 1891, pp. 12, 36; H. Waller to E. Sturge, 13 November 1890, Rhodes House MS. C98; W. Samarin, *The Black Man's Burden: African Colonial Labour on the Congo and Ubangi Rivers, 1880–1900* (Boulder, Colo., 1989), pp. 103–4.
91. *Aborigines' Friend*, December 1890, pp. 89–100.

from being a heartless murderer, [he had exercized] masterful self-control and justice.'[92]

The charges against Stanley were developed in a substantial tract published in 1891 by Henry Fox Bourne, secretary of the Aborigines Protection Society, entitled *The Other Side of the Emin Pasha Relief Expedition*. Not content with the now routine allegations of 'wanton slaughtering and village-burning', Fox Bourne asserted (as historians have since argued) that the covert functions of Stanley's expedition included the acquisition of territory for the British East Africa Company (which, through William Mackinnon, Stanley's chief sponsor, became closely associated with the expedition) and the extension of Leopold's influence in Central Africa, which required negotiations with Tippu Tib.[93] Such criticisms were repeated by many others; not for the first time, Stanley was characterized as a *conquistador*.[94] Radical liberals, socialists and anarchists, including H. M. Hyndman and William Morris, interpreted Stanley's 'empire-making errand' in economic as well as in moral and political terms.[95] Figure 6.4 reproduces an image from a penny socialist pamphlet, published in Aberdeen, which portrays Stanley posing as a benevolent philanthropist while being garlanded by an angel of capitalism; in the background, meanwhile, the actual effects of his 'civilizing mission' are represented by a scene of violence and destruction. Such rhetoric was to become part of the standard armoury of critics of the 'new imperialism' during the next two decades. Leopold's Congo state was represented as the most extreme expression of a system of imperialism based on the forced appropriation of land and labour.[96]

92. [H. Wellcome], 'Draft Ms Notes in Defence of Mr Stanley', Stanley MS. 10/2, RGS Archives; *Aborigines' Friend*, April 1891, pp. 155–64; *The Times*, 13 December 1890, p. 7.
93. H. R. Fox Bourne, *The Other Side of the Emin Pasha Relief Expedition* (London, 1891), pp. 45–6, 75. See also R. Anstey, *Britain and the Congo in the Nineteenth Century* (Oxford, 1962), pp. 212–25; Smith, *Emin Pasha Relief Expedition*; J. S. Galbraith, *Mackinnon in East Africa, 1878–1895: A Study in the 'New Imperialism'* (Cambridge, 1972); Youngs, *Travellers in Africa*.
94. C. Chaillé-Long, *L'Égypte et ses provinces perdues* (Paris, 1892), p. 4, pp. 199–234; *Anti-Slavery Reporter*, February 1878, p. 7.
95. H. M. Hyndman, *General Booth's Book Refuted* (London, 1890), p. 4; W. Morris, *News From Nowhere*, in *Collected Works of William Morris*, 24 vols (London, 1910–15), vol. 16, pp. 94–5; D. J. Nicoll, *Stanley's Exploits: Or Civilising Africa* (Aberdeen, 1890).
96. Samarin, *Black Man's Burden*, pp. 41–60; J. Stengers and J. Vansina, 'King Leopold's Congo, 1886–1908', in R. Oliver and G. Sanderson (eds), *The Cambridge History of Africa*, vol. 6 (Cambridge, 1985), pp. 315–58.

6.4   Frontispiece to D. J. Nicoll, *Stanley's Exploits: Or Civilising Africa* (1890).

By the time Fox Bourne published his indictment of Leopold's state, *Civilisation in Congoland*, in 1903, a much broader campaign was under way to draw public attention to the situation in Central Africa, through the work of the Congo Reform Association and the writings of Edmund Morel, notably his *The Congo Slave State* (1903) and *Red Rubber* (1906). Thirteen years earlier, however, Leopold's Congo state had the official sanction of the international community (at the Berlin and Brussels conferences, for example),[97] as well as the support of the

97.   S. Cookey, *Britain and the Congo Question, 1885–1913* (New York, 1968), pp. 22–5. Nevertheless, the British Foreign Office was aware as early as 1884 of allegations concerning the involvement of Leopold's agents in the business of slavery: see R. Oliver, *Sir Harry Johnston and the Scramble for Africa* (London, 1964), pp. 47–9.

anti-slavery establishment. It was the campaign against Stanley's 'Congo atrocities' in 1890 which marked the turning point in liberal England's attitude towards Leopold's state. The Aborigines Protection and Anti-Slavery Societies were increasingly to argue that slavery, though ostensibly outlawed in the Congo, was being practised under another name, and that beneath its cover of a 'civilizing' mission Leopold's state was becoming a 'vast field of havoc and spoliation'.[98]

Conclusion

> You may say that by our commercial relations with African tribes we must surely have let in light. I reply, if it be so, it is the blaze of the burning village, or the flash of the Winchester rifle – at best it is the glare from the smoke-stack of the Congo steamer bearing away tons upon tons of ivory.[99]

In a letter to William Gladstone written in January 1891, Sir William Harcourt described Stanley's last journey of exploration as one of those 'filibustering expeditions in the mixed guise of commerce, religion, geography and Imperialism, under which names any and every atrocity is regarded as permissible'.[100] For many of his contemporaries, Stanley was the symbol of a much larger phenomenon in the history of exploration. Within the geographical establishment, his style was clearly seen as a threat; it promised a popular, commercial and 'sensational' geography. For his liberal critics, Stanley's methods amounted to what Harcourt termed the 'worst form of piratical jingoism', representing the triumph of force over principle. Stanley's geographical and liberal critics converged at one point, the symbolic centre of so many contemporary debates over exploration and empire: the memory of David Livingstone. To them, in fact, Stanley was everything that Livingstone was not. While Livingstone's tact and moderation had left behind him 'a track of light where the white man who follows ... is in perfect safety', Stanley had surrounded himself with 'an atmosphere of terror created by the free use of fire and the sword'.[101] Even Stanley himself acknowledged the distinction, while placing a characteristically self-serving interpretation on it: 'Each man has his own way. His, I think, had its defects, though the old man, personally, has been almost Christ-like for

98.   H. R. Fox Bourne, *Civilisation in Congoland* (London, 1903), p. 303.
99.   Waller, *Ivory, Apes and Peacocks*, p. 88.
100.   A. G. Gardiner, *The Life of Sir William Harcourt*, 2 vols (London, 1923), vol. i, p. 94.
101.   *Anti-Slavery Reporter*, November 1878, p. 119.

goodness, patience, and self-sacrifice. The selfish and wooden-headed world requires mastering, as well as loving charity; for man is a composite of the spiritual and earthly.'[102] Stanley's methods of exploration seem to blur so profoundly the distinction between geography and warfare as to make it almost unrecognizable; as has been well observed, every one of his expeditions were 'invasions . . . designed to overcome resistance, whether from the terrain or from its inhabitants, and to come back with a trophy'.[103] While his missions were not directly controlled by individual governments (aside from his work for Leopold), he was not slow to associate them with the advancement of strategic interests – the British in East Africa and the Sudan, the Belgians in the Congo and even the Americans in Zanzibar. The sheer variety of the political claims on Stanley suggests that, rather than representing the interests of any empire in particular, he was a pioneer of the new imperialism in general. Like Kurtz in *Heart of Darkness*, 'all Europe contributed' to his making.[104]

While Stanley was undoubtedly a marketable symbol of the new imperialism,[105] his expeditions were subject to an unusual degree of criticism. During the 1870s, as we have seen, the geographical establishment found itself at the centre of a very public controversy over Stanley's treatment of the indigenous peoples of Central Africa; while leading geographers attempted to minimize the intrusion of politics into their proceedings, others insisted that the charges against Stanley raised fundamental questions of principle. This was certainly the position of Exeter Hall, whose condemnation of 'exploration by warfare' found some echoes within the Society itself. By 1890, the contours of controversy had changed shape; the RGS, for example, appears to have played little direct part in the controversies surrounding the Emin Pasha expedition. Elsewhere, however, questions about Stanley's role in the Congo were setting in motion a campaign that would pave the way for a broader critique of imperialism. What Stanley did for the map of Africa was one thing; the controversy his methods of exploration ignited was another. In the course of the campaign over the Congo atrocities, the map of Africa returned to haunt the liberal conscience, a process graphically represented in an illustration to Morel's *Red Rubber* (1906), depicting the course of the River Congo superimposed, in crimson, on

---

102. Stanley, *Autobiography*, p. 295.
103. D. Middleton (ed.), *The Diary of A. J. Mounteney Jephson, Emin Pasha Relief Expedition, 1887–1889* (Cambridge, 1969), p. 8.
104. J. Conrad, *Heart of Darkness*, ed. R. Kimbrough (New York, 1988), p. 50.
105. T. Richards, *The Commodity Culture of Victorian England* (London, 1990), ch. 3.

a map of Europe. For even at the height of geography's imperial past, there were those who refused the easy equation between exploration and progress. The critical response to Stanley's expeditions suggests an altogether different perspective. 'Exploration under these conditions is, in fact, exploration plus buccaneering', warned the *Pall Mall Gazette* in 1878, 'and though the map may be improved and enlarged by the process, the cause of civilisation is not a gainer thereby, but a loser.'[106]

106. *Pall Mall Gazette*, 11 February 1878.

Chapter 7

Making Representations: From an African Exhibition to the High Court of Justice

Between March and November 1890, the Victoria Gallery in London's Regent Street hosted the Stanley and African Exhibition, a popular show designed to celebrate the achievements of white men in the 'Dark Continent'. The exhibition brought together a variety of different interests, representing science, commerce, government, anti-slavery and the missionary movements, in an effort to capitalize on the publicity surrounding Stanley's last major African expedition. Among the huge assortment of ethnographic objects, pictures and trophies on display were two African children, Gootoo and Inyokwana, described in the accompanying literature as 'slave boys'. In contemporary accounts of the exhibition, the children were represented in a number of ways: as living specimens of uncivilized otherness, as faithful domestic servants for the use of Europeans and as physical metaphors for the child-like condition of the African. Such tropes rehearsed established conventions in popular racial discourse and ethnographic display, and in themselves were unremarkable. More unusual, however, was the close scrutiny which the condition of the children attracted once the exhibition had closed. In November 1890, one of the members of the Exhibition committee, Charles Allen (secretary of the British and Foreign Anti-Slavery Society), brought a *habeas corpus* action in the High Court against the putative guardians of the children, claiming that they had been cruelly treated and would be returned to slavery in Africa. Although this failed, a second action (in the Chancery division) resulted in the appointment of new guardians for the boys and a court order providing for their care in South Africa. This outcome, a delicate compromise between the claims of the contending parties, masked deeper confusions which the case had been supposed to resolve. In short, the court proceedings put in question the casual certainties of the exhibition. That the boys had to be represented, that they could not represent themselves (beyond the display of their bodies), was not at issue: but how, and by whom?

The case of the two boys was not regarded as sufficiently important to warrant a mention in either the Law Reports or the legal press, and it did not attract widespread attention in the newspapers (owing to reporting restrictions imposed at an early stage). However, buried in the papers of the Anti-Slavery Society there lies an extensive verbatim record of the court proceedings, a record which documents the multiple confusions and tensions of the case.[1] Reading this text today, in the quietness of Rhodes House in Oxford, is a surprisingly unsettling experience. I am tempted to liken it to opening a long-forgotten window which affords a different perspective on the process of representation, disrupting the view presented in the more public texts associated with the exhibition. But the analogy is too easy, if only because it suggests that the truth hidden in the exhibition hall – the maltreatment of two African children, the dubious status of colonial guardianship, the nature of African slavery – emerges freely and for all to see in the court proceedings. As I have noted, the reporting of the case was restricted; moreover, the exchanges between counsel, witnesses and judges (as traced in the verbatim record) were highly formalized encounters, structured by the rules of law and the conventions of the court. Nevertheless, the contrast in perspective remains. The exhibition hall and the court room were different spaces, articulating distinct logics of production and exchange: the one sensational and commercial, governed by the imperative to sell, the other austere and arcane, subject to the dictates of precedent. By reading the texts of the exhibition alongside those of the court case, and setting both in the wider context of late-Victorian empire-building in Africa, we can explore some more general questions concerning representation, geography and empire.[2]

1. The transcript of the proceedings as well as most of the associated depositions are held in the papers of the Anti-Slavery Society, Rhodes House, Oxford (MSS Brit. Emp. s. 22, G11). There are copies of some affidavits in the Chancery proceedings at the Public Record Office, London.
2. While some readers have described the argument in this chapter as a form of deconstruction, its interpretative strategy is one of historical and geographical contextualization rather than deconstruction in the strict sense. Of course we must acknowledge the constructedness of 'context': it is not some inert background, to which texts can be reduced, but an essential ingredient of any interpretation. Moreover, contexts can and must be treated as multiple, not singular: choosing which context is appropriate for which purpose is part of the job of interpretation. But for a challenging counter-argument, see C. Barnett, 'Deconstructing context: exposing Derrida', *Transactions of the Institute of British Geographers*, 24 (1999), pp. 277–94.

Exhibiting Native Bodies

The Stanley and African Exhibition projected an imaginative geography of the colonial enterprise centred on a binary opposition between British enterprise (embodied in the figure of Stanley himself) and African primitivism. It belongs to a wider tradition of spectacular display through which empire was consumed at home in a vast range of exhibitions, plays, pageants, dioramas and panoramas.[3] A prominent feature of many of the great exhibitions and world's fairs of the second half of the nineteenth century was the representation in miniature form of colonial landscapes, including reconstructions of 'typical' village and street scenes. (This tradition might be said to have come to a fitting climax with the Royal Air Force displays at Hendon during the 1920s, where bombers pulverized carefully reconstructed native villages into dust, before an enthusiastic audience.[4]) Many of these spectacles included not just reconstructions of colonial landscapes, but also representative inhabitants. The display of non-Europeans as authentic specimens of the 'exotic' was not confined to the celebrated international exhibitions of the nineteenth century: groups of 'Zulu warriors', 'Bella Coola Indians', 'Aztec children' and 'African pygmies' appeared periodically in a variety of places, including London's exhibition rooms (such as the Egyptian Hall in Piccadilly or the Cosmorama in Regent Street), musical halls and popular theatres, increasingly vast arenas of spectacular entertainment (such as those at Earls Court and Olympia) and, well into the twentieth century, zoos (in Basle, Hamburg, Budapest and Paris to name a few examples).[5] For all their variety, these enterprises had

3. R. Altick, *The Shows of London* (Cambridge, Mass., 1978); T. Barringer and T. Flynn (eds), *Colonialism and the Object: Empire, Material Culture and the Museum* (London, 1998); A. Coombes, *Reinventing Africa: Museums, Material Culture and Popular Imagination in Late Victorian and Edwardian England* (Yale, 1994); F. Driver and D. Gilbert (eds), *Imperial Cities: Landscape, Display and Identity* (Manchester, 1999); P. Greenhalgh, *Ephemeral Vistas: The Expositions Universelles, Great Exhibitions and World's Fairs, 1851–1939* (Manchester, 1988); I. Karp and S. Lavine (eds), *Exhibiting Cultures: The Poetics and Politics of Museum Display* (Washington, DC, 1991); J. MacKenzie, *Propaganda and Empire* (Manchester, 1984); R. Rydell, *All the World's a Fair: Visions of Empire at American International Expositions, 1876–1916* (Chicago, 1984).
4. D. Omissi, 'The Hendon Air Pageant, 1920–1937', in J. MacKenzie (ed.), *Popular Imperialism and the Military* (Manchester, 1992), pp. 198–220.
5. Altick, *Shows of London*, pp. 235–87; R. Corbey, 'Ethnographic showcases, 1870–1930', *Cultural Anthropology* 8 (1993), pp. 338–69. See also H. Debrunner, *Presence and Prestige: Africans in Europe* (Basel, 1979); C. Feest (ed.), *Indians and Europe* (Aachen, 1987); J. Green, *Black Edwardians: Black People in Britain,*

one thing in common: they represented cultural and racial difference through the display of native bodies.

Timothy Mitchell has suggested that the imperial exhibitions of the late nineteenth century enacted a spectacular way of enframing the world as a collection of objects to be inspected, classified and catalogued.[6] In his portrayal of these exhibitions as exemplars of modern modes of power and experience, Mitchell offers some intriguing ideas about the ways in which a variety of spaces come to be reconstituted in one site, the projection of an imperial geography. In this chapter, however, I am concerned less with the 'world as exhibition' than with the world *of* the exhibition: and here the process of representation appears much more troublesome, more contingent and contested, than it does in the fantasy of the world-as-exhibition. Moreover, where live subjects were on display, there was always the possibility that the exhibits themselves would depart from the script, offering unexpected visions to their audience. Like the spectacular colonial melodramas of the period, the popular ethnographic exhibition promised an exchange of sorts between observers and observed, colonizers and colonized.[7] The performance of cultural difference by both parties to this exchange could not be guaranteed in advance: as there were different ways of seeing such shows, their meanings always threatened to proliferate.[8] Throughout the nineteenth century, in fact, popular ethnographic displays often gave rise to expressions of anxiety. In 1855, for example, John Conolly, the reforming asylum doctor and President of the Ethnological Society, condemned many of the more popular exhibitions as exploitative, complaining that they offered too much sensation and

---

1901–1914 (London, 1998); B. Gregory, 'Staging British India', in J. Bratton et al. (eds), *Acts of Supremacy: The British Empire and the Stage, 1790–1930* (Manchester, 1991), pp. 150–78; B. Lindfors, 'Circus Africans', *Journal of American Culture*, 6 (1983), pp. 9–14; P. Mason, *Infelicities: Representations of the Exotic* (Baltimore, Md., 1998), pp. 110–30; W. Schneider, 'Africans in Paris', in his *An Empire for the Masses* (Westport, Conn., 1982), pp. 125–51; B. Shephard, 'Showbiz imperialism: the case of Peter Lobengula', in J. MacKenzie (ed.), *Imperialism and Popular Culture* (London, 1986), pp. 94–112; B. Street, 'British popular anthropology: exhibiting and photographing the Other', in E. Edwards (ed.), *Anthropology and Photography, 1860–1920* (London, 1992), pp. 122–31.

6. T Mitchell, *Colonising Egypt* (Cambridge, 1988), esp. ch. 1. See also D. Gregory, *Geographical Imaginations* (Oxford, 1994), pp. 34–7; T. Bennett, 'The exhibitionary complex', *New Formations*, 4 (1988), pp. 73–102.

7. Cf. H. Holder, 'Melodrama, realism and empire on the British stage', in J. Bratton et al. (eds), *Acts of Supremacy*, pp. 129–49; M. Booth, *Victorian Spectacular Theatre* (London, 1981); Altick, *Shows of London*, pp. 173–83, 473–7.

8. On the parallel case of the zoo, see R. Jones, ' "The sight of creatures strange to our clime": London zoo and the consumption of the exotic', *Journal of Victorian Culture*, 2 (1997), pp. 1–26.

too little enlightenment. Drawing particular attention to the case of two 'Aztec children' recently displayed in London, he complained of a lack of provision for their care and education: 'The lives of the Aztecs have been insured by their proprietor, to whom they were sold like sheep; but what support is assured to them? Already they are falling into the class of minor shows, and exhibited in the suburbs.'[9] If education were to be distinguished from exploitation, critics like Conolly argued, the popular gaze had to be *contained*: sober science and philanthropy had to replace vulgar sensationalism. Similar anxieties surfaced in two of the most celebrated cases involving the display of exoticized bodies during the nineteenth century, the so-called 'Hottentot Venus' in 1810 and the 'Elephant Man' in 1884.[10] Both episodes highlight the ambivalence of spectatorship, as expressed in the tension between the professional rituals of enlightened scientific observation and the sensationalism of the popular show.

This problem of 'containment' was also evident in the controversy over the Stanley and African Exhibition. While the show itself attempted to reconcile various different colonial interests within a single enterprise, the court case revealed this attempt to be no more than a fragile fiction. The study of such moments of controversy can throw light on the troubled history of colonialism, by highlighting tensions which often seem to be flattened out, decontextualized, in narrowly textual analyses of 'colonial discourse'. Of course, the dispute over the two boys displayed at the Stanley and African Exhibition was soon resolved; in legal terms, at least, there was a determinate outcome. As James Clifford remarks in another context, 'while the court is a theater of dramatic gestures, it is also a machine for producing a permanent document'.[11] But can we speak in this case of a 'permanent document'? We have not one document but many – notably a lengthy verbatim record of court proceedings, which has survived simply by chance. This document, unlike the brief formal statement which constitutes the court's final judgement, is marked by the traces of many different voices. Might it tell a different story?

9. J. Conolly, *The Ethnological Exhibitions of London* (London, 1855), p. 29.
10. S. Gilman, 'Black bodies, white bodies', *Critical Inquiry*, 12 (1983), pp. 204–42; P. Graham and F. Oehlschlaeger, *Articulating the Elephant Man: Joseph Merrick and His Interpreters* (Baltimore, Md., 1992).
11. J. Clifford, 'Identity in Mashpee', in his *The Predicament of Culture* (Cambridge, Mass., 1988), p. 328.

Representing Darkest Africa

An exhibition devoted to the accomplishments of British men in Africa (especially explorers, missionaries, traders and hunters) was well calculated to catch the imperial mood in the spring of 1890. In the words of the geographer John Scott Keltie, Africa was a continent whose 'time had come'.[12] In the twenty years since Stanley's famous encounter with Livingstone, a succession of commercial, missionary and military expeditions had extended European influence throughout the continent, mapping out territory for conquest. In the process, African peoples were reduced, like the landscape, to mere obstacles in the way of European power; in a lecture to the Royal Geographical Society in 1886, Francis De Winton had confidently assured his audience that the inhabitants of the Congo river basin were unlikely to 'offer the least resistance to its occupation by the dual forces of civilisation and commerce'.[13] The Berlin Conference had accelerated the pace of the scramble; as Horace Waller put it, 'lines, boundaries and territories [were taking shape] almost with the rapidity of crystallisation'.[14] In the thick of these competing claims were a number of European explorers, including Carl Peters, Serpa Pinto and Stanley himself. When news reached London at the end of 1889 that Stanley had finally emerged from his quest to relieve Emin Pasha, it was guaranteed to cause a sensation.

The Stanley and African Exhibition was designed to exploit this mood of excitement. In the words of the exhibition catalogue,

> The popular imagination has been touched by the varied story of the Dark Continent to an unprecedented extent. It has been a story which has appealed in trumpet tones to the philanthropist as well as to the mere lover of adventure, to the merchant as well as to the geographer, and to the Christian missionary eager for the spread of Christ's kingdom as well as to the patriotic politician anxious for his nation's aggrandisement. . . . To illustrate some of these varied forms of enterprise in a concrete fashion is the object of the Stanley and African Exhibition, while celebrating what

12. J. S. Keltie, 'Mr Stanley's expedition: its conduct and results', *Fortnightly Review*, 48 (1890), p. 81.
13. F. De Winton, 'The Congo Free State', *Proceedings of the Royal Geographical Society*, 8 (1886), pp. 609–27. De Winton was Stanley's successor in the Congo Free State.
14. H. Waller, *Nyassaland: Great Britain's Case Against the Portuguese* (London, 1890), p. 3.

we may safely conclude to be the culminating point in the romantic history of the Dark Continent.[15]

These 'varied forms of enterprise' were represented in an organizing committee made up of no less than 77 individuals; indeed, the list reads like a catalogue of contemporary British interests in Africa. It included directors of large trading companies,[16] colonial administrators,[17] military men,[18] explorers and travellers,[19] representatives of the missionary and philanthropic communities[20] and a handful of museum professionals.[21] Many of the members of the Committee were closely associated with the Royal Geographical Society, which itself provided a list of potential donors and a collection of maps and diagrams for display.[22] While some influential geographers continued to doubt Stanley's sensational style (which one privately described as 'little short of insulting to those who think of Geography as I do'), the geographical establishment was closely associated with the celebrations surrounding his return from Africa in 1890, not least with the exhibition itself.[23]

According to the catalogue, the exhibits were divided into five main parts: the Native Section (including weapons, implements and adornments collected by explorers), the Geographical Section (consisting of maps and diagrams showing the progress of European knowledge of Africa), the Portraits Section (including pictures and relics of the most famous explorers, missionaries, abolitionists, traders and hunters), the

15. *The Stanley and African Exhibition: Catalogue of Exhibits* (London, 1890), pp. 5–6.
16. Including Sir William Mackinnon and Sir Lewis Pelly of the Imperial British East Africa Company, Sir George Goldie of the Royal Niger Company and the Duke of Fife of the British South African Company.
17. Including Sir John Kirk (then British representative at the African slave trade conference at Brussels), Sir Claude Macdonald (who had served in Egypt, Zanzibar and the Niger territories), Sir Henry Rawlinson (a past Consul at Baghdad and an Orientalist scholar), Sir Henry Barkly and Sir Charles Mills (both of whom held posts in the Cape Colony during the 1870s) and Sir Clement Hill of the Foreign Office.
18. Notably Viscount Wolseley, veteran of the Ashanti and Zulu wars, and Sir Charles Wilson, then Director-General of the Ordnance Survey.
19. Apart from Stanley himself, the list of explorers included Sir Samuel Baker, Sir Richard Burton, Verney Lovett Cameron, Paul Du Chaillu, James Grant, Edward Delmar Morgan and Joseph Thomson.
20. Including Charles Allen, secretary of the Anti-Slavery Society, Archdeacon Farler of the Universities Mission to Central Africa, Robert Ashe of the Church Missionary Society and the ubiquitous Horace Waller.
21. For example Sir Francis Cunliffe-Owen, Director of the South Kensington Museum, and Sir Charles Hercules Read of the British Museum.
22. C. Peek to H. W. Bates, 1 February 1890 (RGS Archives, London).
23. R. Strachey to H. W. Bates, 1890 (RGS Archives). See also chapter 6 above.

Slave Trade Section (exhibiting artefacts and images associated with slavery) and the Department of Pictures and Photographs of African Life.[24] This classification was imperfectly realized in the space of the exhibition itself, where the claims of ethnographic science, commercial gain, missionary endeavour and popular entertainment jostled awkwardly for the same space. The catalogue meanwhile contrived to represent a visit to the exhibition through a hackneyed narrative of exploration: 'The Exhibition is reached through [a] village palisade ornamented with skulls, EN ROUTE FOR THE HEART OF SAVAGE AFRICA'. Beyond lay 'the explorers' first camp': 'Tents pitched. The cook at work. On all sides palm groves, quaint huts, and half-clothed negroes – a foretaste of the feast of marvels in store . . . Meanwhile the traveller makes himself as comfortable as possible, and succeeds wonderfully, thanks to modern ingenuity.'

On one side, according to a report in *The Times*, the visitor was confronted by images of the scenery of the east coast of Africa and the Indian Ocean; on the other the Congo River rushing over Stanley Falls, 'while round the corner, he looks upon the Aruwimi forest, with Mount Ruwenzori in the far distance'. Although from *The Times* the correspondent acknowledged that this layout was 'incongruous', he sensed a larger purpose in the diorama: 'if the visitor keeps in mind that the aim has been to represent some typical African scenery not much harm will be done'.[25]

Beyond the foyer, with its bust of Henry Morton Stanley and a large map of African exploration, there were portraits of the Queen, Stanley and King Leopold, flags of the Congo State and the Chartered Companies associated with the exhibition and various trophies from the Emin Pasha Relief Expedition itself. The rest of the exhibits were displayed in a rectangular hall, with an upper gallery on three sides. In the central space there was a variety of objects, including another bust of Stanley, a model of Theed's African group on the Albert Memorial, a stuffed adult male gorilla from Gabon, four hippopotamus skulls, musical instruments from the Niger, a native hut from Bechuanaland and photographs from the Congo. On the columns of the hall were the heads and horns of antelopes, wart hogs, antelope, buffalo, crocodiles and other wild animals, collections of spears, swords and shields and a variety of costumes, fabrics and religious objects. In panels around the walls, and in the cases below them, were most of the exhibits of the Native Section, dominated by weaponry, crudely classified by

24. See Coombes, *Reinventing Africa*, pp. 70–5.
25. *The Times*, 21 March 1890, p. 14.

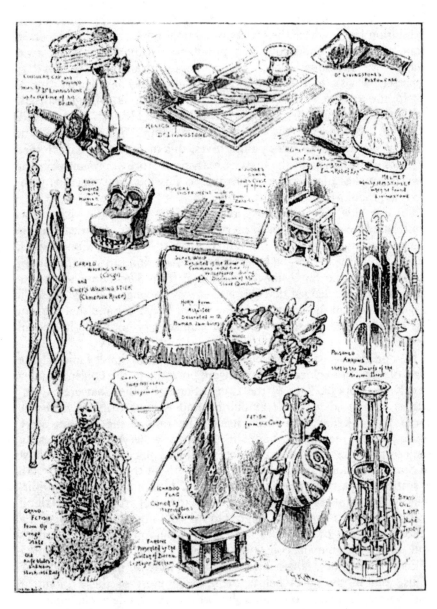

7.1 'Sketches at the Stanley and African Exhibition' (*Illustrated London News*, 29 March 1890).

geographical region.[26] The gallery was devoted mainly to relics – we might say fetishes – of European adventures and campaigns in Africa, including Mungo Park's last journal, Livingstone's teaspoons, a post-card from General Gordon in Khartoum, Bishop Hannington's watch, a set of surveying instruments and a slaver's whip once exhibited in the House of Commons (figure 7.1). There were also portraits of explorers, missionaries and hunters, interspersed with pictures of African land-scapes, wildlife and peoples. Alongside these was a reconstruction of an 'African primeval forest and village', including a slave-raiding scene set against the background of Mount Ruwenzori. Even the ceiling above was colonised for the display of a set of geographical diagrams prepared by John Scott Keltie at the RGS.

What, precisely, was being represented at the Stanley and African Exhibition? In part, it was the British displayed to themselves; the remark by the correspondent from *The Times* that 'Central Africa in most of its aspects is well represented' referred primarily to the breadth of British interests in evidence (notably the numerous portraits of members of the organizing committee) rather than to the authenticity of the ethnographic displays.[27] The image of Africa as the 'Dark Continent' promoted in the exhibition was already a cliché: the poisoned arrows, pygmies' spears, fetishes and idols, the stuffed gorilla, the 'primeval forest' and above all the slave-raiding diorama[28] – all reinforced a marketable vision of Africa widely associated with the name of Henry Morton Stanley.[29] The exhibition was a hybrid affair, part ethnographic show, part popular entertainment; even Barnum's Jumbo the Elephant found a place among the photographs. The very location of the exhibition confirmed its popular and commercial char-acter: the Victoria Gallery, in Regent Street, occupied a site which forty years previously had housed the famous Cosmorama.[30] The cover of the exhibition catalogue showed Stanley at the fringe of the forest,

26.   The regions were: Somaliland and Egyptian Sudan; Emin Pasha's Province and Uganda; Masai-Land; East Central Africa; Central South Africa; Congo Basin; the Middle and Lower Niger; the West Coast of Africa.
27.   *The Times*, 22 February 1890, p. 15.
28.   The slavery exhibits attracted much attention: see 'Sketches at the Stanley and African Exhibition', *Illustrated London News*, 29 March 1890, p. 391; 'The Dark Continent', *Fun*, 2 April 1890, p. 147; A. Bertrand, *Alfred Bertrand, Explorer and Captain of Cavalry* (London, 1926), p. 96.
29.   T. Richards, *The Commodity Culture of Victorian England: Advertising and Spectacle, 1851–1914* (Stanford, Calif., 1990), pp. 119–67.
30.   The Cosmorama's exhibits during the mid-nineteenth century included a 'Zulu chief', three Indians from the 'El Dorado of Sir Walter Raleigh' (British Guiana), an immense human head reconstructed from bones discovered in Louisiana and P. T. Barnum's most lucrative asset, General Tom Thumb.

7.2 Stanley and African Exhibition Catalogue (London, 1890). By permission of the RGS–IBG.

raising his famous peaked white helmet aloft in a distinctly theatrical gesture (figure 7.2). The showman had found another stage; his helmet, needless to say, soon found its way into the exhibition.[31]

Among the most popular attractions at the exhibition were the two African boys said to have been rescued from slavery. Among the souvenirs on sale to visitors were portraits of the children, posed with shields and knobkerries in a composite style which might be characterized as 'ethnographic picturesque'.[32] An accompanying text circulated

31. *The Times*, 10 May 1890, p. 13.
32. Thanks to James Ryan for this suggestion. On the visual representation of racial 'types', see E. Edwards, 'Photographic "types": the pursuit of method', *Visual*

at the exhibition – the 'History of the Two Boys' – described them as natives of Umzila's country in Gazaland, a region to the north-east of the Transvaal, adjoining Portuguese East Africa.[33] According to the 'History', the children – named here as Gootoo and Inyokwana – had been enslaved following the murder of their fathers by native 'chiefs'. An unnamed white trader travelling through the region was said to have 'gained possession' of them; he, in turn, had passed them on to Florence Thorburn, a resident of Swaziland, hundreds of miles further south. While the 'History of the Two Boys' stopped there, it seems that the children were brought to London by Florence Thorburn, and her husband John, in October 1889, a few months before the opening of the Stanley and African Exhibition. Their presence in the Victoria Gallery, alongside 'life-size models of types of representative African peoples', was intended to authenticate the representation of 'Darkest Africa'.

The High Court of Justice

While the 'History of the Two Boys' was designed to be no more than a souvenir, it was to receive much closer scrutiny following the closure of the exhibition, when the case of the two boys reached the High Court of Justice. During the Summer of 1890, complaints about the boys' treatment by the Thorburns (with whom they were lodged at a nearby hotel) began to reach members of the exhibition committee. That these complaints eventually took the form of a legal action may well have reflected a broader shift of opinion about Stanley's expedition. As we have seen in chapter 6, revelations over the Emin Pasha Relief Expedition opened a rift between the anti-slavery lobby and Stanley's supporters; meanwhile, further arguments were raging over the role of chartered companies and the fate of British interests throughout Africa.[34] Leading figures in the Anti-Slavery Society played a prominent

Anthropology, 3 (1990), pp. 235–58; Edwards, *Anthropology and Photography*; J. Ryan, *Picturing Empire: Photography and the Visualization of the British Empire* (London, 1997), pp. 140–82.

33.   For contemporary accounts of the region, see St Vincent Erskine, 'Journey to Umzila's, South-East Africa, in 1871–2', *Journal of the Royal Geographical Society*, 45 (1875), pp. 45–128; A. Anderson, 'Notes on the geography of South Central Africa', *Proceedings of the Royal Geographical Society*, 16 (1884), pp. 19–36; A. M. Cardoso, 'Expedição as terras de Muzilla em 1882', *Boletim da Sociedade Geographia de Lisboa*, 7 (1887), pp. 153–213. (I am grateful to James Sidaway for his help with translation.)

34.   In addition to the references in chapter 6, see J. Mackenzie, 'The expansion of South Africa', *Contemporary Review*, 56 (1889), pp. 753–76; Waller, *Nyassaland*.

role in these controversies, and three of them (Charles Allen, Horace Waller and Robert Felkin) were associated with the Stanley and African Exhibition. It was on Waller's advice that the Society's secretary initiated the High Court action against the Thorburns at the end of October 1890. Applying for a writ of *habeas corpus*, Charles Allen claimed that the boys had been brought to England 'practically in slavery', and were destined to return to slavery in Africa.[35] Although this action failed, a second action concerning the guardianship of the children (in Chancery) was more successful, and in May 1891 the children were made wards of court. Soon afterwards, the judge in this case formally appointed three guardians – Cardinal Manning of Westminster, the Reverend Thomas Seddon (an aide of Manning's) and Florence Thorburn herself – and ordered that the children be sent to an industrial school at Mariannhill, in Natal. They appear finally to have sailed for South Africa with Florence Thorburn on 19 November 1891.

How should the case of the two boys be understood? In legal terms, it might be situated in a larger history of court rulings on the subjects of slavery and child welfare. From one perspective, for example, it looked backwards to the eighteenth century, when *habeas corpus* writs were issued by leading anti-slavery campaigners such as Granville Sharp in order to prevent the forcible return to the West Indies of black slaves brought to Britain as domestic servants or children's companions;[36] or to the 1820s, when a similar case was brought concerning the ill-treatment of Saartje Baartman (the 'Hottentot Venus'). From another perspective, seen in the context of modern family law, the case might be said to have looked forward: it has been suggested, for example, that the 1890s were an important turning-point in the evolution of wardship cases,[37] as the concept of the 'welfare of the child' was clarified by the courts and extended through the campaigns of organizations such as the National Society for the Prevention of Cruelty (formed in 1889).[38]

35.   Queen's Bench, Affidavit of Charles Allen, 29 October 1890, p. 1. This account of the case is based principally on the transcript of proceedings, associated depositions and the papers of the Anti-Slavery Society (see note 1 above). The proceedings are referred to below according to the two divisions of the High Court which considered the case – Queen's Bench (for *habeas corpus*) and Chancery (for guardianship).
36.   F. O. Shyllon, *Black Slaves in Britain* (London, 1974), pp. 40–5, 176.
37.   N. Lowe and R. White, *Wards of Court* (London, 1979), pp. 3–5; A. Manchester, *A Modern Legal History of England and Wales, 1750–1950* (London, 1980), pp. 390–1.
38.   The 1889 Prevention of Cruelty to Children Act placed restrictions on the performance of children in theatres and other places of entertainment. It was used soon afterwards by the NSPCC over the performance of a troupe of cyclists at the Westminster Aquarium: L. Rose, *The Erosion of Childhood: Child Oppression in*

On closer inspection, however, these legal genealogies appear less adequate as guides to the issues at stake in this case. Firstly, the relevance of earlier precedents was (successfully) contested; counsel for the Thorburns, for example, described the action as an anachronism, no more than a calculated attempt to revive the fortunes of the Anti-Slavery Society by recalling its earlier reputation for legal activism. In the event, the *habeas corpus* action failed; the Queen's Bench judge held that the boys were not being held in a state of slavery. Secondly, even though the guardianship proceedings in the Chancery division were successful (to the extent that the children were made wards of court), the concept of the 'welfare of the child' was interpreted here in a very particular way. Rather than being a universal reference point irrespective of class, race and geography, the welfare of children was seen in the context of contemporary racial and colonial assumptions. Far from being closed around a narrowly defined history of legal precedents, then, the case of the two boys articulated a more general ambivalence about the relationships between ideas of liberty, slavery, welfare and protection. This can be demonstrated by a discussion of the three main points at issue: whether the Thorburns had better legal claim (or 'title') to the children than anyone else, whether the children had been ill-treated, and whether they had been or were likely to become slaves.

The first issue was that of 'title'. The term was used throughout the proceedings, even though it was acknowledged that in English law it could not be applied to persons. The simultaneous use and disavowal of the term suggests a kind of double-think: on the one hand, a recognition that people could not be treated as property, on the other, proceeding as if they were. The 'History of the Two Boys' became a key piece of evidence on this point: counsel for the Anti-Slavery Society contended that the document failed to establish the legitimacy of the Thorburns' claim on them. The boys were said in the 'History' to have been passed by a trader to Florence Thorburn, in exchange for treatment of a gunshot wound: a contract, of sorts. In court, the trader was identified as Robert McNab (a name which, one of the barristers quipped, was singularly appropriate).[39] Eventually the boys were made

---

Britain, 1860–1918 (London, 1991), pp. 62–4. The secretary of the Children's Aid Society was in contact with the Anti-Slavery Society during November 1890, but I have been unable to find evidence of formal involvement in the case of the two boys.

39.   McNab, like the Thorburns, was active in the Swaziland concessions boom of the late 1880s. He had a reputation for violence; indeed, his gunshot wound is mentioned in an official report (Chancery, Applicant's Evidence, p. 13; 'Correspondence respecting the Affairs of Swaziland', Parliamentary Papers 1887 [c.5089] LXI, pp. 10–11). See also P. Bonner, *Kings, Commoners and Concessionaires: The*

wards of the High Court (in its capacity as *parens patriae*), a decision which raised the question of who else might be 'entitled' to them.[40] Both sides in the case were required to propose suitable figures of standing as guardians: Arthur Pease and Sir Thomas Fowell Buxton were nominated by the Anti-Slavery Society, and Cardinal Manning by the Thorburns.[41] As these names suggest, sectarian rivalry played a significant part in the dispute, as it did in other cases of contested guardianship during this period. Manning was a committee member of the Anti-Slavery Society, though he eventually resigned over the case. In various ways, therefore, the issue of entitlement remained crucial throughout the proceedings. What was ultimately at issue was not, in fact, the liberty or consent of the subject (as in conventional *habeas corpus* cases), but rather claims to the guardianship of the children.

The second issue in the case concerned the charge of ill-treatment against the Thorburns. The Anti-Slavery Society attempted to prove in court that the children had been neglected and abused, that they had been inadequately clothed while being put on show, and that they had been exploited for financial gain, both at the Stanley and African Exhibition and at various popular theatres and music halls elsewhere in London. These charges, summed up by the claim that they had been 'treated almost as dogs [rather than] human beings',[42] were difficult to prove in court. That the boys were exhibited did not in itself provide sufficient grounds for legal action; according to Baron Pollock (the judge presiding in Queen's Bench), this was 'simply a question of education and feeling'.[43] Likewise, he dismissed the allegations of neglect and cruelty, upholding the Thorburns' claim to have cared for the boys in a manner appropriate to their 'position in life and of their country' – in other words, their age, class and race.[44] Throughout the proceedings, Pollock made pointed comparisons with the treatment of working-class children and ethnic communities in Britain; on claims that the boys had not been provided with footwear, for example, he

---

Evolution and Dissolution of the Nineteenth-century Swazi State (Cambridge, 1983), pp. 225–9; J. Matsebula, *A History of Swaziland*, 3rd edn (Cape Town, 1988), pp. 65–6.

40.   Chancery, Proceedings, 7 May 1891, pp. 128–9.

41.   See the correspondence between Cardinal Manning and Charles Allen in June 1891, and Anti-Slavery Society Minute Book, 6 November and 4 December 1891 (Anti-Slavery Society Archives).

42.   Queen's Bench, Proceedings, 13 November 1890, p. 6.

43.   *Ibid*, 17 November 1890, p. 39.

44.   *Ibid*, p. 40. The judge's constant interjections underlined his point: for example, 'Many people in this country hold to the belief that we educate our own children too highly' (p. 7), and 'Certain people do beat their children with a whip' (p. 39).

interjected: 'Well, well – an Irishman or Scotchman would be very angry if you insisted on his wearing shoes.'[45] At a later stage, he remarked that the treatment of the boys as 'household drudges' provided no basis for intervention, 'otherwise every cabin boy who came home in a ship from the East would get a *habeas corpus* and say "I would rather be sent to Eton College"'.[46] The jocular tone of such exchanges between barristers and the Bench injected a certain levity into the proceedings, no doubt reflecting the legal profession's own assessment of the significance of the case. In his judgement, however, Pollock reiterated his view that notions of welfare and freedom had to be seen in the context of colonial situations: 'Those who have been much abroad, or in the colonies, know perfectly well that it is the natural condition of every dominant race towards the retreating race that they become more or less their servants or under their protection.'[47]

This brings us to the third and most problematic issue in the case: the question of slavery. Counsel for the Anti-Slavery Society claimed in court that the two boys had been purchased in Africa as 'chattels', were being held 'practically in slavery' in England, and were destined to return to a 'slave country', Swaziland.[48] In support of the last of these claims, the court heard evidence from an influential missionary, John Mackenzie. Although he had never been to Swaziland, Mackenzie claimed that his knowledge of the Tswana in Bechuanaland (as resident Commissioner there in 1886–7) entitled him to speak about the entire 'Bantu family', of which – he said – the Swazis formed one 'branch'. (This was a weak argument – even Baron Pollock recognized that 'Bechuanaland and Swaziland are very different places'.)[49] Affidavits from four further 'authorities' on Swaziland along with extracts from popular travel narratives and official reports were read to the High Court during the Chancery proceedings in May 1891.[50] Yet interpretations of what precisely constituted 'slavery' differed widely. When counsel for the Anti-Slavery Society declared simply that 'Slavery is that [condition wherein] you have not freedom', his opponent was quick to point out that similar terms might be applied to 'certain people in the

45. *Ibid*, 13 November 1890, p. 18.
46. *Ibid*, 17 November 1890, p. 34.
47. *Ibid*, 17 November 1890, p. 39.
48. *Ibid*, 13 November 1890, pp. 1, 4, 6, 11.
49. *Ibid*, 17 November 1890, pp. 37–8.
50. Chancery, Proceedings, 7 May 1891, pp. 53–63, 89–109. For the sources of the extracts see E. Mathers, *Golden South Africa*, 4th edn (London, 1889), p. 253; J. Ingram, *The Land of Gold, Diamonds and Ivory* (London, 1889), pp. 172–3; 'Further correspondence respecting the affairs of Swazieland and Tongaland', Parliamentary Papers 1890 [c.6200] LII, pp. 229–32.

East of London', who were often said to be 'living in a state of slavery'.[51]

Historians have identified a variety of forms of unfree labour operating in Swaziland and its neighbouring territories during the late nineteenth century. These forms of labour control (which included tribute, raiding, apprenticeship and domestic service) were available to different groups on different terms.[52] Whether they amounted to slavery or not is (and was) a question of interpretation. An expert witness in the case of the two boys, for example, drew a distinction between slave ownership (which he insisted did not exist anywhere in southern Africa) and the taking of captives subsequently treated as 'wards' of their adopted tribe or nation.[53] Philip Bonner provides considerable evidence of captive-raiding in his modern history of the Swazi polity (which he describes as 'the principal captive-trading state in South-Eastern Africa' during the 1860s), although he argues that these captives did not strictly constitute a classic slave class.[54] British government correspondence during the 1880s suggests that children and cattle were occasionally brought back to Swaziland from raids on neighbouring kraals, to be sold 'for the price of £20 or less'.[55] In addition, there was increasing demand from both the Boers and newly arrived Europeans for domestic labour. Florence Thorburn herself acknowledged that children were effectively traded by men such as McNab, although she preferred to describe them as apprentices rather than slaves: 'We say to anyone "We can't get servants here. If you will get us some we will pay you." They go and get us some from the chief.' Even so, she denied that McNab was known as a slave-dealer, claiming somewhat implausibly that 'He may do it for the love of it.'[56] Another witness in the case described the children as 'of the type commonly employed by English Residents in the Colonies as goat or calf herds, junior nurses, or for light domestic service, or as messengers, and at wages of from 2/6 to 6/- per month which is periodically collected not by the boys but by their natural

---

51. Chancery, Proceedings, 7 May 1891, pp. 124, 132–4.
52. P. Harries, 'Slavery, social incorporation and surplus extraction: the nature of free and unfree labour in South-East Africa', *Journal of African History*, 22 (1981), pp. 318–30; Bonner, *Kings, Commoners and Concessionaires*, pp. 80–4, 90–2; J. Crush, *The Struggle for Swazi Labour, 1890–1920* (Kingston, Ont., 1987), pp. 24–5.
53. Chancery, Respondent's Evidence (Affidavit of William Campbell, 5 November 1890), p. 5.
54. Bonner, *Kings, Commoners and Concessionaires*, p. 80.
55. Chancery, Applicant's Evidence (Affidavit of John Mackenzie, 2 December 1890), p. 9.
56. Chancery, Deposition of Florence Thorburn, 2 March 1891, p. 2.

Guardians'. The important point here is that these terms were contested; as counsel for the Anti-Slavery Society put it, 'some people call it apprenticeship, but I call it slavery'.[57]

Making Representations

If the Stanley and African Exhibition attempted to present a coherent picture of British imperialism in Africa, the proceedings in the High Court exposed some of the imaginative work which had gone into its composition. The 'History of the Two Boys' circulated at the exhibition, for example, was subjected to the rigours of a legal examination, and found wanting. In the process, attention was focused less on the children themselves than on the claims of those who represented them. The 'History of the Two Boys' had said nothing about their self-appointed guardians, the Thorburns, who were prominent figures in Swaziland during the concessions boom of the late 1880s; John Thorburn's influence in Swaziland was such that the King's residence itself had been dubbed 'Thorburnsville'.[58] It became apparent during the case that they had come to London in 1889 in order to trade in some of their concessions.[59] Such adventurers had created turmoil in Swaziland during the late 1880s, when the Swazi King had been persuaded to sell concessions for 'the monopoly of almost everything required for the use of man, except sunlight and air'.[60] Late in 1889, recognizing the instability of the situation, the Transvaal and British governments had appointed a joint commission to investigate the administration of Swaziland.[61] The region was to remain in the public eye in London throughout 1890, with some (including Charles Dilke and Rider Haggard) calling for the extension of formal British influence.[62]

57. Queen's Bench, Proceedings, 13 November 1890, p. 6.
58. T. Griffithes, *From Bedford Way to Swazieland* (London, 1890), p. 22.
59. Concessions granted to the Thorburns had included rights to printing, gas manufacture, advertising, surveying, mining and grazing land. John Thorburn donated concession documents, as well as a collection of axes and a hippopotamus skull, to the Stanley and African Exhibition: J. Thorburn, *Struggles in Africa* (London, 1890), p. 36; *Stanley and African Exhibition Catalogue*, pp. 19, 39.
60. H. Robinson, 'The Swaziland question', *Fortnightly Review*, 47 (1890), p. 288. See also Bonner, *Kings, Commoners and Concessionaires*, pp. 182–207; 'Report on Swaziland by Colonel F. De Winton', Parliamentary Papers 1890 [c.6201] LII, pp. 59–65.
61. N. Garson, 'The Swaziland question and a road to the sea, 1887–1895', *Archives Yearbook for South African History*, 2 (1957), pp. 267–434.
62. C. Dilke, *Problems of Greater Britain*, vol. i (London, 1890), pp. 548–53; H. Rider Haggard, 'The fate of Swaziland', *New Review*, 2 (1890), pp. 64–75.

The Thorburns' involvement in the Stanley and African Exhibition thus needs to be seen in the context of wider debates over the future of British imperialism in Southern Africa. If the Anti-Slavery Society could represent Swaziland as a lawless country, in which concession-hunters like Thorburn wielded excessive power over people and property, this would do more than win a case in the High Court; it could also strengthen the case for an extension of British influence there. Counsel for Florence Thorburn argued in the High Court that the appointment of a British representative to the government of Swaziland in 1890 would *ipso facto* protect the two boys: 'we cannot doubt, the place being under English control, that it would be a very mild form of slavery, which would not interfere with their freedom'.[63] This piece of sophistry (which incidentally misconstrued the new constitutional position in Swaziland) was designed to exploit the founding myth of the British anti-slavery movement: the very air and soil of England (and her dominions) was inimical to slavery. It was assumed by all sides that, by definition, slavery could not exist within British dominions: the dispute on this point thus revolved around whether Swaziland was a 'slave country'. The point was lost by the Thorburns: the Court ordered the children to be sent to an industrial school in South Africa (rather than Swaziland) in order to keep them within the jurisdiction of the British crown. Yet the assumption on which it was based remained intact.

The anti-slavery cause was a vital element of the British imperial self-image during the late nineteenth century, enabling the British to represent themselves as Livingstone's heirs in the protection of the 'native'. The issue of guardianship raised in the case of the two boys might thus be seen as emblematic of a more general process, by which British justice was interposing itself as *parens patriae* on behalf of black Africans. Such claims were not in themselves new. During the 'Venus Hottentot' case of the 1820s, for example, the British governor at the Cape had been described as a 'guardian over the Hottentot nation under his government, by reason of their general imbecile state'.[64] Moreover, the metaphorical association of black slaves and working-class children had had a particularly significant, though complex and contested, place in the history of British philanthropy since at least the early nineteenth century.[65] The development of evolutionary racism and scientific theories of recapitulation added a new dimen-

---

63.   Chancery, Proceedings, 7 May 1891, p. 136.
64.   Chancery, Proceedings, 7 May 1891, p. 146.
65.   See especially H. Cunningham, *The Children of the Poor: Representations of Childhood Since the Seventeenth Century* (Oxford, 1991), pp. 60–83, 97–101.

sion to these associations: Alfred Russel Wallace, for example, asserted in 1864 that 'the relationship of a civilised to an uncivilised race, over which it rules, is exactly like that of parent to child'. Forty years later, Alfred Milner, High Commissioner at the Cape, characterized Africans as 'children, needing and appreciating a just paternal government'.[66] British imperialism was increasingly represented as a mission of protection (hence 'protectorates') of indigenous peoples against the intrusions of others, whether these others were Arab slave-traders, Portuguese explorers, German adventurers, Boer farmers or (occasionally) irresponsible British concession hunters. This was the position of an increasing number of missionary and anti-slavery activists, such as the members of the South Africa Committee during the 1880s.[67] Missionaries like John Mackenzie 'inserted themselves as cultural brokers between the blacks and the whites', urging the extension of imperial rule in the language of guardianship; a case, as has been pointed out, of 'the ultimate imperial hegemony, . . . overrule as a kindness to the colonized'.[68]

To adopt the role of guardian over natives or children is also to speak for them. Philanthropic pressure groups like the Anti-Slavery Society and the Aborigines Protection Society claimed the right to speak on behalf of their wards, slaves and indigenous peoples, throughout the world; indeed, when Africans attempted to speak for themselves, these societies found their *raison d'être* under threat.[69] In the case of Gootoo and Inyokwana, the boys found themselves spoken for in three senses: as Africans, as 'slaves' and as legal minors. In contrast to other *habeas corpus* cases, those involving the guardianship of children did not turn on the issue of consent. In these cases, as Lord Justice Kay explained in 1893, 'the practice has been that the judge himself saw the child, not for the purpose of obtaining the consent of the child, but for the purpose, and as one of the best modes of, determining what was really for the welfare of the child'.[70] Thus the two boys in this case were seen

---

66. D. Lorimer, *Colour, Class and the Victorians* (Leicester, 1978), p. 148; B. Porter, *The Lion's Share: A Short History of British Imperialism, 1850–1983*, 2nd edn (London, 1984), p. 181.

67. See for example, H. Fox Bourne, 'South Africa and the Aborigines Protection Society', *Contemporary Review*, 56 (1889), pp. 346–60.

68. J. Comaroff and J. Comaroff, *Of Revelation and Revolution: Christianity, Colonialism and Consciousness in South Africa* (Chicago, 1991), pp. 303–8; A. J. Dachs, 'Missionary imperialism: the case of Bechuanaland', *Journal of African History*, 13 (1972), pp. 647–58.

69. B. Willan, 'The Anti-Slavery and Aborigines' Protection Society and the South African Natives' Land Act of 1913', *Journal of African History*, 20 (1979), p. 87.

70. Law Reports: R. v. Gyngall [1893] 2 QB, p. 250.

by a judge (Baron Pollock) for twenty minutes in November 1890; having been on public display at the Stanley and African Exhibition, they were now subjected to a private view. 'They do not look unhappy boys', Pollock reported to the Court. 'They were very cheerful with me, and I think they spoke the truth. . . . I can judge from the boys' own faces and manner how far they have been fairly treated.'[71] The judge's words reveal much about the conduct of the case: throughout, the boys were represented, they did not represent themselves. Their bodies, in a sense, spoke for them. It was thus fitting that the Court should eventually consign them to Mariannhill, a Catholic industrial school attached to a Trappist monastery near Durban, where they would be trained in the disciplines of manual labour: in the words of the Abbott, 'We do not want the kaffirs to be inspectors on the railways, but we want them to become good artisans and trustworthy agricultural labourers.'[72]

The proceedings in court demonstrated that not all representations carried equal weight; indeed, the purpose of the case was precisely to judge between them. The boys' own testimony about their treatment by the Thorburns, as reported by guides at the exhibition, was quickly discredited; words, it was said, had been put into their mouths.[73] (Similar arguments were to be used by critics of Roger Casement's 1903 report on atrocities in the Congo, which relied partly on evidence from Africans: 'Truth in the eyes of a native is not what is or has been, but what ought to be, what he wishes, what he thinks one wishes or what is expected of him.')[74] If the boys' evidence was doubly suspect – as children and as Africans – so too was that of the guides at the exhibition, many of whom were women: their evidence was simply disregarded by Judge Pollock. The Anti-Slavery Society itself received considerable support from women, though they were not represented on its national committee. Significantly, the case of the two boys may have originated in the complaint of a woman, identified only as Miss P. Wilshere of Welwyn, who brought the condition of the boys to the

71. Queen's Bench, Proceedings, 17 November 1890, pp. 36, 40.
72. W. Brown, *The Catholic Church in South Africa* (London, 1960), p. 245. See also F. Schimlek, 'New ways in the missions of South Africa', in *Mariannhill and Its Apostolate* (Reimlingen, 1964), pp. 65–84. Ironically, Mariannhill was later to play a quite different role: the black consciousness movement of the late 1960s was closely associated with its graduates, including Steve Biko.
73. Queen's Bench, Proceedings, 13 November 1890, pp. 26–7.
74. *The Congo: A Report of the Commission of Enquiry* (1906), quoted in J. Osborne, 'Wilfred G. Thesiger, Sir Edward Grey and the British campaign to reform the Congo, 1905–9', *Journal of Imperial and Commonwealth History*, 27 (1999), 59–80 [p. 61].

attention of Horace Waller via her contacts with the Universities Mission to Central Africa. From her private correspondence with officers of the Anti-Slavery Society, it is clear that she wished to remain out of public view, though she kept a keen interest in the welfare of the children, even offering at one point to look after them herself. Following Baron Pollock's initial judgement in November 1890, she questioned his confident assertion that he could tell 'from the boys' own faces and manner' whether they had been mistreated, insisting that 'a woman would have soon seen which way the boys' dislike lay, men do not understand children'.[75] Such an argument clearly had its limits: she did not, for example, extend it to Florence Thorburn. Differences of class and religion played a part here: in an attempt to secure her own claim to the guardianship of the children, Florence Thorburn had arranged for their baptism in the Catholic Church in November 1890.[76] While these differences over gender and denomination further complicated the politics of representation, they did not fundamentally alter the terms of the case. The issue was representation, not voice: the children them-selves remained mute witnesses throughout, their bodies standing in for their words.

* * *

The Stanley and African Exhibition was an attempt to represent the identities of the colonizer and the colonized, and the boundaries which defined them, in a coherent form, to fix in the space of the exhibition hall an imaginative geography which in retrospect appears far more unstable. The case of the two boys, I have argued, raised troubling questions about the politics of representation: just who was entitled to speak on their behalf? By setting the texts of the exhibition against those of the court-room, we can unsettle the loud assertions that accompanied such spectacular displays of colonial achievement; and what might otherwise appear as a seamless discourse of white power in

75. P. Wilshere to C. Allen, 10 May 1892 (Anti-Slavery Society Archives). Her interest in the boys' welfare outlasted that of Anti-Slavery Society officials, who were subsequently more concerned with the substantial legal costs of the case: P. Wilshere to C. Allen, 16 October 1891; P. Wilshere to ?, n.d.; P. Wilshere to C. Allen, 13 August (1894); H. Waller to C. Allen, 15 May 1891 (Anti-Slavery Society Archives).
76. The boys' names (though not their parents') were recorded in the Baptisms Book of the Church of St Mary of the Angels, Bayswater, on 30 November 1890. The baptism certificate was an exhibit in the case. I am grateful to Father Michael Hollings for enabling me to consult the original.

the Dark Continent begins to unravel.[77] While this methodology might be construed as an historicized form of deconstruction, it has also involved a kind of remapping: an imaginative movement between the sites of the exhibition hall in London's West End, the High Court of Justice in the Strand and the contested territories of South-East Africa. In the process, we have encountered not one form of representation, but many; and beyond the court-room, at least, they appear difficult to reconcile. What were the limits of slavery and anti-slavery? Did ideas of child welfare extend to black Africans? While judgements were delivered, the verdict of the court was itself contested.

In much of this chapter, I have treated the case of the two boys as an exemplar of contemporary attitudes towards anti-slavery and child welfare, paying particular attention to the tensions between the contending parties to the action. In another perspective, however, the case might also be seen as a paradigm of a larger process in which the language of guardianship was appropriated in the service of empire. Henry Morton Stanley himself argued in 1890 that the government of Africa required a firm but fair parental hand: 'In order to rule them, and to keep one's life amongst them, it is needful resolutely to regard them as children.'[78] In the present context, Stanley's sensational claims about the pygmies of the inner Congo on his return from the Emin Pasha expedition have a wider significance. The suggestion that a child-like people without a history, perhaps the descendants of a diminutive race mentioned by Herodotus, had been discovered deep within the central African forest, had a powerful and enduring impact.[79] The two children at the Stanley and African Exhibition appear in fact to have been last-minute substitutes for a pygmy which Stanley had intended to bring back from Africa; indeed, in other appearances at popular music halls and theatres in London during 1890, they were billed incongruously as 'Dwarfs from the Dark Forest' and 'Swaziland Pygmies'.[80] While Stanley's *In Darkest Africa* portrayed pygmies as cunning and

77. A metaphor borrowed from D. Haraway, 'Teddy bear patriarchy: taxidermy in the Garden of Eden', in his *Primate Visions: Gender, Race and Nature in the World of Modern Science* (London, 1989), p. 46.

78. D. Stanley (ed.), *The Autobiography of Henry Morton Stanley* (London, 1909), p. 377.

79. G. Casati, *Ten Years in Equatoria* (London, 1891), pp. 155–62. See also J. Vansina, 'Do pygmies have a history?', *Sprache und Geschichte in Afrika*, 7 (1986), pp. 431–45; J. Vansina, *Paths in the Rainforests: Toward a History of Political Tradition in Equatorial Africa* (London, 1990).

80. *The Times*, 27 February 1890, p. 5; Chancery, Applicant's Evidence (Affidavits of N. Reynolds and H. Applegarth) pp. 1, 13.

EMIN PASHA

AND THE

REBELLION AT THE EQUATOR

A STORY OF NINE MONTHS' EXPERIENCES IN THE LAST OF THE SOUDAN PROVINCES

BY

A. J. MOUNTENEY-JEPHSON

(Late Stanley's Officer)

WITH THE REVISION AND CO-OPERATION OF

HENRY M. STANLEY, D.C.L. &c., &c.

WITH MAP AND NUMEROUS ILLUSTRATIONS

LONDON

SAMPSON LOW, MARSTON, SEARLE, & RIVINGTON

7.3 Frontispiece to A. J. Mounteney-Jephson, *Emin Pasha and the Rebellion at the Equator* (1890).

resourceful,[81] to others they were innocent and child-like. In this respect, it is telling that the frontispieces of two other accounts of Stanley's expedition bore tiny illustrations of little cherubic Africans, drawn by Dorothy Tennant, an artist known for her images of 'street arabs' from the London streets (figure 7.3).[82] An exhibition of her pictures was held in Regent Street at the same time as the Stanley and African Exhibition; and, as if to complete the circle, she was married to Stanley in July 1890.

81. H. M. Stanley, *In Darkest Africa* (London, 1890), vol. i, pp. 351–3; vol. ii, pp. 92–6, 150–1.
82. A. J. Mounteney-Jephson, *Emin Pasha and the Rebellion at the Equator* (London, 1890); T. H. Parke, *My Personal Experiences in Equatorial Africa* (London, 1891). See also D. Tennant, *London Street Arabs* (London, 1890).

Chapter 8

Exploring 'Darkest England': Mapping the Heart of Empire

As there is a darkest Africa is there not also a darkest England?[1]

The rhetoric of Geography Militant was exploited in a variety of different contexts during the nineteenth and twentieth centuries. The figure of the intrepid explorer was found not only in the pages of exotic travel narratives, but also in juvenile fiction, scouting manuals and, perhaps above all, the literature of social investigation. 'General' William Booth, founder of the Salvation Army and the author of *In Darkest England and the Way Out* (1890), was by no means the first social reformer to employ the language of imperial exploration in the context of missionary work at home, though his calculating appropriation of Henry Morton Stanley's sensational title provides the most celebrated instance of this process at work.[2] It was already a cliché of the Victorian literature of urban investigation that another world lay beyond the fine frontages and thoroughfares of the metropolis, waiting to be explored, colonized and civilized. *In Darkest England* may thus be read, in part, as a continuation of earlier efforts to map the moral geographies of the Victorian city. In other respects, however, William Booth's project – like Stanley's – marked something new: a sensational publicity campaign, focused on a charismatic individual, which at the same time relied on distinctly modern methods of organization and salesmanship.

This chapter considers projects of social exploration, mapping and

1. W. Booth, *In Darkest England and the Way Out* (London, 1890), p. 11.
2. Stanley's title was borrowed by authors writing on a variety of themes, from Darkest Russia to Darkest New York: D. Stanley (ed.), *The Autobiography of Henry M. Stanley* (London, 1909), p. 411.

colonization at the heart of empire, focusing especially on the literature of urban investigation at the *fin-de-siècle*. It is indeed tempting to read *In Darkest England* symptomatically, as the product of a wider discourse of urban investigation replete with references to intrepid exploration in unknown regions, travels among savage tribes, and calls to colonization. For William Booth, as for many of his contemporaries, the city was a landscape to be mapped and colonised; furthermore, the 'way out' of moral and social decay in the metropolis, he argued, lay ultimately in colonial emigration. In order to sustain such a symptomatic reading, however, it is important to recognise that the discourse of urban exploration, like that of imperial travel writing, was far from homogeneous. Booth's *In Darkest England* negotiated a distinctive path between various strains of writing: on the one hand, for example, the synoptic mapping of the urban poor repre-sented in the work of his contemporary Charles Booth, and on the other, a tradition of urban ethnography often associated with Henry Mayhew.[3] Moreover, such a symptomatic reading has its limits, if only because texts are never merely instances of discursive formations: they are also tactical interventions which shape those formations in particular historical moments. It is necessary therefore to give close consideration to the contexts in which such texts were written and read. William Booth's militant geography, like Stanley's, had its critics: indeed, the critical response to *In Darkest England* tells us much about the heterogeneity of the discourse of urban exploration at the *fin-de-siècle*. There was more than one way to explore the imperial city.

Geography Militant in Darkest England

William Booth described his 'Darkest England' scheme as the product of 'a huge Campaign carried on for many years against the evils which lie at the roots of all the miseries of modern life'.[4] *In Darkest England* was an instant best-seller: within a month, 115,000 copies had been sold, catapulting the 'General' and his Salvation Army onto the public stage. Booth was, course, far from unique in his concern with the social and moral condition of the urban poor in late-Victorian Britain: during

---

3.   The contrast between these modes of urban exploration reflects similar distinc-tions made in recent work on imperial travel writing: see especially M. L. Pratt, *Imperial Eyes: Travel Writing and Transculturation* (Routledge, 1992).
4.   W. Booth, *In Darkest England and the Way Out* (London, 1890), preface.

the previous decade, in particular, a host of social reformers, urban investigators, charity workers, socialists, novelists and missionaries had covered much the same territory. But as many of his critics pointed out, *In Darkest England* paid little attention to the work of other agencies and individuals. Like Stanley, Booth presented his work as that of a pioneer in the field, while in fact relying heavily on the labours of others. The knowing appropriation of Stanley's rhetoric thus served more than one purpose: in particular, it allowed Booth to present himself as a militant explorer in the darkness. 'May we not find a parallel at our own doors, and discover within a stone's throw of our cathedrals and palaces similar horrors to those which Stanley has found existing in the great Equatorial forest?' Warming to his theme, Booth compared the slave traders and ivory raiders in Stanley's writings to publicans and other predators on the urban poor, and drew analogies between the pygmies of equatorial Africa and the stunted specimens of 'Darkest England'. While Stanley's account of the interminable forest enabled Booth to emphasize the sheer extent of urban poverty, it was the swamp and its poisonous atmosphere which provided the most potent environmental metaphor: 'A population sodden with drink, steeped in vice, eaten up by every social and physical malady, these are the denizens of Darkest England'.[5]

In Darkest England was divided into two parts, entitled 'The Darkness' and 'Deliverance'. In the first, Booth began with what he described as a scientific account of 'the submerged tenth'. Drawing selectively on Charles Booth's recently published survey of poverty in East London (discussed below), he estimated the population of 'Darkest England' as three million people living in a state of absolute destitution or chronic poverty, 'nominally free but really enslaved'.[6] Having established the extent of the problem, he then painted a series of vivid portraits of the homeless poor (the 'nomads of civilisation'), the unemployed, the destitute ('on the verge of the abyss'), the vicious, the criminal and the abandoned children ('the rakings of the human cesspool'). Booth's scheme for social regeneration combined an emphasis on the reform of character with the improvement of social conditions: to reach individuals, social bridges had to be provided across the town swamps. The key to the scheme lay in a network of colonies: first, what Booth called a 'city colony', consisting of various institutions – food depots, night shelters, workshops and labour bureaux – which together would act as 'Harbours of Refuge for all and any who have been shipwrecked in life,

5. Booth, *In Darkest England*, pp. 11–12, 14–15.
6. Booth, *In Darkest England*, p. 23.

character or circumstances'.[7] These were supplemented by the 'farm colony', designed as a means of moral and industrial training in preparation for a new life. Finally, there was the 'over-sea colony' which would provide the ultimate destination for much of the destitute population of 'Darkest England'.

Accompanying *In Darkest England* was a fold-out chart, described as a birds-eye view of the scheme as a whole (figure 8.1). It depicts the 'submerged tenth' struggling to survive in a torrential sea, illuminated only by a Salvation Army lighthouse, while lifeboats are despatched in an organized rescue effort. The saved are led into a plethora of institutions in the city colony, including workshops, shelters, labour bureaux and children's homes. From there, another column of humanity can be seen making its way to the farm colony, far away from the chaos of urban life. In the distance, steamers provide passage for emigrants to the proposed colony across the sea, as well as to settlements in the British colonies and elsewhere. This imaginative geography is framed by an arch whose pillars display the statistics of crime, vice and destitution in 'Darkest England'. Above, the figures of a baker and a laundress symbolically affirm the Salvation Army's gospel of work as a means of social reclamation. The image as a whole depicts Booth's 'Great Machine' in action, turning the waste material of urban England into productive and useful citizens. To set this machine in motion, to establish these colonies, expeditions had to be organized in a militant spirit: 'It needs each of us to be as indomitable as Stanley,' Booth argued, 'to burst through all obstacles, to force our way right to the centre of things, and then to labour with the poor prisoner of vice and crime with all our might.'[8]

Booth's scheme attracted criticism from all sides. To liberals, such as Thomas Huxley, its quasi-collectivist solution to the problem of poverty came far too close to socialism; to socialists, such as H. M. Hyndman, it represented the last gasp of philanthropic charity.[9] In the present context, what is particularly striking about the critical response to *In Darkest England* is the common charge of 'sensationalism'. Huxley's distrust of the 'rowdy self-advertisement' of the scheme was shared by critics within and beyond the established Church. In one sermon, for

7. Booth, *In Darkest England*, p. 92.
8. Booth, *In Darkest England*, p. 156.
9. T. Huxley, *Social Diseases and Worse Remedies* (London, 1891); H. M. Hyndman, *General Booth's Book Refuted* (London, 1890). On attitudes towards the scheme within the labour movement, see especially V. Bailey, 'In Darkest England and the Way Out: the Salvation Army, social reform and the labour movement, 1885–1910', *International Review of Social History*, 29 (1984), pp. 133–71.

8.1 Chart from William Booth's *In Darkest England, and the Way Out* (1890).

example, the book was dismissed as 'only a big advertisement': 'it suits the age in which we live because it is big; and in our age we have, to a certain extent, in England become coloured by an American enthusiasm for everything which is great'. Another minister connected the book with the spectacular street campaigns of the Salvation Army: 'its disciples are taught to court publicity, . . . to get up sensational meetings, mountebank performances, and make a great fuss and show'. Meanwhile, the free-thinker G. W. Foote likened Booth's sensational methods to the showmanship of P. T. Barnum.[10] Such complaints echoed critical responses to best-selling exploration narratives, preeminently those of Henry Morton Stanley himself. Booth's readiness to model himself on Stanley provided ready ammunition for his critics; as one put it, 'both are past masters in the art of advertising themselves'.[11] Figure 8.2, in which Booth is depicted dancing enthusiastically on stage in female costume, bears more than a passing resemblance to a caricature of Stanley published the previous year (cf. figure 6.2).[12] While Stanley's helmet is exchanged for a tambourine, and Booth himself takes on the role of chorus-girl, the effect of the theatrical setting in both these images is to undermine the credibility of sensational appeals for public attention by associating them with the fickle world of popular entertainment. Mocking the manliness of the explorer is a means of questioning his trustworthiness: in the world of show business, nothing is what it seems.

Such criticisms mark out *In Darkest England* as a more modern text than it might otherwise appear. While Booth's phantasmagoric rendering of the evils of the city reworked well-worn evangelical themes, the methods he used both to organize his scheme and to market his message were more novel. In this context, it is significant that Booth concluded his preface to *In Darkest England* with a fulsome acknowledgement of 'valuable literary help from a friend of the poor' in the preparation of

10. R. Eyton, *A Rash Investment: A Sermon on the Salvation Army Scheme of Social Reform* (London, 1890), pp. 13–14; Anon, *'In Darkest England': A Reply to 'General' Booth's Sensational Scheme for Social Salvation* (London, 1890), pp. 13, 33; G. W. Foote, *Salvation Syrup, or Light on Darkest England: A Reply to General Booth* (London, 1891).
11. R. B. Roxby, *General Booth Limited: A Limelight on the 'Darkest England' Scheme* (London, 1892), p. 83.
12. The costume and rituals of the Salvation Army – especially the tambourine itself – provided a source of ridicule. 'Their services', wrote one Wesleyan in 1885, 'are frequently a travesty of a music-hall entertainment': K. S. Inglis, *Churches and the Working Classes in Victorian England* (London, 1963), p. 188. Figure 8.2 is reproduced in P. Walker, '"I live but not yet I for Christ liveth in me": men and masculinity in the Salvation Army, 1865–1890', in M. Roper and J. Tosh (eds), *Manful Assertions: Masculinities in Britain since 1800* (London, 1991), pp. 92–112.

8.2 William Booth on Stage: A Caricature of Sensational Showmanship (*St Stephens Review*, 1892).

the manuscript. Several historians have identified the celebrated journalist W. T. Stead as Booth's assistant, or even his co-author.[13] Stead

13. Booth, *In Darkest England*, preface; G. Stedman Jones, *Outcast London: A Study in the Relationship between Classes in Victorian Society* (London, 1971), p. 311 n. 20; R. Samuel, *Island Stories: Unravelling Britain* (London, 1998), p. 307. See also F. Whyte, *The Life of W. T. Stead*, vol. 2 (London, 1925), p. 13; H. Begbie, *The Life of General William Booth*, vol. ii (London, 1920), pp. 87–8.

was the central figure in the 'new journalism' of this period.[14] As editor of the *Pall Mall Gazette*, he had helped to initiate the public debate over *The Bitter Cry of Outcast London*, published in 1883. His subsequent exposé of child prostitution, in the 'Maiden Tribute of Modern Babylon', has justly been described as 'one of the most success-ful pieces of scandal journalism of the nineteenth century'.[15] While Stead did not invent sensational journalism, he made it mainstream, capitalising on the changing nature of the press and its expanding markets. Indeed, he was the main target of conservative critics of the new journalism, such as Matthew Arnold, who complained that its sensationalism owed more to American methods than to English.[16] As Judith Walkowitz and others have shown, Stead's reporting did much to shape the public debate over the social question in the 1880s: his vision of the *Pall Mall Gazette* as an 'engine of social reform and collective moral renewal' was realized in a series of highly effective publicity campaigns.[17] This vision, coupled with his own brand of purity politics, brought Stead into close contact with William Booth and the Salvation Army.[18] Booth's own son, Bramwell, later described Stead as 'a Salvationist in Mufti':[19] Bramwell was himself involved in the legal case arising from the 'Maiden tribute', which ended with Stead spending three months in Holloway jail, a martyr to the cause of social justice. While the narrative voice of *In Darkest England* was distinctive, its debt to the sensationalism of contemporary reportage is clear.

Many of the critics of *In Darkest England* directly associated its sensationalism with the evangelical methods of the 'General' and his followers. For critics within the Church, the Salvation Army's 'street manoeuvrings and skirmishings' represented 'a parody on the Christian way of salvation', placing far too much weight on expressions of ecstatic emotion and the charismatic authority of the preacher.[20] According to one historian, the key moment of conversion was itself represented by

14. R. Schults, *Crusader in Babylon: W. T. Stead and the Pall Mall Gazette* (Lincoln, Nebr., 1972); J. H. Wiener (ed.), *Papers for the Millions: The New Journalism in Britain, 1850s to 1914* (New York, 1988).
15. J. Walkowitz, *City of Dreadful Delight: Narratives of Sexual Danger in Late-Victorian London* (London, 1992), p. 29.
16. J. H. Wiener, 'How new was the new journalism?', in Wiener, *Papers for the Millions*, pp. 47–8.
17. Walkowitz, *City of Dreadful Delight*, p. 95.
18. Stead published biographies of both the 'General' and his wife Catherine.
19. Bailey, 'In Darkest England', p. 150.
20. P. Dwyer, *General Booth's 'Submerged Tenth', or the Wrong Way to do the Right Thing* (London, 1891), pp. 38, 67. Another critic explicitly linked Booth's 'sensational appeals' with the 'the wild methods of religious fanaticism' (Eyton, *A Rash Investment*, p. 29).

salvationists as 'sensational; it was a dramatic, ecstatic, bodily experience'.[21] So it is hardly surprising that the methods of the Salvation Army were denounced as vulgar and irrational by middle-class intellectuals: Huxley described them as organized fanaticism, while Hyndman ridiculed 'the grotesque fetishism of the Salvation Army, with its strange semi-barbarous songs and dances'.[22] (Such responses suggest that what was at stake here was more than political or religious principles, narrowly defined: Salvationist methods, like Stanley's expeditions, presented a challenge to orthodox models of masculinity and whiteness.) Within the established Church, critics drew parallels between the autocratic methods of the Salvation Army and those of messianic religious sects led by a single charismatic individual.[23] The 'General' himself claimed inspiration from the Wesleyan tradition, especially its emphasis on organization and leadership, portraying the Salvation Army as an instrument of redemption ordained by God to bring about the Kingdom of God on earth. He pointed to biblical precedents which licensed the use of military imagery in the missionary cause: the idea of the Church Militant not only had deep historical roots, it animated religious practice across the denominational spectrum, as indicated by the popularity of hymns like 'Onward Christian Soldiers'.[24]

Booth was unapologetic about the quasi-military discipline of the Salvation Army; indeed, he described it as 'one great secret of its success'. Expeditions into 'Darkest England', as much as Stanley's in Africa, required organization, discipline and above all obedience. Field officers had to submit to the authority of their commander-in-chief: 'A telegram from me', he claimed, 'will send any of them to the uttermost parts of the earth'.[25] If Stanley provided a serviceable model for Booth, it was not merely because of his skills as a publicist; it also reflected his presentation of the work of exploration as a sustained exercise in the application of will-power. Indeed, the more one looks for parallels between the two men, the more they seem to multiply: in their emphasis on the moral virtue of labour, their challenges to what they regarded as an obstinate establishment and their attempts to mobilize popular opinion. Like Stanley, as we have seen, Booth represented himself as a pioneer: and one can perhaps detect in his lack of acknowledgement of the work of others a similar degree of self-confidence, verging on

21. Walker, 'I live but not yet I', p. 100. See also Inglis, *Churches and the Working Classes*, pp. 180–194.
22. Huxley, *Social Diseases*, p. 58; Hyndman, *General Booth's Book Refuted*, p. 12.
23. Dwyer, *General Booth's 'Submerged Tenth'*.
24. Inglis, *Churches and the Working Classes*, pp. 181–2.
25. Booth, *In Darkest England*, p. 243.

megalomania.[26] It is now generally recognized by historians that the 'Darkest England' scheme was in fact the work of more than one hand, and that Booth – like Stanley – was something of an opportunist, borrowing liberally from others while presenting himself as a pioneer. Keenly aware of the declining levels of support for the Salvation Army in East London during the late 1880s, he had hoped to regenerate the organization by means of a sensational publicity campaign. In the process, as his critics loudly complained, he failed to acknowledge the extent of his borrowings from rival organizations like the Church Army and socialist agitators like Henry George.[27]

In the foregoing account of the content and reception of the Darkest England scheme, I have emphazised aspects of the work which received the greatest attention from its many critics: namely, the promotion of the scheme by means of a recognizably 'sensational' publicity campaign, and its reliance on a strictly hierarchical structure of authority, centred on William Booth himself. On both counts, as we have seen, the debate over *In Darkest England* echoed critical responses to the style and methods of contemporary explorers such as Stanley, who self-consciously embraced the style and methods of the new imperialism. In other respects, however, the idea of 'Darkest England' appeared much more conventional: in representing the nether-regions of the metropolis as spaces to be explored and colonized, Booth was appropriating a well-established trope in the writings of Victorian and Edwardian social investigators. In what follows, I focus on two key features of this discourse of urban exploration as it developed in the later nineteenth century: the technique of social mapping and the project of the domestic colony. The former was to be realized most famously in the work of Charles Booth, while the latter loomed large in debates over social policy well into the Edwardian era. The question for William Booth and his contemporaries was not whether to map or to colonize the spaces of 'Darkest England', but how to do so.

26. There is an uncanny resemblance between Booth's confession that in the writing of *In Darkest England* 'I have more constantly used the first personal pronoun than ever before in anything I have written' (p. 277) and Stanley's that 'I have also used the personal pronoun first person singular, "I", oftener, perhaps, than real modesty would admit . . . Ego is first and foremost in this book' (*How I Found Livingstone* (London, 1872), pp. xxii, 69).
27. The Church Army had proposed a similar scheme for city, farm and overseas colonies in a pamphlet published in March 1890. Henry George's ideas had influenced the Social Reform wing of the Salvation Army: see N. Murdoch, 'William Booth's In Darkest England and the Way Out: a reappraisal', *Wesleyan Theological Journal*, 25 (1990); Bailey, 'In Darkest England', pp. 146–58.

Mapping *Terra Incognita*

'There is nothing new in the book, except for a map at the beginning,
which for its exquisite humour might have been produced by a
Hogarth', complained one of *In Darkest England*'s fiercest critics.[28] The
purpose of the 'map' was clearly less analytic than symbolic: rather
than to provide the basis for a statistical account of the geography of
destitution, its function was to synthesize William Booth's vision of the
moral landscape of 'Darkest England' and the 'way out'. The iconography of this landscape owed much to Booth's millennialism, especially in
the form it took after the mid-1880s, when he came to regard salvation
as a matter of social regeneration as well as of personal sanctification.
In other respects, however, the 'map' reworked long-established
assumptions about the nature of modern urbanism. The notion that
urban living might be associated with the co-existence of poverty and
plenty, that even at the heart of the wealthiest city in the world there
might be found the most wretched conditions of life, was in itself far
from novel. Furthermore, Booth's analogy with the exploration of
unknown lands was hardly new: indeed, 'there is barely an area of
nineteenth-century fictional and non-fictional prose in which the central
attitudes and terminology of social exploration do not appear'.[29] As
Peter Keating has argued, it is the sheer adaptability of the language of
exploration which made it so attractive to novelists, social investigators
and reformers throughout the nineteenth and early twentieth centuries.

In some respects, Booth's presentation of himself as a social explorer
in the darkness of the modern city would have been familiar to an
earlier generation. While the metaphors varied – the swamp, the forest
and the labyrinth proved particularly popular – the poorer regions of
the metropolis were repeatedly represented by mid-Victorians as
dangerous landscapes to be explored.[30] What particularly concerned
social reformers was their own lack of control over such spaces, hence
their overriding obsession with hidden recesses, narrow turnings, dark
alleys and shadowy corners. The 'rookeries' of London, for example,
were often portrayed during the middle decades of the nineteenth
century as beyond the public gaze, outside the ambit of official surveil-

28. Roxby, *General Booth Limited*, p. 18.
29. P. Keating, *Into Unknown England, 1866–1913: Selections from the Social
Explorers* (London, 1976), p. 13.
30. Walkowitz, *City of Dreadful Delight*, pp. 17–19. See also F. Driver, 'Moral
geographies: social science and the urban environment in mid-nineteenth century
England', *Transactions of the Institute of British Geographers*, 13 (1988),
pp. 275–87.

lance; indeed, this was said to be one of their defining features.[31] They were diseased spaces, threatening the health of the social body as a whole: 'fever dens', 'plague spots', 'hot-beds of moral pestilence', 'rendezvous of vice', 'nurseries of felons', 'colonies of paupers', 'seed-beds of revolution', the 'nuclei of the disaffected'.[32] The task of the social explorer – the novelist and social scientist alike – was to map out the moral geography of these localities. As George Godwin put it in his *Town Swamps and Social Bridges* (1859): 'We must dive, then, into the back-slums of London – the social morasses – the shadowy corners.' Godwin's appeal to the consciences of his affluent readers was framed in terms William Booth would have recognized. (Another of his works opened with the question, 'Do you ever go East, good Reader?') And his solution, though lacking the evangelical temper of *In Darkest England*, was otherwise described in remarkably similar terms: 'Drain the swamps and increase the bridges.'[33] Godwin's social bridges included reformatories, hospitals, missions, ragged schools, model dwellings, nurseries and public parks: these weapons of mid-Victorian ameliorism would reappear a generation later in the 'Darkest England' scheme.

William Booth's rhetorical question 'As there is a darkest Africa is there not also a darkest England?' was by 1890 something of a cliché. Seven years earlier, George Sims had characterized his sensational *How the Poor Live* (1883) as a journey 'into a dark continent that is within easy walking distance of the General Post Office'. Sims's ironic intent was made clear in the sentence that followed: 'This continent will, I hope, be found as interesting as any of those newly-explored lands which engage the attention of the Royal Geographical Society – the wild races who inhabit it will, I trust, gain public sympathy as easily as those savage tribes for whose benefit Missionary Societies never cease to appeal for public sympathy.'[34] A similar trope was employed to much sharper effect in Charles Dickens's satire on 'telescopic phil-anthropy' in *Bleak House* (1853), in which Mrs Jellyby's all-consuming concern with the natives of 'Borrioboola-Gha' is contrasted unfavoura-bly with the chaotic state of her own household. Dickens's accounts of

31.   H. J. Dyos, 'The slums of Victorian London', in D. Cannadine and D. Reeder (eds), *Exploring the Urban Past: Essays in Urban History* (Cambridge, 1982), pp. 129–53; R. Evans, 'Rookeries and model dwellings: English housing reform and the moralities of private space', *Architectural Association Quarterly*, 10 (1978), pp. 24–35.

32.   T. Beames, *The Rookeries of London* (London, 1851).

33.   G. Godwin, *Town Swamps and Social Bridges* (Leicester, 1972; orig. 1859), pp. 12, 102; G. Godwin, *Another Blow for Life* (London, 1864), p. 1.

34.   Keating, *Into Unknown England*, p. 14.

his own numerous journeys through the poorer districts of London portrayed their inhabitants as above all individuals, degraded perhaps, but ultimately as redeemable as any savage or barbarian; in fact, as he made clear in a virulently racist essay on the 'Noble savage' published in the same year, far more so.[35]

Of all William Booth's predecessors, it was Henry Mayhew who deployed the analogy of the urban investigator-as-explorer in the most sustained fashion. His mid-century reports for the *Morning Chronicle*, collected together in *London Labour and the London Poor*, had famously represented the street-folk of London as 'wandering tribes', with their own distinctive languages, physiognomies, customs and moral codes. Taking his cue from the ethnologist James Cowles Prichard, Mayhew styled himself as a 'traveller in the undiscovered country of the poor'.[36] In his social investigations with John Binny, he presented the metropolis as 'essentially a city of antithesis – a city . . . where the very extremes of society are seen in greater force than anywhere else'.[37] London was imagined as a miniature globe in itself, Hampstead and Sydenham its north and south poles, while at the equator lay 'the whole line of Oxford Street, Holborn, and Cheapside scorching under the everlasting summer of what would then be the metropolitan torrid zone; and while it was day at Kensington, night [would be] reigning at Mile End'.[38] For all Mayhew's attention to plurality and heterogeneity, he – like so many other social investigators – often reverted to the contrast between East and West, represented here (as so often) by Mile End and Kensington. So often too, the poorer districts were characterized as existing in an almost perpetual darkness, in the shadows of the 'nether world', in need of the light of civilization: 'in passing from the skilled operative of the West-end to the unskilled workman of the eastern quarter of London', wrote Mayhew, 'the moral and intellectual change is so great that it seems as if we were in a new

35. C. Dickens, 'The noble savage', *Household Words*, 11 June 1853, reprinted in D. Pascoe (ed.), *Selected Journalism, 1850–1870* (Harmondsworth, 1997), pp. 560–5.
36. D. E. Nord, 'The social explorer as anthropologist: Victorian travellers among the urban poor', in W. Sharpe and L. Wallock (eds), *Visions of the Modern City* (Baltimore, Md., 1987), pp. 122–34; M. Cowling, *The Artist as Anthropologist: The Representation of Type and Character in Victorian Art* (Cambridge, 1989), esp. pp. 185–206.
37. H. Mayhew and J. Binny, *The Criminal Prisons of London* (London, 1862), pp. 28, 7, quoted in Cowling, *The Artist as Anthropologist*, p. 186.
38. J. Ryan, *Picturing Empire: Photography and the Visualization of the British Empire* (London, 1997), p. 179.

land, and among another race'.[39] This opposition between East and West reappeared in many subsequent works, including *London: A Pilgrimage* (1872) by Jerrold and Doré and *Street Life in London* (1878) by Thomson and Smith.[40] Here, as in Mayhew's writings, it functioned less as a description of the variety of urban life than as a metaphorical device through which the heterogeneity of the metropolis could be grasped.

While this distinction between East and West London was not wholly without material referents in the geography of employment, pauperism and wealth,[41] it sustained a powerful imaginative geography. The bifurcated language of East and West, as Walkowitz puts it, 'reinforced an imaginative distance between investigators and their subjects, a distance that many urban explorers felt nonetheless compelled to transgress'.[42] It also enabled the binary imaginaries of empire and race – of civilization and barbarism, of progress and degradation, of light and dark – to be mapped onto the city. In the context of the social crisis of the 1880s, outcast London came to be perceived much more as a threat than a spectacle: as Stedman Jones has argued, the predominant middle-class reaction to the rediscovery of poverty in the 1880s was not so much guilt as fear – of degeneration, of revolution, of contamination.[43] The repetition of older tropes (East and West, dark and light) alongside newer ones (especially the increasingly prevalent image of the abyss) took on new meanings in this context of social crisis. The metaphor of the abyss turned the spectacle of exotic difference into something infinitely more threatening: a gaping chasm in the social landscape, undermining the very basis of existing institutions.[44]

It is important to recognize that the language used by social investigators was itself open to investigation. The proliferation of metaphors in works such as *In Darkest England* attracted attention, providing fertile ground for criticism and parody. Bernard Bosanquet, for example, complained that William Booth's florid terminology – the 'sea

---

39. D. Green, *From Artisans to Paupers: Economic Change and Poverty in London, 1790–1870* (Aldershot, 1995), p. 140.
40. On the former, see G. Pollock, 'Vicarious excitements: *London: A Pilgrimage* by Gustave Doré and Blanchard Jerrold, 1872', *New Formations*, 4 (1988), pp. 25–50; on the latter, J. Ryan, *Picturing Empire*, pp. 173–80.
41. For the earlier Victorian period, see Green, *From Artisans to Paupers*; for the later, see Stedman Jones, *Outcast London*.
42. Walkowitz, *City of Dreadful Delight*, p. 20.
43. Stedman Jones, *Outcast London*, esp. pp. 281–314.
44. Keating, *Into Unknown England*, pp. 20–2. See also E. Woods, *A Darkness Visible: Gissing, Masterman and the Metaphors of Class, 1880–1914* (PhD thesis, University of Sussex, 1988).

of human misery', the 'quagmire of human sludge' – betrayed an indiscriminate and fundamentally unscientific approach to the problem of poverty.[45] This criticism was echoed by others: one churchman suggested that *In Darkest England* treated a whole class 'in the same fashion as you might proceed if you were draining an Irish bog'.[46] In this respect, Bosanquet and others drew a contrast between *In Darkest England* and Charles Booth's *Life and Labour in East London*, published in 1889. The first fruits of this project (which was eventually to result in the multi-volume survey of *Life and Labour of the People in London*) were reported in a paper to the Royal Statistical Society in May 1887: 'every social problem', Charles Booth had argued, 'must be broken up to be solved or even to be adequately stated'.[47] This was not simply an appeal for analysis. In the context of contemporary debates over the social question, it served to focus attention on the differences within the working class, especially between the respectable poor and the residuum. 'The hordes of barbarians of whom we have heard,' wrote Booth, 'who, issuing from their slums, will one day overwhelm modern civilization, do not exist. There are barbarians, but they are a handful, a small and decreasing percentage: a disgrace, but not a danger.'[48]

Charles Booth presented his own survey as a riposte to the sensational exposés of urban poverty during the 1880s, and in many ways it anticipated some of the critical response to *In Darkest England*. As he explained in the conclusion to the 1889 volume, entitled 'Point of View':

> East London lay hidden from view behind a curtain on which were painted terrible pictures: Starving children, suffering women, overworked men; horrors of drunkenness and vice; monsters and demons of inhumanity; giants of disease and despair, Did these pictures truly represent what lay behind, or did they bear to the facts a relation similar to that which the pictures outside a booth at some country fair bear to the performance or show within?[49]

'The writers of this book', continued Charles Booth, 'have each of them at different points, tried to lift this curtain and to see for themselves the

45. B. Bosanquet, '*In Darkest England*' *on the Wrong Track* (London, 1891), pp. 8–9. See also C. S. Loch, *An Examination of General Booth's Social Scheme* (London, 1891).
46. Eyton, *A Rash Investment*, p. 14.
47. Keating, *Into Unknown England*, p. 24.
48. C. Booth (ed.), *Life and Labour in East London*, vol. i: *East London* (London, 1889), p. 39. See also Stedman Jones, *Outcast London*, pp. 319–21.
49. Booth, *Life and Labour in East London*, pp. 591–2.

world it hid.' The sober observations of the social scientist were more trustworthy than the sensational methods of the showman, simply because they relied on a different way of seeing: conscientious, disinterested, objective. Booth's *Life and Labour* series was the fruit of a large team of researchers (including Beatrice Potter, Clara Collet and Hubert Llewellyn Smith, but also a host of lesser-known figures) rather than of one charismatic individual, and this sense of a collaborative project played an important part in the published accounts of their investigations.[50] Yet by using the metaphor of the curtain in this way, Charles Booth himself was imagining himself as the impresario of another kind of theatre, opening up the hidden truths of the city to the light of cool reason. 'What I have endeavoured to present to my readers', Booth wrote in one of the volumes in the series, 'is a picture or a way of looking at things, rather than a doctrine or an argument.'[51]

In this context, Charles Booth's celebrated descriptive maps of London poverty substituted for the 'terrible pictures' painted by journalists, novelists and agitators. The first was published with the 1889 volume on East London; and two years later, it was followed by a map of the whole of London in four sheets. These maps were designed to replace the garish, phantasmagoric imagery of the sensational exposé with a comprehensive and objective survey of the geography of urban poverty across London. Based primarily though not exclusively on the analysis of interviews with School Board visitors, their purpose was to represent in graphic form the fruits of a huge and otherwise inaccessible amount of information; indeed, they were exhibited to the public, in London and elsewhere.[52] Throughout Charles Booth's work, graphic representations (maps, charts and diagrams) were designed to serve a dual purpose, as both analytical instruments and means of communication. In his published writings, he often emphazised his desire to 'add life and warmth' to the statistical data his team had amassed, which by themselves were 'somewhat colourless and cold'.[53] Although his 'buttoned-up' prose was clearly designed to differentiate his writings from

50. See especially R. O' Day and D. Englander, *Mr Charles Booth's Inquiry: Life and Labour of the People in London Reconsidered* (London, 1993), pp. 10–19; K. Bales, 'Charles Booth's survey of Life and Labour of the People in London, 1889–1903', in M. Bulmer, K. Bales and K. Sklar, *The Social Survey in Historical Perspective* (Cambridge, 1991), pp. 66–110.
51. C. Topalov, 'The city as terra incognita: Charles Booth's poverty survey and the people of London, 1886–1891', *Planning Perspectives*, 8 (1993), pp. 395–425 (p. 409).
52. Booth, *Life and Labour in East London*, p. 24.
53. Booth, *Life and Labour in East London*, p. 156.

the highly wrought rhetoric of more sensational accounts,[54] he was keenly aware of the need to add colour to his descriptions. Sometimes this involved the use of sensitive accounts of the character of particular districts, sometimes insights into the experience of individuals. 'I cannot hope to make the rows of figures in this table as luminous and picturesque to every eye as they are to mine', Booth had warned his audience at the Royal Statistical Society in 1887; 'and yet I am not content without making an attempt to do so'.[55] In a different way, the maps themselves performed a similar function, by turning numbers into pictures: however, in Booth's eyes, at least, they were not curtains, but mirrors.

The rhetorical power of the descriptive maps becomes still more significant when the cumbersome arrangement and sheer scale of Booth's *Life and Labour* series is taken into account: seventeen volumes in three editions, it represented more of a compendium than a guide. Writing in 1902, Charles Masterman expressed his sense of disorientation:

> We perused nine bulky volumes, mazes of statistics, ordered and classi-
> fied, maps of picturesque bewilderment of colour, infinite detail of streets
> and houses and family lives. And at the end of it all the general impression
> left was of something monstrous, grotesque, inane; something beyond the
> power of individual synthesis; a chaos resisting all attempts to reduce it
> to orderly law. We are little nearer at the end than at the beginning to
> the apprehension of the conditions of Abysmal London.[56]

The maps of London poverty were designed to make the results of the surveys readily accessible to 'the power of individual synthesis'. They were based on assessments of the condition of areas (streets or parts of streets) rather than individual households or families. Each street was classified into one of eight classes, denoted by a code (A–H) summarizing the condition of its inhabitants. The maps represented these classes by a scheme of colours, from black (for the 'very poor, lowest class', including the 'vicious and semi-criminal') to yellow ('upper middle class'). They depicted a heterogeneous landscape: while the East–West contrast was evident, there were also numerous local

---

54. In their discussion of the more austere Industry Series, O' Day and Englander suggest that there is 'a disjuncture between the buttoned-up Booth of the printed survey – very grave and very eminent – and the more approachable Booth of the published notebooks': *Mr Charles Booth's Inquiry*, p. 156.
55. Walkowitz, *City of Dreadful Delight*, p. 34.
56. C. Masterman, 'The social abyss', *Contemporary Review*, 81 (1902), p. 25, cited in O' Day and Englander, *Mr Charles Booth's Inquiry*, p. 23.

variations. 'Each district has its character – its peculiar flavour', wrote Charles Booth of East London. 'One seems to be conscious of it in the streets. It may be in the faces of the people, or in what they carry – perhaps a reflection of it is thrown in this way from the prevailing trades – or it may lie in the sounds one hears, or the character of the buildings.'[57] More generally, there was also a distinct social gradient extending from the overcrowded neighbourhoods of East and Central London to the wealthier suburbs, swelled by the centrifugal movement of the better-off from the poorer districts, resulting in 'curious resemblances between opposite sides or corners of the social map'.[58] Overall, these patterns were used to support a distinctive social ecology of the city: local patches of black lay in seas of blue and pink, while the currents and eddies of migration were reflected in broader, concentric patterns across the city.[59]

Charles Booth's maps, then, had a number of functions. As analytical tools, they developed his arguments about the social geography of urban life, mapping a taxonomy of social classes onto spaces at the scale of the street; as illustrative devices, they provided a synthetic overview of the results of the project, exhibiting them in a form which could be readily comprehended; and as guides to action, they served as Baedekers for a generation of social reformers dedicated to the projects of modern urban planning.[60] Yet the epistemology of the social map was in theory far removed from that of the narrative of urban explorer: it relied on the detachment of the observer, on the cool analytical gaze of the social scientist. It built on an already existing tradition of social survey, dramatically extending and intensifying the view from above.[61] While Charles Booth adopted the language of exploration at certain points in his writings, and lived incognito in lodgings in the East End for short periods in order to observe the poor first hand, the maps themselves represented a different angle of vision. As Christian Topalov puts it, 'The era of the pioneer expedition was over; it was time to take

---

57. Booth, *Life and Labour in East London*, p. 66.
58. C. Booth, *Life and Labour of the People in London*, final volume, *Notes on Social Influences and Conclusion* (London, 1903), pp. 182–3.
59. On Booth's urban ecology, see D. Reeder, 'Introduction', in his *Charles Booth's Descriptive Map of London Poverty 1889* (London, 1984); D. Reeder, 'Representations of metropolis: descriptions of the social environment in *Life and Labour*', in D. Englander and R. O'Day (eds), *Retrieved Riches: Social Investigation in Britain, 1840–1914* (Aldershot, 1995), pp. 323–38.
60. S. Koven, 'The dangers of castle building: surveying the social survey', in Bulmer, Bales and Sklar, *The Social Survey*, p. 370.
61. For an account of Booth as the inheritor of a well-established 'survey habit of mind', see E. Yeo, 'The social survey in social perspective, 1830–1930', in Bulmer, Bales and Sklar, *The Social Survey*, pp. 49–65.

possession of the territory by a complete representation of it. Just as the statistical table could not tolerate a gap, the map could not tolerate a blank space, a terra incognita.'[62]

Colonizing and Cultivating

If the map enabled late-Victorian social explorers to negotiate their way through 'Darkest England', the planting of a colony or settlement was commonly regarded as a means of both introducing civilization to its demoralized inhabitants and promising a 'way out'. Proposals for the establishment of 'colonies' at home played a significant part in the schemes for the alleviation of poverty proposed by both William Booth and Charles Booth, as well as many of their contemporaries. The notion of the domestic colony as an instrument of social reform did not of course originate in this period: it appears in a variety of guises through-out the nineteenth century, in the writings of utopian socialists, Poor Law reformers, reformatory campaigners, asylum doctors, urban plan-ners and advocates of land reform.[63] Yet its imaginative appeal to intellectuals and reformers during the late-Victorian and Edwardian period is particularly striking. To the social imperialists (who counted 'General' Booth among their number), the idea of the colony was closely linked with theories of urban degeneration. Their anxieties about rural depopulation, combined with their diagnosis of the pathology of

62. Topalov, 'The city as terra incognita', p. 412. In her account of urban spectatorship, Walkowitz makes more of Booth's own forays into the East End, arguing that his masquerade as an inhabitant reflected an unresolved ambivalence towards the working-class other (*City of Dreadful Delight*, pp. 36–7). But his accounts of these expeditions were quite unlike those of his contemporaries W. T. Stead or William Booth; furthermore, Booth represented himself as an observer of 'specimens' of the poor, not a communicator with them, though this distinction may not apply so readily to his unpublished writings. It has been argued that female investigators were more likely to employ aural rather than visual means of observation on their travels through the city: see D. Nord, *Walking the Victorian Streets: Women, Representation and the City* (Ithaca, New York, 1995), pp. 189–93, 217–19; E. Ross, *Love and Toil: Motherhood in Outcast London, 1870–1918* (Oxford, 1993), ch. 1.
63. For some examples, see W. Armytage, *Heavens Below: Utopian Experiments in Britain, 1560–1960* (London, 1961); F. Driver, 'Discipline without frontiers? Representations of the Mettray reformatory colony in Britain, 1840–1880', *Journal of Historical Sociology*, 3 (1990), pp. 272–93; J. Radford, 'Sterilisation versus segregation: control of the "feeble-minded", 1900–1938', *Social Science and Medicine*, 33 (1991), pp. 449–58; J. Rockey, 'From vision to reality: Victorian ideal cities and model towns', *Town Planning Review*, 54 (1983); P. Gould, *Early Green Politics* (Brighton, 1988).

urbanism, led many to support schemes for land 'colonies' at home as well as abroad. In a collection of essays entitled *Social Arrows* (1886), for example, Reginald Brabazon (the Earl of Meath) described London in terms William Booth would have been proud of, as 'a Babylon of which the world has never dreamt'.[64] Brabazon (the President of the Church Army) advocated a range of schemes, including the provision of parks and playgrounds in large cities, physical training for the poor and programmes of state-aided colonization and emigration for the casual poor. Like William Booth, he was convinced that the 'way out' of social problems lay ultimately in colonization, both within and beyond the city.

The 'Darkest England' scheme was presented by many of its supporters as a manifesto for emigration and colonization. W. T. Stead certainly thought so: accompanying the copy of *In Darkest England* that he sent to Lord Milner, then in Cairo, was a note expressing his satisfaction at its advocacy of social imperialism. 'You will be delighted to see that we have got the Salvation Army solid not only for Social Reform but also for Imperial Unity. I have written to Rhodes about it and we stand on the eve of great things.'[65] Stead's conspiratorial tone should not mislead us into thinking that the promotion of state-aided emigration or support for the 'Darkest England' scheme was the prerogative of a small clique. To the contrary: as Victor Bailey has shown, many elements of Booth's programme won support from liberals and labour activists who were otherwise increasingly critical of the activities of the Salvation Army.[66] The idea of colonization, though it took a variety of different forms, appealed to reformers across the political spectrum.

William Booth's tripartite colonization scheme synthesized different aspects of the idea of the colony as a means of social reform 'at home': the town colony as a bridgehead or series of bridgeheads in the city itself, bringing light into the darkness of the slums; the farm colony as a means of training the residuum in the ways of work and character; and the overseas colony as a safety-valve for overpopulation in the crowded cities at home, a 'New Britain'. The last of these schemes, and perhaps the most ambitious, was effectively shelved by the Salvation Army during the 1890s, although it was revived momentarily during

64. R. Brabazon, 'Great cities and social reform', in his *Social Arrows* (London, 1886), pp. 223–50 (p. 224). See also F. Aalen, 'Lord Meath, city improvement and social imperialism', *Planning Perspectives*, 4 (1989), pp. 127–52; B. Semmel, *Imperialism and Social Reform: English Social Imperial Thought* (London, 1895–1914); Stedman Jones, *Outcast London*, pp. 308–12.
65. Bailey, 'In Darkest England', p. 151.
66. Bailey, 'In Darkest England', esp. pp. 151–6.

the early-twentieth-century debate over physical deterioration and national efficiency. But even Henry Rider Haggard's favourable report on Booth's scheme for overseas colonization, commissioned by the Colonial Secretary in 1905, failed to overcome official reluctance to endorse the scheme, and subsequently the Salvation Army focused its efforts to promote the overseas aspect of the 'Darkest England' scheme mainly on sponsored emigration, becoming what one historian calls 'a sort of Cook's agency for the respectable working class'.[67]

In contrast, Booth's schemes to establish colonies at home won more support. The city colonies were effectively assemblages of institutions, including workshops, shelters and industrial homes, all of them stepping stones on the path to regeneration. In this respect, Booth's language, if not the details of his 'Darkest England' scheme, echoed that of other social reformers, including the founders of the settlement houses which proliferated in the East End of London, following the establishment of Toynbee Hall in a disused industrial school in Whitechapel in 1884.[68] At the heart of the settlement ethos, as articulated by Canon Barnett and others, was a diagnosis of social crisis in terms of the polarized social geography of cities: what was needed, it was argued, was the establishment of permanent bases within working-class districts in order to foster a sense of community and of individual worth. In the words of one clergyman,

> The dwellers in the East End of our towns will not be converted by missionaries and tracts sent by dwellers in the West End. The dwellers in the West End must go to the dwellers in the East themselves, share with the East those pleasures which give interest and delight to the dwellers in the West, and make up the fulness of their life. When the dwellers in the West go thus to the dwellers in the East they will be themselves converted, for they will have turned to Christ and accepted His yoke of personal service, and the dwellers in the East, recognizing the true helpfulness of the Christian life, will be converted too.[69]

The character of the better-known settlements, such as Toynbee Hall, reflected the ethos of disinterested service, which animated a rising generation of liberal intellectuals. The role of Oxford and Cambridge in supplying Toynbee Hall was reflected in the fabric of the buildings, notably its dining hall complete with a set of college shields, as well as

---

67. Bailey, 'In Darkest England', p. 164.
68. See S. Meacham, *Toynbee Hall and Social Reform* (London, 1987).
69. W. Moore Ede, *The Attitude of the Church to Some of the Social Problems of Town Life* (London, 1896), cited in Inglis, *Churches and the Working Classes*, p. 143.

in the somewhat rarefied educational programme: university life trans-planted in the East End. While the direct impact of the settlement house experiment was limited, it attracted much attention: many of the most prominent social reformers of the period (including William Beveridge, who was a sub-warden at Toynbee Hall in 1903) were directly associ-ated with it, while others (like Charles Booth and Beatrice Potter) used the settlements as bases for their own social survey work. As this suggests, settlements ought not to be seen as the consequence of the discovery of 'Darkest England': as with the settlement houses in the United States and elsewhere, they preceded and accompanied the work of social mapping, in all its guises.[70] Indeed, the very idea of settlement reflected assumptions about the relation between class separation and the demoralization of the poor which may be traced back to the 1860s.[71]

From a modern perspective, the language of 'settlement' contains more than an echo of the colonizing spirit of works such as *In Darkest England*: in both cases, the 'planting' of a colony is portrayed as the first step towards the regeneration of a demoralized population. These parallels between settlement houses and the Salvation Army's town colonies should certainly not be stretched too far: the sources of inspiration and means of operation of these institutions were as distinct as their clientele. Barnett himself drew a sharp distinction between the way of missions and the way of the settlement: characterizing the mission as a proselytizing venture, inspired by zealous – and often sensational – campaigns of conversion, he portrayed the settlement project as a sober effort to foster mutual understanding through neigh-bourly association between the rich and the poor.[72] Yet there was also common ground between William Booth and the liberal philanthropists, perhaps most evident in the third element of his 'Darkest England' Scheme – the proposals for a farm colony. Organized on quasi-military lines, the farm colony was intended to be settled by colonists selected from Salvation Army shelters and workshops in London. Booth argued that it would provide a training which was simultaneously reformatory and industrial (in the Victorian sense):

70. See especially K. Sklar, 'Hull-House maps and papers: social science as women's work in the 1890s', in Bulmer, Bales and Sklar (eds), *The Social Survey in Historical Perspective*, pp. 111–47; D. Ward, *Poverty, Ethnicity and the American City, 1840–1925: Changing Conceptions of the Slum and the Ghetto* (Cambridge, 1989).
71. For this argument, see Stedman Jones, *Outcast London*, pp. 258–61.
72. S. Barnett, 'The ways of "settlements" and of "missions"', *Nineteenth Cen-tury*, 42 (1897), 975–84.

> Every person in the Farm Colony will be taught the elementary lesson of
> obedience, and will be instructed in the needful arts of husbandry, or
> some other method of earning his bread. . . . It is a Training School for
> Emigrants, a place where those indispensably practical lessons are given
> which will enable the Colonists to know their way about and to feel
> themselves at home wherever there is land to till, stock to rear, and
> harvests to reap.[73]

A farm colony was soon established at a large estate at Hadleigh, in
Essex, overlooking the Thames estuary. By 1892, two hundred colonists
were employed there in market gardening, animal husbandry and brick
manufacture.[74] The very location provided its promoters with ample
opportunity not only for metaphorical play on the theme of reclamation, but also for imaginative associations with the circulation of
imperial trade:

> From the Tudor Tower that commands the Thames you can see the food
> of the nation passing up the silent highway in a ceaseless procession of
> steamers from all parts of the world. . . . Below, the waste marshes, richly
> grassed, await rescue for higher purposes than pasture by the wastrel men
> and town refuse that the city parishes can supply in any quantity
> required.[75]

Accounts of the early years of the colony present it as a landscape of
industrious reclamation, both moral and environmental. 'It is not as an
ordinary dispenser of alms that the Salvation Army is succeeding',
reported one convert to the scheme: 'It succeeds as a process of rescue,
not only by the restoration of self-respect to the mind, and muscle to
the body, but also by the subjugation of sensual appetites and bestial
tastes.'[76]

The Hadleigh colony attracted the attention of many social reformers
and politicians, including those who were otherwise critical of aspects
of the Salvation Army's work. The Guardians of the Poplar Union,
led by socialist George Lansbury, thought it a suitable place to send
their able-bodied paupers, while more willing visitors also included
W. T. Stead, Cecil Rhodes and Beatrice Webb. Their support for labour
colonies needs to be situated in a wider context: similar schemes had

---

73. Booth, *In Darkest England*, p. 134. See also F. Booth-Tucker, *In Darkest
India* (Bombay, 1891). For an argument about Salvation Army reformatories in
India, see R. Tolen, 'Colonizing and transforming the criminal tribesman: the
Salvation Army in British India', *American Ethnologist*, 18 (1991), pp. 106–25.
74. Bailey, 'In Darkest England', p. 160.
75. A. White, *Truth About the Salvation Army* (London, 1892), p. 14.
76. White, *Truth About the Salvation Army*, p. 16.

been widely canvassed during the 1880s, not merely by social imperialists like Brabazon, but also by liberal progressives like Canon Barnett
and Alfred Marshall. Charles Booth had also expressed support for the
use of labour colonies, which he described as a form of 'limited
Socialism', principally in order to segregate his Class B (the casual
poor), about one-tenth of the total, from the rest of the working class.
'The difficulty' he argued in 1889, 'lies solely in inducing or driving
these people to accept a regulated life.'[77] Subsequently, Booth revised
his initial enthusiasm for labour colonies, restricting their application to
a rather smaller class. Even so, he described Hadleigh in 1902 as 'a
very useful institution': indeed, 'as an experiment, its value has been
even greater, justifying all the money and zeal expended on it'.[78] In the
context of Edwardian debates over the Poor Laws, the colony was
heralded by some reformers as a model of what should be done with
the residuum, the 'unemployables'. The 1904 Inter-Departmental Committee on Physical Deterioration visited Hadleigh, and recommended
the establishment of labour colonies on the same lines (with additional
powers of compulsory detention) 'for the reclamation of some of the
waste elements of society'.[79] Again, such schemes met with support
across the political spectrum, though it was insufficient to result in
legislation. Similar proposals formed part of both the Minority and
Majority Reports of the Royal Commission on the Poor Laws in 1909.[80]

The idea of the colony thus played an important role in debates over
the urban poor during the late-Victorian and Edwardian period. As we
have seen, proposals for land colonies found support across the political
spectrum: far from there being an unbridgeable gap between, say, the
writings of William and Charles Booth, or between Brabazon and
Barnett, we find in this respect at least some striking points of convergence. This is not at all to deny the differences; it is merely to suggest
that conventional accounts of the late-Victorian and Edwardian 'discovery' of the problem of poverty in general, and unemployment in
particular, often fail to explain the points of convergence. And perhaps
the most important of these was the view that a certain part of the
problem of poverty – opinions varied as to how large the part was –

---

77. Booth, *Life and Labour in East London*, p. 166; Stedman Jones, *Outcast
London*, pp. 303–8; J. Brown, 'Charles Booth and labour colonies', *Economic
History Review*, 21 (1968), pp. 349–60.
78. C. Booth, *Life and Labour of the People in London*, third series, *Religious
Influences*, vol. 6 (London, 1902), p. 181. See also Booth, *Life and Labour of the
People in London*, final vol., pp. 206–8.
79. Quoted in Bailey, 'In Darkest England', p. 165.
80. Royal Commission on the Poor Laws and Relief of Distress, Parliamentary
Papers 1909 [cd. 4499] XXXVII, pp. 427–31, pp. 1117–23, 1199–201.

could be described in moral terms, in terms of patterns of conduct. Once patterns of moral conduct were seen to be the problem, moral training was naturally the solution. In other words, the idea of the colony that was being canvassed by these social reformers – liberals and conservatives alike – was essentially reformatory in spirit. This was a model that could be applied to children at home as well as to natives abroad, to the morally unfit and the residuum alike. It required segregation, preferably out of the city, industrial training, usually on the land, and, above all, reformatory discipline.[81]

The Heart of the Empire: from Colonization to Citizenship

In deploying the language of exploration in the context of social investigation at home, 'General' Booth styled himself after a very particular model: the explorer as a campaigner. As commander of a quasi-military organization, his rule – like Stanley's – was supposed to be absolute; and as the impresario of a sensational publicity campaign, he promoted his scheme with all the vigour he could muster. Perhaps what most distinguished *In Darkest England* from both the picturesque descriptions of urban explorers like Henry Mayhew and the 'buttoned-up' prose of social scientists like Charles Booth, was its sense of urgency: here was a call to action, not an exotic travel narrative or a statistical treatise. 'Darkest England' was portrayed as nothing less than a cancer within the imperial organism, a place of degeneration offering a pathetic contrast to the glamour of British enterprise overseas. For 'General' Booth, as for many social imperialists, the city was the problem and the empire was part of the solution; the 'way out' of moral and social decay in the metropolis lay ultimately in the establishment of colonies at home and abroad. For some of Booth's liberal contemporaries, however, the empire – or at least the popular culture of imperialism – was actually part of the problem. In this context, Charles Masterman's edited volume of essays on *The Heart of the Empire* (1901), which appeared in the midst of the Boer War, is a paradigm.[82]

81. On the relation between the ideas of colonizing, cultivating and reforming, see Driver, 'Discipline without frontiers?'; Tolen, 'Colonizing and transforming'.
82. The following paragraph draws on F. Driver and D. Gilbert, 'Heart of empire? Landscape, space and performance in imperial London', *Environment and Planning D: Society and Space*, 16 (1998), pp. 11–28. The idea of the city as a 'cancer' at the heart of the imperial body was common in discourses of public health and civic improvement across Europe: for another example, see J. MacKenzie, 'The second city of the empire: Glasgow, imperial municipality', in F. Driver and D. Gilbert

With Masterman, the rhetoric of social exploration finds its limit: the threat of 'Darkest England' is replaced by the mediocrity of the crowd as the problem of the age.

Masterman begins his own contribution to *The Heart of the Empire*, an essay entitled 'Realities at Home', by contrasting the social crusades of the 1880s with what he regards as the apathy of his own time. The widespread disenchantment with domestic social reform, following the failure of panaceas like Booth's 'Darkest England' scheme, had produced a kind of moral void; and this was being filled with 'other and noisier enthusiasms – the lust of domination, the stir of battle, the pride in magnitude of Empire; delight in the rule over alien nations, commercial aggrandisement, and dissatisfaction with anything short of predominance in the councils of the world'.[83] Meanwhile, argued Masterman, the very nature of social problems at home had undergone a profound transformation; nowhere was this clearer than in London itself, where the silent, yet inexorable, growth of the working-class 'ghetto' threatened to encircle the imperial city.[84] The problem Masterman describes is no longer that of the notorious slums, the 'isolated pools' or 'black spots' explored and mapped by previous generations of social reformers, up to and including Charles Booth; it is now a problem of the mass, of 'grey streets, grey people, a drab monotony'. By some 'subtle alchemy', Masterman warned, a new 'city type' had come into being: 'stunted, narrow-chested and easily wearied; yet voluble, excitable, with little ballast, stamina or endurance – seeking stimulus in drink, in betting, in any unaccustomed conflicts at home or abroad'.[85] In this context, the growth of popular imperialism was not merely a diversion; it was a positively demoralizing force, appealing to the most 'primitive' instincts of the urban masses. This attitude was most clearly expressed in liberal anxieties about outbreaks of 'jingoism' during the Boer War. While J. A. Hobson portrayed jingoism as the return of the primitive in modern life, Masterman developed the theme in a polemical work entitled *From the Abyss*:

> Our streets have suddenly become congested with a weird and uncanny people. They have poured in as dense black masses from the eastern railways; they have streamed across the bridges from the marshes and

---

(eds), *Imperial Cities: Landscape, Display and Identity* (Manchester, 1999), pp. 215–37 (esp. pp. 218–19).
83. C. Masterman 'Realities at home', in C. Masterman (ed.), *The Heart of the Empire* (London, 1901), p. 4.
84. Masterman, 'Realities at home', pp. 13–14.
85. Masterman 'Realities at home', pp. 16, 7–8. See also C. Masterman, *In Peril of Change* (London, 1905).

desolate places beyond the river; they have been hurried up in incredible number through tubes sunk in the bowels of the earth, emerging like rats from a drain, blinking in the sunshine.[86]

In this extraordinarily resonant passage, Masterman opens up the dark side of the imperial city: a place where unknown forces and uncontrollable desires come to the surface, threatening to engulf the very moral and physical fabric of society.

For Masterman and his colleagues, then, the social problem could no longer be adequately described in the language of social mapping. To be sure, he argued, there were scattered pools and patches of social squalor – remnants of the residuum – to be found across the urban landscape. 'This class is continually being broken up', wrote Masterman: 'polluted areas are cleared and rebuilt; the black aggregations disappear from the chart of poverty in the central districts'. Perhaps he was thinking of the London County Council's wholesale redevelopment of the notorious Old Nichol or Boundary Street area in Bethnal Green, the setting for Arthur Morrison's novel, *A Child of the Jago*. Contemporary accounts of the LCC scheme drew unambiguously on the iconography of 'Darkest England', as figure 8.3 suggests. But as far as Masterman was concerned, such piecemeal efforts merely redistributed the problem: 'It is as if one washed out an ink-spot on a picture with water; the blot vanishes, but the whole neighbourhood sensibly becomes coloured a darker hue.'[87] While Masterman used this image in the context of the particular problem of chronic and criminal poverty (Charles Booth's Class A), it serves as a fitting metaphor for his vision of modern urban life more generally: the less visible, but more intractable, problem of the mass.

'Each age is confronted by its own problem', wrote Masterman's close colleague Reginald Bray in his book *The Town Child* (1907): 'Today, we are confronted by the problem of the town.' Bray's diagnosis of the social question had much in common with Masterman's: for both, the process of urbanization had quietly and irreversibly transformed the landscape of modern society. 'The town, like Frankenstein's monster', wrote Bray, 'has slipped from the control of its creator and developed automatic processes of growth and acquired a separate existence of its own.' The combination of the natural and the monstrous

---

86.   C. Masterman, *From the Abyss* (London, 1902), p. 2. See also J. A. Hobson, *The Psychology of Jingoism* (London, 1901); J. A. Hobson, *Imperialism: A Study* (London, 1902).

87.   Masterman, 'Realities at home', p. 21. On the Boundary Street scheme, see R. Steffel, 'The Boundary Street estate', *Town Planning Review*, 47 (1976), pp. 161–73.

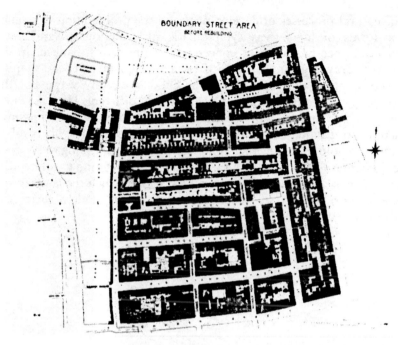

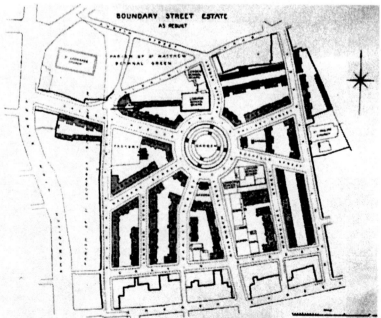

8.3 The Transformation of the Boundary Street Estate: Before and After (London County Council, *Housing of the Working Classes*, 1900).

– of natural processes of development and the proliferation of strange new forms of life – was symptomatic of evolutionary (and more specifically neo-Lamarckian) conceptions of modern urbanism. In the country, Bray argued, nature proved a 'benignant teacher', shaping the body, mind and character of the child in healthy ways. But the psychology of modern urban life was entirely different. Here the child was presented instead with 'a confused torrent of chaotic perceptions': 'there is no definite centre round which these thousand sights revolve, nothing to hold them together and give them unity, nothing to produce the consciousness of cause and effect: all is bewilderingly different'.[88] Such diagnoses as these ushered in a new age, in which the language of social exploration was to be displaced by that of modern sociology; calls to citizenship rather than colonization.

88. R. A. Bray, *The Town Child* (London, 1907), pp. vii, 54, 16–17.

Chapter 9

Geography Militant and its After-life

It is over. Bertrand Piccard and Brian Jones have circumnavigated the world by balloon non-stop, and a depression being felt among the world's professional adventurers will grow even harder to shake off. Every explorer with a book to sell has been asked the same question: What's left? What are you going to do next?[1]

In 1904, the geographer Halford Mackinder famously announced the passing of the 'Columbian' era of exploration and expansion which had structured the pattern of world politics for five hundred years: with the mapping out and carving up of the globe almost complete, the epoch of closed space was at hand.[2] While Mackinder was concerned with the shifting balance of power between land and sea, his sense of an irreversible change in the geographical order of things was shared by many of his contemporaries. According to Joseph Conrad, for example, the forces of modernization – we would say globalization – had swept away the conditions for authentic exploration: 'The days of heroic travel are gone; unless, of course, in the newspaper sense, in which heroism like everything else in the world becomes as common, if not as nourishing, as our daily bread.' For Conrad, the epoch of Geography Militant had been superseded by an altogether less noble age of global tourism, in which sham-explorers trod well-worn paths: 'the glance of

1. E. Douglas, 'What's left now for the world's frustrated daredevils?', *Observer*, 21 March 1999, p. 18.
2. H. Mackinder, 'The geographical pivot of history', *Geographical Journal*, 23 (1904), pp. 421–44. See also G. Kearns, 'Closed space and political practice: Frederick Jackson Turner and Halford Mackinder', *Environment and Planning D: Society and Space*, 2 (1984), pp. 23–34; S. Kern, *The Culture of Time and Space, 1880–1918* (Cambridge, Mass., 1983).

the modern traveller contemplating the much-surveyed earth beholds in fact a world in a state of transition ... Nothing obviously strange remains for our eyes now.'[3] Similar themes were subsequently reworked in avowedly more critical texts, including Lévi-Strauss's *Tristes Tropiques*, in which the modern business of exploration is treated with scorn: what could be more ignoble, asks Lévi-Strauss, than delivering illustrated tales to an audience of 'children accompanied by their mothers or nursemaids, some eager for a free change of scene, others weary of the dust and noise outside'?[4] (The horror, the horror . . .) The lantern-slide show and the glossy picture book are interpreted here as signs of a degenerate modernity: the explorer is nothing more than a showman – a purveyor of entertainment for a passive public, pointedly figured as both feminized and infantile.

Amid the media circus which accompanies the business of adventure in our own time – a solitary walk to the South Pole, an unaided ascent of Everest, a circumnavigation of the globe by balloon – one frequently finds similar laments for the passing of an age of innocent exploration. True explorers, the argument goes, had no need for either lucrative sponsorship or instant publicity; they simply went fearlessly into the unknown, in search of truth. Yet such paeans to the heroism of the lone explorer are utterly partial, not least because the accomplishments of figures such as Captain Cook or David Livingstone depended on far more than their own resourcefulness and courage. Their projects of exploration involved not merely the labours of many others in the field, but also the support of intermediaries, if not as sponsors and patrons, then as reporters, publishers or image-makers; and their presentation to the public relied on a variety of communicative media, from letters, books and government reports to popular magazines, newspapers and displays. In fact, the very image of a lone individual, struggling against the elements in order to advance the frontier of knowledge, is telling evidence of the power of such media to re-present the experience of exploration. As I have argued throughout this book, travel narratives were but one manifestation of a wider culture of exploration which embraced many other sorts of writing and image-making.

The purpose of this final chapter is to trace the worldly after-life[5] of

3. J. Conrad, 'Travel' (1923), reprinted in *Last Essays* (London, 1926), pp. 121–34.
4. C. Lévi-Strauss, *Tristes Tropiques* (London, 1973), p. 18.
5. I have borrowed this term from J. MacKenzie: 'David Livingstone and the worldly after-life: imperialism and nationalism in Africa', in *David Livingstone and the Victorian Encounter with Africa* (National Portrait Gallery, 1996), pp. 201–19.

Geography Militant, a figure regenerated in a variety of guises, from the pages of popular magazines to the sales rooms of auction houses. In the modern age, the culture of exploration lives on in a variety of forms: far from simply being eradicated from the map by the forces of modernity, the frontier has been reinstalled in other spaces, both material and imagined. Conrad's tribute to a lost age of heroic exploration was, in its own way, as much a part of a wider culture of exploration as the travel narratives he celebrated. That is to say, its nostalgic vision of geographical enterprise, apparently uncompromised by worldly associations with commerce or empire, has long been a feature of European discourses on exploration. This vision was an essential ingredient of the myth of the heroic explorer as it developed during the nineteenth century, and has also exerted a profound influence throughout the twentieth. In this context, we should do well to recall that Conrad's celebrated essay on 'Geography and some explorers' was reprinted in the *National Geographic* in 1924, alongside lurid accounts of 'Adventures among the lost tribes of Islam in Eastern Darfur' (by a district commissioner), 'Australia's wild wonderland' and 'The conquest of the Sahara by the automobile'. The announcement of the passing of Geography Militant was to say the least premature: even as Conrad wrote, it was being resurrected in a multitude of forms.

Geography Militant Regenerated

Traditions in the history of ideas, as in the history of popular culture, are best conceived as dynamic, rather than inert: they have to be constructed and re-enacted in order to live on.[6] In what follows, I am concerned with the reproduction of the motifs of Geography Militant within the realms of public culture. Here, Victorian myths of heroic exploration are given new life: far from being residual hangovers from the nineteenth century, or merely repetitions of well-worn tropes, they are regenerated in new, often camped-up, guises. In order to understand the ways in which such traditions are embedded in a range of cultural forms (such as advertising, photography, tourist guidebooks or film), we have to enlarge our vision of what geographical traditions are. Until recently, historians of geography have tended to restrict their focus to

6.   The debate which followed the publication of David N. Livingstone's influential account of *The Geographical Tradition* (1992) highlighted different ways in which such 'traditions' may be conceived: see F. Driver (ed.), 'Geographical traditions: rethinking the history of geography', *Transactions, Institute of British Geographers*, 20 (1995), pp. 403–22.

more refined, scholarly texts, a perspective that casts into shadow many of those worldly realms in which geographies are imagined, produced and consumed.[7] In this final chapter, I want to show why it is necessary to travel beyond the cabinet and into the field of public culture.

In this context, it should be emphasized that the question of geography's public image preoccupied the representatives of the Royal Geographical Society throughout the nineteenth century, and this itself involved the construction of a specific kind of tradition. For its founders, the Society was the natural heir to traditions of exploration which had characterized British history since the sixteenth century; John Barrow, for example, described the English as a 'travelling people', and he unhesitatingly affirmed 'that bold and masculine spirit of discovery which, disdaining danger, seeks to extend the knowledge and dominion of man to the utmost limits of the globe he inhabits'.[8] As we saw in chapter 2, Barrow's imperial vision was bequeathed to Roderick Murchison, who wholeheartedly embraced a more expansive vision of the Society's public role, especially in the promotion of exploration. The cumulative effect of his efforts was to strengthen the public image of a distinctive 'tradition' of British geography, so that by 1870 it would have seemed impossible to imagine that the Society had come into being only forty years earlier. But perhaps the most assiduous of all those involved in constructing this tradition was Clements Markham, secretary of the Society from 1863 to 1888 and president from 1893 to 1905. Markham, who wrote the first official history of the Society, increasingly styled himself as the guardian of its past. He promoted his interest in the history of travel through a series of public events to celebrate notable events in the history of exploration and discovery, such as the 400th anniversary of Columbus's trans-Atlantic crossing, the 500th anniversary of Prince Henry 'the navigator' and the fiftieth anniversary of the departure of Franklin in his ill-fated voyage to the Arctic.[9] Above all, Markham was the driving force behind the revival of the Society's role in promoting polar exploration, culminating in his mobilization of official support for Scott's expeditions to the Antarctic.

7. For some recent work on the history of popular geographies, see I. Cook and P. Crang, 'The world on a plate', *Journal of Material Culture*, 1 (1996), pp. 131–53; C. Lutz and L. Collins, *Reading National Geographic* (Chicago, 1993); R. Phillips, *Mapping Men and Empire: A Geography of Adventure* (London, 1997); J. Ryan, *Picturing Empire: Photography and the Visualization of the British Empire* (London, 1997).
8. [J. Barrow], 'Continental travelling and residence abroad', *Quarterly Review*, 38 (1828), pp. 145–72 (p. 152).
9. H. R. Mill, *The Record of the Royal Geographical Society, 1830–1930* (London, 1930), p. 230.

None laboured more energetically than he to associate the history of exploration with the contemporary myth of the imperial explorer; rarely has antiquarianism been more worldly-wise.

Many of the presidents of the RGS during the first half of the twentieth century – notably Goldie, Curzon, Holdich, Younghusband and Close – had held high military or political office, and were happy to endorse the public image of the geographical tradition bequeathed to them by Markham and his predecessors. The involvement of the Society in the provision of military intelligence during the First World War, in the promotion of further polar exploration and finally in the organization of a series of expeditions to the Himalayas, suggests that the moment of Geography Militant was far from past.[10] The 'conquest' of Everest in 1953 was a sensational media event, scooped by James Morris for *The Times*, which published the story on the day of the coronation of Elizabeth II. Here, as before, leading figures at the RGS were keen to use the public interest in exploration to secure prestige: arguments from national honour were as prominent in 1953 as they had been a century before. Visual technologies accessible to a wide audience, most notably film and colour photography, offered new possibilities for the promotion of exploration at home. The Society's new lecture hall, adjoining its house at Lowther Lodge, Kensington Gore, was fitted with a projection room designed to meet the requirements of the London County Council, 'which [H. R. Mill complained] does not discriminate between the private hall of a scientific society composed of rational persons and the public theatre of any degree'.[11] Whether Mill's irritation with officialdom was justified or not, the distinction between private hall and public theatre was difficult to detect in reports of many of the public meetings organized by the RGS from the mid-nineteenth century onwards (figure 9.1). The lecture hall opened in 1930 could accommodate over 860 people, and its panelled walls were decorated with the names of famous explorers, from Hakluyt to Scott. Today it is used regularly for public meetings of all kinds, and lectures on travel and exploration continue to attract large audiences.

10. M. Heffernan, 'Geography, cartography and military intelligence: the Royal Geographical Society and the First World War', *Transactions, Institute of British Geographers*, 21 (1996), pp. 504–33; K. Dodds, 'Antarctica and the modern geographical imagination, 1918–1960', *Polar Record*, 33 (1997), pp. 47–62; P. Hansen, 'The dancing lamas of Everest: cinema, orientalism and Anglo-Tibetan relations in the 1920s', *American Historical Review*, 101 (1996), pp. 712–47; G. Stewart, 'Tenzing's two wrist-watches: the conquest of Everest and late imperial culture in Britain, 1921–1953', *Past and Present*, 149 (1995), pp. 170–97; and the ensuing debate with Peter Hansen, *Past and Present*, 157 (1997), pp. 159–90.
11. Mill, *Record of the Royal Geographical Society*, pp. 143–4.

ENTERTAINMENTS AT WHICH WE HAVE NEVER ASSISTED.

9.1 Exhibition of Globe-Trotting at the Royal Geographical Society (*Punch*, 14 November 1928).

Notwithstanding the role of the RGS in promoting a certain vision of travel and exploration during the twentieth century, it was certainly not the sole source of Geography Militant *redivivus*. The history of geography during the twentieth century, as much as the nineteenth, is not merely a history of institutions or professional bodies. It also embraces a variety of knowledges and practices in the realm of popular geographies: the geographies which are learned in school playgrounds, youth movements, the popular press, tourist brochures, commodity advertising and film. And in many of these places the culture of Geography Militant continues to thrive.

Recent work on the history of geographical education, for example, points to a striking degree of inertia in the curriculum; the imperial attitudes of the nineteenth century, it seems, really did live on in the text-books of the first half of the twentieth.[12] Furthermore, as Teresa Ploszajska has shown, fieldwork within and beyond the school grounds

---

12. T. Ploszajska, *Geographical Education, Empire and Citizenship: Geographical Teaching and Learning in English Schools, 1870–1944* (1999); A. Maddrell, 'Discourses of race and gender and the comparative method in geography school texts, 1830–1918', *Environment and Planning D: Society and Space*, 16 (1998), pp. 81–103; W. Marsden, 'Rooting racism into the educational experience of childhood and youth in the nineteenth and twentieth centuries', *History of Education*, 19 (1990), pp. 333–53; J. Mangan (ed.), *The Imperial Curriculum: Racial Images and Education in the British Colonial Experience* (London, 1993).

was often conceived of as an exercise in exploration: the space of the frontier could be inhabited at home as well as abroad. One early-twentieth-century London teacher devised a 'colonization game' for pupils on Hampstead Heath; another portrayed the girls in her field classes as 'discoverers – Stanleys, Livingstones'.[13] As Ploszajska shows, the history of fieldwork in schools consists of much more than merely a repetition of such imperial tropes; yet their reappearance in this context is surely telling, given the regeneration of the idea of exploration in contemporary discourses of youth training. While some have pointed to straightforward continuities between Baden-Powell's reputation as a hero of imperial masculinity and the Scouting movement, especially prior to the First World War,[14] the continuing attractions of exploration as a form of *play* should not be forgotten. Contemporary children's books exploit much the same theme: one modern example, in the 'Make and play' series, encourages children to become latter-day explorers in their own homes, courtesy of a few survival tips and a kit which includes pencils, scissors, glue, string and 'snake-bite lotion'.[15] The attractions of adventure playgrounds for older children also stem, to some degree, from their imaginative associations with exploration in dangerous 'frontier' environments.[16] In the virtual world of the CD-ROM, meanwhile, the rhetoric of adventurous exploration has been given a new lease of life.[17]

The iconography of exploration also deserves consideration in this context. The use of photography within the classroom has been a distinctive feature of geographical education throughout the twentieth

13. T. Ploszajska, 'Down to earth? Geography fieldwork in English schools, 1870–1944', *Environment and Planning D: Society and Space*, 16 (1998), pp. 757–74. On the relation between the culture of exploration and the arts of citizenship, see D. Matless, *Landscape and Englishness* (London, 1998), ch. 2; F. Driver and A. Maddrell (eds), 'Geographical education and citizenship', *Journal of Historical Geography*, 22 (1996), pp. 371–442.
14. R. H. MacDonald, *Sons of the Empire: The Frontier and the Boy Scout Movement, 1890–1918* (Toronto, 1993); A. Warren, 'Popular manliness: Baden-Powell, scouting and the development of manly character', in J. Mangan and J. Walvin (eds), *Manliness and Morality: Middle-class Masculinity in Britain and America, 1800–1940* (Manchester, 1987), pp. 199–217; J. Bristow, *Empire Boys: Adventures in a Man's World* (London, 1991).
15. H. Songhurst, *Explorers* (London, 1992).
16. One children's playground in the London borough of Richmond is explicitly designed as an 'explorer's challenge': each assemblage of wooden frames, rope swings and ladders is accompanied by display boards devoted to noted explorers, from David Livingstone to Ranulph Fiennes.
17. J. Light, 'The changing nature of nature', *Ecumene*, 4 (1997), pp. 181–95; F. Driver, 'Visualising geography: a journey to the heart of the discipline', *Progress in Human Geography*, 19 (1995), 123–34.

century. The Geographical Association, the major professional body for school-teachers in the UK, was founded in 1893 partly as a response to calls to exploit the educational potential of photography. Halford Mackinder, himself closely associated with the foundation of the Association, often described the discipline of geography as a kind of visualization. As James Ryan has pointed out, Mackinder's vision was quintessentially imperial; in his view, the purpose of geographical education was to bestow upon citizens of the empire 'the power of roaming at ease imaginatively over the vast surface of the globe'.[18] Ryan's account of Mackinder's role in the Colonial Office Visual Instruction Committee (established in 1902) indicates that this was far from empty rhetoric, for Mackinder saw in photography the opportunity to capture the scenes and sights of empire for a mass audience. The Committee sent an artist-turned-photographer on a journey around the world – a modern voyage of exploration – to obtain suitable imperial images for use in lantern-slide lectures and in textbooks. Mackinder himself instructed the photographer to represent in vivid form both 'the native characteristics of the country and its people, and the super-added characteristics due to British rule', a classic colonial formula which in practice proved difficult to sustain.[19]

Beyond the lecture hall and the classroom, popular geographical magazines provided further vehicles for the circulation of images of exploration. While such magazines proliferated in the nineteenth century (*Le Mouvement Géographique*, published from 1884 by the Belgian Geographical Institute, being one example), it is in the twentieth that they have come to be genuinely popular. In their critical history of the *National Geographic*, Lutz and Collins argue that the magazine promoted an exoticized and aestheticised vision of the ethnic other which in some respects perpetuated colonial stereotypes about the peoples of the Third World. This argument has not gone unchallenged, and it could be argued that the authors' conception of the photograph as an 'intersection of gazes' opens a space for a different interpretation.[20]

Such magazines have undoubtedly played an important role in the

18. Cited in Ryan, *Picturing Empire*, p. 209. On Mackinder's obsession with visualization, see also G. Ó. Tuathail, *Critical Geopolitics: The Politics of Writing Global Space* (Minneapolis, Minn., 1996), pp. 75–110.
19. Ryan, *Picturing Empire*, p. 190.
20. C. Lutz and J. Collins, *Reading National Geographic* (Chicago, 1993). See also S. Montgomery, 'Through a lens, brightly: the world according to *National Geographic*', *Science as Culture*, 4 (1993), pp. 4–46; S. Schulten, 'The perils of *Reading National Geographic*', *Reviews in American History*, 23 (1995), pp. 521–7.

recycling of images of exploration and encounter during the twentieth century. The smaller-circulation *Geographical Magazine*, first published in 1935 in association with the Royal Geographical Society, provides a notable example. Early issues of the magazine contained numerous illustrated articles about travel and exploration, including Aldous Huxley on religion in Central America and Compton Mackenzie on Paris in springtime, as well as a photographic essay by Henri Cartier-Bresson on the Moslems of Kashmir. As these names suggest, the magazine had a somewhat literary and aesthetic temper during its first twenty years, reflecting the intellectual tastes and social networks of its founder, Michael Huxley. Huxley had joined the diplomatic service in 1922, and subsequently served in Tehran, Washington and London; his brother Gervase had directed publicity campaigns at the Empire Marketing Board.[21] While the neo-colonial presentation of non-western cultures is evident in its early years, as much in the advertising as the articles themselves, the *Geographical* was also concerned with the 'exploration' of different parts of Britain – its natural regions, commercial cities, literary landscapes and ancient relics. As well as bringing exotic worlds into the English home, the magazine was designed to picture anew the familiar landscapes of Britain. This was exploration, though not always of the militant kind. Since the 1960s, the magazine has undergone a number of significant shifts, reflecting editorial changes, commercial pressures and the changing nature of academic geography. Yet exploration remains an important reference point. Writing in the *Geographical* on the sixtieth year of its publication, the then Director of the RGS, John Hemming, described the 1990s as 'the golden age of discovery': 'We are constantly learning more about how the great ecosystems function. And there is plenty more still to be discovered.'[22]

It is in the literature of advertising and tourism that one finds the most unabashed exploitation of the motifs of Geography Militant: by picturing the commodity on the frontiers of knowledge and power, the glamour of overseas exploration could be associated with consumption at home. Visual references to the British imperial frontier in general, and explorers in particular, are common in late-Victorian advertisements for commodities such as soap, tea and pills; explorers like Stanley and Livingstone thus found themselves represented as models of English

---

21. R. W. Clark, *The Huxleys* (London, 1968), pp. 249–51.
22. J. Hemming (October 1995), quoted in an advertisement for 'The Changing World', 'the indispensable geographical video' produced to celebrate the sixtieth anniversary of the founding of the Magazine: *Geographical Magazine*, January 1996, p. 4.

9.2 'Dr Livingstone I presume!' (*Tailor and Cutter*, September/October 1872).

gentlemanly fashion (figure 9.2).[23] As Thomas Richards has argued, 'the commodity was represented as the bulwark of Empire – as both a stabilising influence and a major weapon in England's struggle against a bewildering variety of enemies': nowhere was this clearer than in the many advertisements which exploited images of Stanley's Emin Pasha Expedition in 1890.[24] While Richards suggests that the 1890s marks a

23.   On the significance of dress for the assertion of imperial identity, see H. Callaway, 'Dressing for dinner in the bush: rituals of self-definition and British imperial authority', in R. Barnes and J. B. Eicher (eds), *Dress and Gender: Making and Meaning in Cultural Contexts* (Oxford, 1992), pp. 232–47.
24.   T. Richards, *The Commodity Culture of Victorian England, 1851–1914* (London, 1991), p. 142. See also J. MacKenzie, *Propaganda and Empire* (Manchester, 1984); R. Opie, *Rule Britannia: Trading on the British Image* (Harmond-

significant turning point – the moment of 'jingo kitsch' – the imaginative association of the commodity with the idea of the expanding imperial frontier was not in itself new. One advertising card for the patent medicines manufactured by Thomas Holloway, for example, presents a striking picture of imperial progress: boxes of pills and ointment are piled up on quays from Constantinople to Canton, signifiers of the global reach of commercial civilization (figure 9.3).

The veneration of the commodity as an agent of globalization could reach dizzy heights: 'In the wilds of Tartary, the Siberian Desert, the celestial empire, yea in the very mountains of the moon, are the praises of the great pilular deity Holloway sung, and his name blessed in every known and unknown tongue as the "mighty healer".'[25] Yet the tone here is knowing, even mocking: the sensational methods of the modern advertiser were always vulnerable to satire. In a story published in 1873, for example, the traveller Winwood Reade turned the success of the Holloway marketing machine to a different use. The 'hero' of this story is Archibald Potter, an English gentleman who develops a phobia about the advertisements for Holloway's pills, which he sees 'every hour of the day, in every newspaper he read, in every omnibus he entered, at every railway station, on every boarding'. Seeking refuge from their spell, he escapes abroad, and eventually plunges into Africa, only to find himself once more tormented by Holloway posters. He travels further and further into the interior, finally arriving in a remote village deep in the heart of Africa. But to his horror, he finds that its inhabitants have turned Holloway's poster into a fetish: 'the beautiful crimson colour, the great black stripes, the crisp rustling of the paper, which they supposed to be the voice of the demon from within, [had] powerfully affected their imagination'.[26] In Reade's tale – part parable, part parody – the spell of the commodity is transformed into a curse, reducing Englishmen to the level of savages. While the story hardly develops a sophisticated critique of commodity fetishism, as in Marx, it does anticipate the critique of modern consumerism that one finds in Haggard, and indeed in Conrad. In the present context, it also reminds us that exploration could be represented as an escape as much as a voyage of discovery.

In late-Victorian advertisements, the commodity itself – a biscuit tin,

sworth, 1985); S. Constantine, ' "Bringing the empire alive": the Empire Marketing Board and imperial propaganda, 1926–33', in J. MacKenzie (ed.), *Imperialism and Popular Culture* (Manchester, 1986), pp. 192–231.

25. *Stockport Advertiser*, n.d., cited in A. Harrison-Barbet, *Thomas Holloway: Victorian Philanthropist* (Egham, 1994), p. 75.

26. W. Reade, 'Hollowayphobia', in his *The African Sketch-Book*, vol. i (London, 1873), pp. 169–201.

9.3 Advertising card for Holloway's Pills and Ointments, c. 1882. By permission of Royal Holloway, University of London.

a package of pills, a bar of soap – was intended to function as a sign of reassurance: the fact that Holloway's pills were consumed even at the frontiers of the known world was a measure of the global reach of the values of civilized commerce, and their immunity to difference. However, during the twentieth century, images of the exotic have been put to a different use, exploiting fantasies of escape from the routines of modern urban living, though here too motifs of exploration are knowingly regenerated. Modern adventure tourism thrives on these sorts of associations. In this mood, and with sufficient money, one can today explore 'wild and exotic locations' with the British tour operator Adrift, 'stepping beyond the bondages of modern life, brewing coffee over an open fire and venturing boldly into the unknown', or take a 'rail safari' through the 'savage beauty' of the South African landscape.[27] The modern tourist can trace the journeys of explorers up the Nile, the Amazon or the Yangtze, and even 'follow in Captain Scott's footsteps' at Discovery Point, Dundee, where the *Discovery* is now berthed. Travellers in style can today cruise around Polynesia on the *Paul Gauguin*, a luxury vessel 'expressly designed to harmonise with the beauty of the South Seas and the richness of their culture'.[28]

The motifs of Geography Militant are also to be found nearer to home, especially in the pages of weekend newspaper supplements: high-performance sandals 'for the seasoned explorer' are promoted by Ranulph Fiennes, and Sri Lankan lager is marketed under the name of Samuel Baker, 'explorer, adventurer and Victorian hero'. Meanwhile, the 'colonial style' makes a reappearance in interior design, alongside tribal and tropical collections, associations with the Raj being a reliable selling point: 'Almost 50 years after the wrenching departure of the British from India, the colonial furniture which they abandoned on the verandahs and in the living rooms of their stockbroker Tudor houses from Kashmir to Kerala, is fashionable again, reabsorbed into the English country house look'.[29] The absorption, or rather regeneration, of fantasies of the imperial frontier within the global fashion industry is another case in point. Memories of colonial adventure, filtered through the lens of Hollywood, are thus recycled into a fashion shoot in the pages of a women's magazine, under the predictable title 'Out of Africa': 'From the heart of Kenya, designerwear for a wildlife:

27. Adrift, *Explore Your Imagination* (brochure for 1997–8, London, 1996); Rovos Rail advertisement, South Africa Travel.
28. Sunset, *Exotic Holidays* (brochure for 2000, London, 1999), p. 133.
29. F. Murphy, 'Lost and found', *Guardian Weekend*, 16 December 1995, p. 56; C. McGhie, 'The empire strikes back', *Independent on Sunday Magazine*, 12 December 1993, pp. 76–8.

dresses echoing tribal body paint, safari suits, animal prints and suede skirts and hipsters.' This is not so much jingo kitsch as a fantastical, fetishistic rendering of colonial chic: in the fine print, we read that the party from *Marie Claire* 'stayed with Royal African Safaris at the exclusive Borana Lodge and Kipsing Camp'.[30]

Fantasies of a more adventurous kind of exploration were reworked in a menswear catalogue produced by the River Island Clothing Company in 1993 (figure 9.4). The cover shows two bronzed figures, supposedly hard at work in the rigging of a sailing vessel; superimposed on the image is the title of the catalogue, 'The spirit of adventure', accompanied by a portentous phrase: 'without adventure civilisation is in decay'. Together, words and image evoke a familiar fantasy, a camped-up version of Geography Militant for the late twentieth century. Below this is the logo of the Royal Geographical Society, used here as in other advertising campaigns in exchange for corporate sponsorship of the Society. The catalogue makes the link clear, refashioning yet again the conventional opposition between the field and the study:

> At River Island we have never felt isolated from the real world. Fashion doesn't hide in ivory towers; by definition it's out on the edge of existence seeking new frontiers of style and taste. For us, the spirit of adventure of a tangible aspect of all we do. . . . It is to celebrate that spirit of adventure that River Island has dedicated this brochure to the work of the Royal Geographical Society.

The contents of the catalogue contain the sort of stylish blend of homoeroticism and exoticism typically reworked in men's fashion magazines of the 1990s, though this time with a difference: this catalogue juxtaposes fashion shoots with photographic depictions of modern-day field-work in the Karakoram, Jordan, Oman, Brunei and Utah. The introductory text explains: 'The story of British expeditions didn't end with Scott at the South Pole or when Hillary and Tensing were the first men to scale Everest. Every year dozens of young men and women continue the tradition begun by the Royal Geographical Society nearly 160 years ago.'[31]

30. *Marie Claire*, March 1996, pp. 190–203. The price of the goods displayed (including a snake-print leather jacket and matching skirt at over £4,000) suggests that for most readers the experience of consumption was primarily one of voyeurism. On the reinvention of the exotic within fashion advertising, see J. Craik, *The Face of Fashion* (London, 1994), esp. ch. 2.

31. River Island Clothing Company, *The Spirit of Adventure: Menswear Summer 1993* (London, 1993). I am grateful to David Pinder for drawing this to my attention.

9.4 'The Spirit of Adventure', Summer 1993. By permission of the River Island Clothing Company.

Exploration and Travel: Trading in Memory

relic: object once belonging to or associated with a saint, esp. part of his body, preserved and revered as holy; object treasured in memory of the past; something kept or surviving from long ago.

fetish: inanimate object worshipped or feared by savages for its magical powers and used as an amulet; object supposed to be inhabited by a spirit; anything exaggeratedly reverenced or loved; object rousing undue interest by its sexual associations.[32]

Traditions are not merely inherited, or even recycled: they can also be traded. Twice a year, the London auction house Christie's organizes a sale on the theme of 'exploration and travel'. These sales, like similar specialist auctions devoted to maritime paintings, natural history or wildlife art, offer a glimpse into the world of the collector, a world in which memories of exploration do not come cheap: the total value of the 108 lots sold in the April 1999 sale, for example, was over £1.2 million. The lots are organized for the purposes of the sale into geographical regions – the Pacific and Australasia, the Middle East and Asia, the Americas, Africa, the Arctic and Antarctica (the cultural products of travel within Europe itself evidently have a different market). On view to prospective purchasers are first editions of rare books, maps, sketches, prints, photographs, lantern slides and paintings associated with European and American explorers and travellers (especially naval officers), manuscript letters, journals, notebooks and diaries, a few ethnographic objects collected by travellers, some twentieth-century paintings of non-European landscapes, and, finally, what are usually described as 'relics', including expedition equipment, clothing, medals, furniture and in fact any memorabilia whose provenance might be connected with well-known European explorers.

The 279 lots of the September 1999 sale, for example, included a selection of the private letters and papers of David Blackburn, master of one of the vessels on the First Fleet to Australia, offered at between fifty and eighty thousand pounds (a cat o' nine tails presumed to have been used by Blackburn was also up for auction), an early nineteenth-century oil painting attributed to Samuel Daniell ('A Korah Hottentot Village on the left bank of the Orange River'), together with many other paintings, watercolours and sketches, a harmonium used for religious services on the *Discovery* during Scott's voyage to the Antarc-

---

32. *The Penguin English Dictionary*, 2nd edn (London, 1978).

tic and numerous books, manuscripts and photographs associated with a motley collection of travellers and explorers, including George Anson, John Barrow, Stamford Raffles, David Livingstone, Thomas Baines, Joseph Hooker, Roald Amundsen and Ernest Shackleton. The African explorers John Hanning Speke and James Grant were represented by a single autographed letter and a marble bust respectively, while a manuscript of a lecture apparently delivered by Henry Morton Stanley in 1891 was offered at between eighteen and twenty-five thousand pounds. At the other end of the price spectrum was a photograph of a model of Mount Everest made for a fancy dress competition in Lewisham in 1953, the base of which was signed by Hillary, Tenzing, Hunt and ten other members of the Everest expedition. A photograph of signatures on a model of a mountain: Geography Militant regenerates itself in the most unlikely ways!

But pride of place on this occasion was given to the 'Scott relics', including a collection of items taken from a small brown suitcase consigned to a bank vault fifty years ago: among them were many of Scott's personal possessions found in his tent in November 1912, described here as 'the most poignant of all the relics from the "heroic age" of Antarctic exploration'.[33] The catalogue reproduced sumptuous photographs of Scott and his team, alongside a series of full-colour portraits of each one of the relics: watch, compass, panama hat, gentleman's dressing box, pipes, Bible, diary, telegraph code book, sledging goggles, ration bag, hip flask, silk flags. Related items in the sale included Scott's riding boots, a tea caddy ('a reminder of the very British nature of the expedition') and a single Huntley and Palmer biscuit. The painstaking description of the dimensions, condition and provenance of the biscuit lingered over every detail: 'Messrs. Huntley & Palmers (suppliers), A rectangular sledging biscuit, [1910]. 7.5 × 9 × 1 cm. Stamped in blind *H. & P.* (Lower right hand corner broken away.) Loosely wrapped in grease-proof paper, titled in early hand in ink on outer layer "Antarctic Biscuit Captain Scott's Expedition 1910," all contained within a 1937 *Player's Navy Cut* cigarette tin.' The biscuit eventually sold at auction to the explorer Sir Ranulph Fiennes for almost £4,000: he was reported to have pledged that it would be put on display by the UK Antarctic Heritage Trust.[34]

The sale of the Scott relics provides us with striking evidence of the imaginative reach of the culture of exploration in our own time, here

33. Christie's, *Exploration and Travel: Friday 17 September 1999* (London, 1999), p. 201.
34. 'Scott's South Pole biscuit auctioned for £4,000', *Guardian*, 18 September 1999, p. 11.

installed in a variety of objects, from books to biscuits, whose market value depends precisely on their association with histories and memories. 'From Scott's splendid sledging flags to the shrunken leather washers', the catalogue informs potential buyers, 'all of the following items help to tell the tale of Scott's last expedition, a story whose telling both traumatized and inspired the Nation on the eve of the First World War.'[35] It is as though the relics can put their owners in touch with that past which otherwise has been lost, a time of national greatness, heroic endeavour, the world before the Fall. The dictionary distinction between the relic and the fetish, that most problematic of terms,[36] seems particularly difficult to uphold in this context: to possess these objects is to be possessed by them. Like art-works, moreover, they are increasingly treated as investments: one thus finds articles on the latest sales in the financial pages of the weekend press.[37] But the investment is not simply a matter of financial planning: the commodity here takes the form of a treasured relic, a site of memory. And the power of the objects resides as much in their display as in their ownership, whether this is display for private pleasure or public consumption. Among the memorabilia on display at Christie's most recent sale were Stanley's helmet and Livingstone's cap, borrowed from the Royal Geographical Society especially for the occasion. These decaying pieces of Victorian headgear, in which so much history is absorbed and invested, are amongst Geography Militant's most revered relics (or fetishes). In 1890, they were on show at the Stanley and African Exhibition in Regent Street; just over a century later, they formed an intriguing exhibit at the Serpentine Gallery in Hyde Park. Once at the frontiers of exploration, now in the *avant-garde* of art?[38]

To view such displays today, whether in a museum, a gallery or an auction-room, is to enter into a dialogue between our senses of the past and the present. While the relics themselves may be archaic, the investments in them – financial, emotional, aesthetic – are thoroughly modern. In this context, it is interesting to note how frequently the discourse on exploration has been construed as a narrative of loss: Conrad's tribute to Geography Militant was thus written *in memoriam*, while Lévi-Strauss portrays *Tristes Tropiques* as an act of selective

35. Christie's, *Exploration and Travel*, p. 202.
36. A. Shelton, *Fetishism: Visualising Power and Desire* (London, 1995).
37. S. Dalby, 'Shackleton comes in from the cold: the Americans have discovered our most heroic failure and the demand for memorabilia is taking off', *Guardian Money*, 18 September 1999, pp. 14–15.
38. See F. Driver, 'Old hat, I presume? History of a fetish', *History Workshop Journal*, 41 (1996), pp. 230–4.

remembering.[39] In this chapter, however, I have begun to tell a different story, concerned less with mourning than with creation: only by recognizing its modernity, I suggest, can we begin to grasp the vitality of this culture and its continuing hold on our imagination. Geography Militant has thus not merely survived the processes of modernization and globalization: it has been regenerated in a variety of ever-proliferating forms, from the pages of fashion magazines to the sale-rooms of auction houses. Rather than simply reactivating forgotten histories of imperial exploration, these enterprises are engaged in the business of producing memories: of making the past meaningful for people in the present. This memory work takes place in many different sites, often far removed from the pedagogy of the classroom or the esoteric knowledge of the library, in objects, images, buildings, places, the flotsam and jetsam of everyday life: these are what Raphael Samuel called 'theatres of memory', those realms where 'unofficial' histories evolve and circulate.[40]

Clarence Glacken once famously observed that the historian of geography 'who stays within the limits of his discipline sips a thin gruel';[41] much the same could be said of the geographer who fails to consider the influence of geographical ideas and practices beyond the academy. Throughout this book, I have treated geographical knowledge as a heterogeneous field rather than a tightly defined enclave: an ensemble of practices, institutions and concepts. Seen in this perspective, the notion of geographical knowledge as the preserve of a modern university-based profession (the 'discipline' of geography) is clearly anachronistic for the nineteenth century, and I would suggest that it is also inappropriate for the twentieth. On the one hand, specialist geographical knowledge continues to be produced in a variety of institutional sites beyond academic geography departments: the role of commercial cartographers and the military was and remains especially significant in this context. The prestige of the modern university clearly bestows upon the professional geographer a certain kind of authority; but the technical expertise on which the discipline depends may well be located outside the university sector. On the other, the mobilization of

39. His recent *Saudades do Brasil* is explicitly conceived as an exercise in nostalgia, ironically rendered in the form of a glossy picture book: C. Lévi-Strauss, *Saudades do Brasil: A Photographic Memoir* (Seattle, 1994).
40. See R. Samuel, *Theatres of Memory* (London, 1994), especially the superb polemic on 'Unofficial knowledge', pp. 3–48; and the essays on place as a site of memory, in his *Island Stories: Unravelling Britain* (London, 1998).
41. C. Glacken, *Traces on the Rhodian Shore: Nature and Culture in Western Thought from Ancient Times to the End of the Eighteenth Century* (Berkeley, Calif., 1967), p. xiii.

geographical rhetoric and imagery beyond the academy itself deserves to be treated more seriously as an object of study in its own right. As the case of Geography Militant suggests, this is more than a matter of the 'diffusion' of specialist knowledge through the channels of popular culture: it is perhaps better understood as a process of circulation and regeneration. The general case against a naive diffusionist model of the popularization of science is considerable, not least because it takes for granted a distinction between the active producers and passive consumers of knowledge; it is particularly inappropriate in the case of fields like geography and history, in which expertise and authority are not necessarily equivalent terms.[42]

In many ways, the culture of exploration is today better represented outside the academy than within: indeed, the development of geography as an academic discipline during the twentieth century involved a parting of the ways between the two. The formation of the Institute of British Geographers (IBG) in 1933, for example, provided academic geographers in the UK with a new, more 'modern' institutional vehicle for the expression of their professional interests. In this context, the merger between the Institute and the Royal Geographical Society in 1993 unexpectedly reunited academic geography with what might be called 'geography at large', reactivating memories of earlier differences and raising new concerns, most notably the troubled issue of corporate sponsorship.[43] It is precisely the Society's associations with a recognizable tradition of exploration, as well as with modern environmental research, that make it attractive to potential sponsors; yet within the academic community, attitudes towards this tradition are ambivalent at best. The dispute over Shell's patronage of the Society, which hit the headlines briefly in January 1996, had far-reaching implications: in the words of one journalist writing for the *Spectator*, 'When the nation's academic geographers, not usually the most militant of lobby groups, rise in anger, something is amiss.'[44]

The merger of the RGS with the IBG did not bring academic geography face to face with its past, as many critics contended: it confronted the discipline with the public image of geography at large.

42. R. Cooter and S. Pumfrey, 'Separate spheres and public places: reflections on the history of science popularization and science in popular culture', *History of Science*, 32 (1994), pp. 237–67; B. Lightman (ed.), *Victorian Science in Context* (Chicago, 1997).
43. D. Gilbert, 'Introduction: a forum on Shell, the Ogoni dispute and the Royal Geographical Society (with the Institute of British Geographers)', *Ethics, Place and Environment*, 2 (1999), pp. 219–28.
44. A. McElvoy, 'The moral daze', *The Spectator*, 13 January 1996, pp. 9–12 (p. 9).

Beyond the cabinet, as it were, the culture of Geography Militant continues to regenerate: in the field of public culture, memories of heroic exploration and fantasies of the frontier are alive and well. In this context, the geographical archive is not merely a repository of evidence or even a treasured relic: it has also become, quite literally, an asset. The unique photographic collection held by the merged geographical society, for example, has in recent years become an important source of income. A remarkable selection of these photographs was published in 1997, under the title *Royal Geographical Society Illustrated* ('a unique record of exploration and photography'), accompanied by short essays 'by such famous names as Wilfred Thesiger, Richard Leakey and Edmund Hillary'. Lavishly produced, this was described on the jacket as 'a book to treasure – a unique view of the world in all its variety, and a pictorial reminder of some of the greatest achievements in exploration'.[45] More fetish than relic, the magic of the picture-book stems less from its authenticity as a record of the past than from its presentation as a source of pleasure. The archive of exploration, whether in the form of texts, pictures or objects, continues to exert an influence on our experience and imagination of the world in which we live: it, too, is 'a place of dreams'.[46]

45. *Royal Geographical Society Illustrated* (London, 1997).
46. C. Steedman, 'The space of memory: in an archive', *History of the Human Sciences*, 11 (1998), pp. 65–83 (p. 67).

Manuscripts

Bodleian Library (including Rhodes House), Oxford
    Anti-Slavery and Aborigines Protection Society papers
    Horace Waller papers
    Universities Mission to Central Africa papers
    Lytton–Reade correspondence

British Library, London
    Henry Morton Stanley papers
    David Livingstone correspondence
    Robert Brown correspondence
    Peel papers

Cambridge University Library
    Darwin papers

Geological Society of London
    Murchison papers

Huntington Library, San Marino
    Fields papers

Imperial College, London
    Huxley papers

King's College, Cambridge
    Houghton papers

Museum of Mankind, London
    Anthropological Society archive

News International, London
    The Times archive

Public Record Office, London
  Foreign Office papers
  Chancery court records

Royal Botanic Gardens, Kew
  Hooker papers

Royal Geographical Society, London
  Council and Committee Minutes
  Additional papers
  Henry Morton Stanley collection
  Fellows correspondence
  Journal manuscripts
  Raleigh Club minute book

St Mary of the Angels, Bayswater
  Baptisms book

Southampton City Archives
  Medical Officer of Health records

Unilever PLC, London
  United Africa Company archive (Reade–Swanzy correspondence)

University College London
  Galton papers
  Routledge archive

Wellcome Institute, London
  Henry Wellcome archive

West Sussex Record Office, Chichester
  Maxse papers

Yale University Divinity School, New Haven
  Waller papers

Bibliography

Aalen, F., 'Lord Meath, city improvement and social imperialism', *Planning Perspectives*, 4 (1989), pp. 127–52

Aborigines Protection Society, *First Annual Report* (London, 1838)

Altick, R., *The Shows of London* (Cambridge, Mass.: Harvard University Press, 1978)

Anderson, A., 'Notes on the geography of South Central Africa', *Proceedings of the Royal Geographical Society*, 16 (1884), pp. 19–36

Anon, 'The traveller's oracle', *Blackwood's Magazine*, October 1827, pp. 445–65

Anon, 'Race in history', *Anthropological Review*, 3 (1865), pp. 233–48

Anon, *'In Darkest England': A Reply to 'General' Booth's Sensational Scheme for Social Salvation ... by an East London 'Watchman'* (London: John Kensit, 1890)

Anstey, R., *Britain and the Congo in the Nineteenth Century* (Oxford: Clarendon Press, 1962)

Anstruther, I., *I Presume: Stanley's Triumph and Disaster* (London: Geoffrey Bles, 1956)

Armytage, W., *Heavens Below: Utopian Experiments in Britain, 1560–1960* (London: Routledge & Kegan Paul, 1961)

Bailey, V., 'In Darkest England and the way out: the Salvation Army, social reform and the labour movement, 1885–1910', *International Review of Social History*, 29 (1984), pp. 133–71

Baker, J. N. L., *A History of Geographical Discovery and Exploration*, 2nd edn (London: Harrap, 1937)

Bales, K., 'Charles Booth's survey of life and labour of the people in London, 1889–1903', in M. Bulmer, K. Bales and K. Sklar (eds), *The Social Survey in Historical Perspective* (Cambridge: Cambridge University Press, 1991), pp. 66–110

Banton, M., 'Galton's conception of race in historical perspective', in M. Keynes (ed.), *Sir Francis Galton, FRS: The Legacy of His Ideas* (London: Macmillan, 1993), pp. 170–9

Barnett, C., 'Impure and worldly geography: the Africanist discourse of the Royal Geographical Society, 1831–1873', *Transactions of the Institute of British Geographers*, 23 (1998), pp. 239–51

Barnett, C., 'Deconstructing context: exposing Derrida', *Transactions of the Institute of British Geographers*, 24 (1999), pp. 277–94

Barnett, S., 'The ways of "settlements" and of "missions"', *Nineteenth Century*, 42 (1897), pp. 975–84

Barringer, T., 'Fabricating Africa: Livingstone and the visual image, 1850–1874', in *David Livingstone and the Victorian Encounter with Africa*, exhibition catalogue (London: National Portrait Gallery, 1996), pp. 171–200

Barringer, T. and T. Flynn (eds), *Colonialism and the Object: Empire, Material Culture and the Museum* (London: Routledge, 1998)

[Barrow, J.], 'Continental travelling and residence abroad', *Quarterly Review*, 38 (1828), pp. 145–72

Beaglehole, J. C. (ed.), *The Journals of Captain James Cook on His Voyages of Discovery*, vol. i (Cambridge: Cambridge University Press, 1955)

Beaglehole, J. C., *The Life of Captain James Cook*, (London: Black, 1974)

Beames, T., *The Rookeries of London* (London: Thomas Bosworth, 1850)

Becker, B., *Scientific London* (London: King, 1874)

Beer, G., 'Four bodies on the *Beagle*: touch, sight and writing in a Darwin letter', in G. Beer, *Open Fields: Science in Cultural Encounter* (Oxford: Oxford University Press, 1996), pp. 13–30

Begbie, H., *The Life of William Booth* (London: Macmillan, 1920)

Belcher, E., *A Treatise on Nautical Surveying* (London: Pelham Richardson, 1835)

Bell, L., 'To see or not to see: conflicting eyes in the travel art of Augustus Earle', in J. F. Codell and D. S. Macleod (eds), *Orientalism Transposed: The Impact of the Colonies on British Culture* (Aldershot: Ashgate, 1998), pp. 117–39

Bell, M., Butlin, R. and Heffernan, M. (eds), *Geography and Imperialism, 1820–1940* (Manchester: Manchester University Press, 1995)

Bell, M. and McEwan, C., 'The admission of women fellows to the Royal Geographical Society, 1892–1914', *Geographical Journal*, 162 (1996), pp. 295–312

Bennett, T., 'The exhibitionary complex', *New Formations*, 4 (1988), pp. 73–102

Bertrand, A., *Alfred Bertrand, Explorer and Captain of Cavalry* (London: RTS, 1926)

Bierman, J., *Dark Safari: The Life Behind the Legend of Henry Morton Stanley* (London: Hodder and Stoughton, 1991)

Bingle, R. J., 'Henry Yule: India and Cathay', in R. Bridges and P. Hair (eds), *Compassing the Vaste Globe of the Earth: Studies in the History of the Hakluyt Society, 1846–1996* (London: Hakluyt Society, 1996), pp. 143–63

Blain, V., 'Rosina Bulwer-Lytton and the rage of the unheard', *Huntington Library Quarterly*, 53 (1990), pp. 211–36

Blanckaert, C. (ed.), *Le terrain des sciences humaines, XVIIIe–XXe siècle* (Paris: Harmattan, 1996)

Blunt, A., *Travel, Gender and Imperialism: Mary Kingsley and West Africa* (New York: Guilford Press, 1994)

Bonner, P., *Kings, Commoners and Concessionaires: The Evolution and Dissolution of the Nineteenth-century Swazi State* (Cambridge: Cambridge University Press, 1983)

Booth, C. (ed.), *Life and Labour in East London*, vol. i, *East London* (London: Williams and Norgate, 1889)

Booth, C., *Life and Labour of the People in London*, third series, vol. vi, *Religious Influences* (London: Macmillan, 1902)

Booth, C., *Life and Labour of the People in London*, final volume, *Notes on Social Influences and Conclusion* (London: Macmillan, 1903)

Booth, M. R., *Victorian Spectacular Theatre* (London: Routledge and Kegan Paul, 1981)

Booth, W., *In Darkest England and the Way Out* (London: Salvation Army, 1890)

Booth-Tucker, F., *Darkest India: A Supplement to General Booth's 'In Darkest England and the Way Out'* (Bombay: Bombay Gazette, 1891)

Bosanquet, B., *'In Darkest England' on the Wrong Track* (London: Swan Sonnenschein, 1891)

Botting, D., *Humboldt and the Cosmos* (London: Joseph, 1973)

Bourguet, M.-N., 'The explorer', in M. Vovelle (ed.), *Enlightenment Portraits* (Chicago: Chicago University Press, 1997), pp. 257–315

Bourguet, M.-N. and Licoppe, C., 'Voyages, mesures et instruments: une nouvelle expérience du monde au siècle des lumières', *Annales Histoire, Sciences Sociales*, 52 (1997), pp. 1115–51

Bowler, P., *The Invention of Progress: The Victorians and the Past* (Oxford: Blackwell, 1989)

Brabazon, R. (the Earl of Meath), 'Great cities and social reform', in R. Brabazon, *Social Arrows* (London: Longman, 1886), pp. 223–50

Brantlinger, P., 'Victorians and Africans: the genealogy of the myth of the Dark Continent' *Critical Inquiry*, 12 (1985), pp. 166–203

Bravo, M., 'Ethnographic navigation and the geographical gift', in D. Livingstone and C. Withers (eds), *Geography and Enlightenment* (Chicago: Chicago University Press, 1999), pp. 199–235

Bravo, M., 'Ethnological encounters', in N. Jardine, J. Secord and E. Spary (eds), *Cultures of Natural History* (Cambridge: Cambridge University Press, 1996), pp. 338–57

Bray, R. A., *The Town Child* (London: Fisher Unwin, 1907)

Bridges, R., 'The sponsorship and financing of Livingstone's last journey', *African Historical Studies*, 1 (1968), pp. 79–104

Bridges, R., 'Europeans and East Africans in the age of exploration', *Geographical Journal*, 139 (1973), pp. 220–32

Bridges, R., 'W. D. Cooley, the RGS and African geography in the nineteenth century', *Geographical Journal*, 142 (1976), pp. 27–47, 274–86

Bridges, R., 'The historical role of British explorers in East Africa', *Terrae Incognitae*, 14 (1982), pp. 1–21

Bridges, R. and Hair, P. (eds), *Compassing the Vaste Globe of the Earth:*

Studies in the History of the Hakluyt Society, 1846–1996 (London: Hakluyt Society, 1996)

Brightfield, M., *John Wilson Croker* (Berkeley: University of California Press, 1940)

Bristow, J., *Empire Boys: Adventures in a Man's World* (London: Unwin Hyman, 1991)

Broc, N., *La Géographie des philosophes: géographes et voyageurs français au XVIIIᵉ siècle* (Paris: Éditions Ophrys, 1974)

Brock, W. H., 'Humboldt and the British', *Annals of Science*, 50 (1993), pp. 365–72

Brockway, L. H., *Science and Colonial Expansion: The Role of the British Royal Botanic Gardens* (New York: Academic Press, 1979)

Brodie, F., *The Devil Drives: A Life of Sir Richard Burton* (London: Eyre & Spottiswoode, 1967)

Brown, J., 'Charles Booth and labour colonies', *Economic History Review*, 21 (1968), pp. 349–60

Brown, W. E., *The Catholic Church in South Africa* (London: Burns and Oats, 1960)

Browne, J., *Charles Darwin: Voyaging* (London: Jonathan Cape, 1995)

Browne, J., 'Biogeography and empire', in N. Jardine, J. Secord and E. Spary (eds), *Cultures of Natural History* (Cambridge: Cambridge University Press, 1996), pp. 305–32

Browne, J., 'I could have retched all night: Charles Darwin and his body', in C. Lawrence and S. Shapin (eds), *Science Incarnate: Historical Embodiments of Natural Knowledge* (Cambridge: Cambridge University Press, 1998), pp. 240–87

Brunt, P., 'Clumsy utopians: an afterword', in N. Thomas and D. Losche (eds), *Double Vision: Art Histories and Colonial Histories in the Pacific* (Cambridge: Cambridge University Press, 1999), pp. 257–74

Burchell, W. J., *Travels in the Interior of Southern Africa*, 2 vols (London: Longman, 1822–4)

Burnand, F. C., *A New Light Thrown Across the Keep it Quite Darkest Africa*, 6th edn. (London: Trischler, 1891)

Burnand, F. C., 'Across the Keep-it-Dark Continent, or How I Found Stanley', in F. C. Burnand (ed.), *Some Old Friends* (London: Bradbury and Agnew, 1892), pp. 339–416

Burnard Owen, H., 'Missionary successes and negro converts', *Journal of the Anthropological Society*, 3 (1865), pp. clxxxiv–cciv, ccxliv–ccxlvi

Burton, I., *The Life of Captain Sir Richard Burton* (London: Chapman & Hall, 1893)

Burton, R. F., *The Lake Regions of Central Africa* (London: Longman, 1860)

Burton, R. F., 'Notes on certain matters connected with the Dahoman', *Memoirs of the Anthropological Society of London*, 1 (1863–4), pp. 308–21

Buzard, J., *The Beaten Track: European Tourism, Literature and the Ways to 'Culture', 1800–1918* (Oxford: Clarendon Press, 1993)

Cain, P. J. and Hopkins, A. G., *British Imperialism: Innovation and Expansion, 1688–1914* (London: Longman, 1993)

Cairns, H. A. C., *Prelude to Imperialism: British Reactions to Central African Society, 1840–1890* (London: Routledge & Kegan Paul, 1965)

Callaway, H., 'Dressing for dinner in the bush: rituals of self-definition and British imperial authority', in R. Barnes and J. B. Eicher (eds), *Dress and Gender: Making and Meaning in Cultural Contexts* (Oxford: Berg, 1992), pp. 232–47

Camerini, J., 'Evolution, biogeography, and maps: an early history of Wallace's line', *Isis*, 84 (1993), pp. 700–27

Camerini, J., 'Wallace in the field', in H. Kuklick and R. Kohler (eds), *Science in the Field* (Chicago: Chicago University Press, 1996), pp. 44–65

Camerini, J., 'Remains of the day: early Victorians in the field', in B. Lightman (ed.), *Victorian Science in Context* (Chicago: Chicago University Press, 1997), pp. 354–77

Cameron, I., *To the Farthest Ends of the Earth: The History of the Royal Geographical Society* (London: Macdonald and Jane, 1980)

Cameron, J., 'Agents and agencies in geography and empire: the case of George Grey', in M. Bell, R. Butlin and M. Heffernan (eds), *Geography and Imperialism, 1820–1940* (Manchester: Manchester University Press, 1995), pp. 13–35

Cameron, J., 'Sir John Barrow as a *Quarterly* Reviewer', *Notes and Queries*, 241 (1996), pp. 34–7

Campbell, T., 'R. H. Major and the British Museum', in R. Bridges and P. Hair (eds), *Compassing the Vaste Globe of the Earth: Studies in the History of the Hakluyt Society, 1846–1996* (London: Hakluyt Society, 1996), pp. 81–140

Cannon, S., *Science in Culture: The Early Victorian Period* (Folkestone: Dawson, 1978)

Cannon, W., 'John Herschel and the idea of science', *Journal of the History of Ideas*, 22 (1961), pp. 215–39

Cardoso, A. M., 'Expedição as terras de Muzilla em 1882, *Boletim da Sociedade Geographia de Lisboa*, 7 (1887), pp. 153–213

Carey, D., 'Compiling nature's history: travellers and travel narratives in the early Royal Society', *Annals of Science*, 54 (1997), pp. 269–92

Carter, P., *The Road to Botany Bay: An Essay in Spatial History* (London: Faber, 1987)

Cartwright, F., 'The left arm of David Livingstone', *King's College Hospital Gazette* (1979), pp. 136–7

Casati, G., *Ten Years in Equatoria* (London: Warne, 1891)

Cawood, J., 'The magnetic crusade: science and politics in early Victorian Britain', *Isis*, 70 (1979), pp. 493–518

Chaillé-Long, C., *L'Égypte et ses provinces perdues* (Paris: Nouvelle Revue, 1892)

Clark, R. W., *The Huxleys* (London: Heinemann, 1968)

Clayton, D., *Islands of Truth: The Imperial Fashioning of Vancouver Island* (Vancouver: University of British Columbia Press, 1999)

Clifford, J., *The Predicament of Culture* (Cambridge, Mass.: Harvard University Press, 1988)

Clifford, J., *Routes: Travels and Translation in the Late Twentieth Century* (Cambridge, Mass.: Harvard University Press, 1997)

Clodd, E., 'Memoir', in H. W. Bates, *The Naturalist on the River Amazons* (London: John Murray, 1892), pp. xvii–lxxxix

Clodd, E., *Memories* (London: Chapman & Hall, 1916)

Colenso, J. W., 'On the efforts of missionaries among savages', *Journal of the Anthropological Society*, 3 (1865), pp. ccxlviii–cclxxxii

Collini, S. and Vannoni, A. (eds), *Viaggere per le Conoscere: Le Istruzioni per Viaggiatori e Scienziati Tra Sette e Ottocento* (Florence: Gabinetto Vieusseux, 1995)

Collins, R. O., 'Samuel White Baker', in R. Rotberg (ed.), *Africa and Its Explorers* (Cambridge: Harvard University Press, 1970), pp. 141–73

Comaroff, J. and Comaroff, J., *Of Revelation and Revolution: Christianity, Colonialism and Consciousness in South Africa* (Chicago: Chicago University Press, 1991)

Conolly, J., *The Ethnological Exhibitions of London* (London: John Churchill, 1855)

Conrad, J., 'Geography and some explorers', in R. Curle (ed.), *Last Essays* (London: Dent, 1926), pp. 1–31

Conrad, J., 'Travel', in R. Curle (ed.), *Last Essays* (London: Dent, 1926), pp. 121–34

Conrad, J., *Heart of Darkness*, ed. R. Kimbrough (New York: Norton, 1988)

Constantine, S., ' "Bringing the empire alive": the Empire Marketing Board and imperial propaganda, 1926–33', in J. MacKenzie (ed.), *Imperialism and Popular Culture* (Manchester: Manchester University Press, 1986), pp. 192–231

Conway, M., *Autobiography, Memoirs and Experiences* (London: Cassell, 1904)

Conway, M., 'The martyrdom of man', in M. Conway, *Addresses and Reprints, 1850–1907* (Boston, Mass.: Houghton Mifflin, 1909)

Cook, I. and Crang, P., 'The world on a plate', *Journal of Material Culture*, 1 (1996), pp. 131–53

Cookey, S., *Britain and the Congo Question, 1885–1913* (London: Longman, 1968)

Cooley, W. D., *Dr Livingstone and the Royal Geographical Society* (London: privately printed, 1874)

Coombes, A., *Reinventing Africa: Museums, Material Culture and Popular Imagination in Late Victorian and Edwardian England* (New Haven, Conn.: Yale University Press, 1994)

Cooper, A., 'From the Alps to Egypt (and back again): Dolomieu, scientific voyaging and the construction of the field in eighteenth-century natural history', in C. Smith and J. Agar (eds), *Making Space for Science: Territorial Themes in the Shaping of Knowledge* (Basingstoke: Macmillan, 1998), pp. 39–63

Cooter, R. and Pumfrey, S., 'Separate spheres and public places: reflections on the history of science popularization and science in popular culture', *History of Science*, 32 (1994), pp. 237–67

Corbey, R., 'Ethnographic showcases, 1870–1930', *Cultural Anthropology*, 8 (1993), pp. 338–69

Coupland, R., *Kirk on the Zambesi: A Chapter of African History* (Oxford: Clarendon Press, 1928)

Coupland, R., *The Exploitation of East Africa, 1856–1890* (London: Faber, 1939)

Cowling, M., *The Artist as Anthropologist: The Representation of Type and Character in Victorian Art* (Cambridge: Cambridge University Press, 1989)

Craik, J., *The Face of Fashion* (London: Routledge, 1994)

Crary, J., *Techniques of the Observer: On Vision and Modernity in the Nineteenth Century* (Cambridge, Mass.: MIT Press, 1992)

[Croker, J. W.], 'How to observe – morals and manners', *Quarterly Review*, 58 (1839), pp. 61–72

Crush, J., *The Struggle for Swazi Labour, 1890–1920* (Kingston, Ont.: McGill-Queen's University Press, 1987)

Cunningham, A. and Jardine, N. (eds), *Romanticism and the Sciences* (Cambridge: Cambridge University Press, 1990)

Cunningham, H., *The Children of the Poor: Representations of Childhood Since the Seventeenth Century* (Oxford: Blackwell, 1991)

Curtin, P., *The Image of Africa: British Ideas and Action, 1780–1850* (London: Macmillan, 1965)

Dachs, A. J., 'Missionary imperialism: the case of Bechuanaland', *Journal of African History*, 13 (1972), pp. 647–58

Darwin, C., 'Geology', in J. Herschel (ed.), *A Manual of Scientific Enquiry: Prepared for the Use of Officers in Her Majesty's Navy; and Travellers in General* (London: John Murray, 1849), pp. 156–65

Davis, D. B., *Slavery and Human Progress* (Oxford: Oxford University Press, 1984)

Day, A., *The Admiralty Hydrographic Service, 1795–1919* (London: HMSO, 1967)

De Winton, F., 'The Congo Free State', *Proceedings of the Royal Geographical Society*, 8 (1886), pp. 609–27

Debrunner, H. W., *Presence and Prestige: Africans in Europe* (Basel: Basler Afrika Bibliographien, 1979)

Desmond, A., 'The making of institutional zoology in London, 1822–1836', *History of Science*, 23 (1985), pp. 153–85, 223–50

Dettelbach, M., 'Global physics and aesthetic empire: Humboldt's physical portrait of the tropics', in D. P. Miller and P. H. Reill (eds), *Visions of Empire: Voyages, Botany and Representations of Nature* (Cambridge: Cambridge University Press, 1996), pp. 258–92

Dettelbach, M., 'Humboldtian science', in N. Jardine, J. Secord and E. Spary (eds), *Cultures of Natural History* (Cambridge: Cambridge University Press, 1996), pp. 287–304

Dickens, C., 'The noble savage' (1853), in D. Pascoe (ed.), *Selected Journalism, 1850–1870* (Harmondsworth: Penguin, 1997), pp. 560–5

Dilke, C., *Problems of Greater Britain* (London: Macmillan, 1890)

Dodds, K., 'Antarctica and the modern geographical imagination, 1918–1960', *Polar Record*, 33 (1997), pp. 47–62

Domosh, M., 'Towards a feminist historiography of geography', *Transactions of the Institute of British Geographers*, 16 (1991), pp. 95–104

Drayton, R., 'Science and the European empires', *Journal of Imperial and Commonwealth History*, 23 (1995), pp. 503–10

Dreyer, J. and Turner, H. (eds), *History of the Royal Astronomical Society, 1820–1920* (London: Royal Astronomical Society, 1923)

Driver, F., 'Moral geographies: social science and the urban environment in mid-nineteenth century England', *Transactions of the Institute of British Geographers*, 13 (1988), pp. 275–87

Driver, F., 'Discipline without frontiers? Representations of the Mettray reformatory colony in Britain, 1840–1880', *Journal of Historical Sociology*, 3 (1990), pp. 272–93

Driver, F., 'Geography's empire: histories of geographical knowledge', *Environment and Planning D: Society and Space*, 10 (1992), pp. 23–40

Driver, F. (ed.), 'Geographical traditions: rethinking the history of geography', *Transactions, Institute of British Geographers*, 20 (1995), pp. 403–22

Driver, F., 'Visualising geography: a journey to the heart of the discipline', *Progress in Human Geography*, 19 (1995), pp. 123–34

Driver, F., 'Old hat, I presume? History of a fetish', *History Workshop Journal*, 41 (1996), pp. 230–4

Driver, F. and Gilbert, D., 'Heart of empire? Landscape, space and performance in imperial London', *Environment and Planning D: Society and Space*, 16 (1998), pp. 11–28

Driver, F. and Gilbert, D. (eds), *Imperial Cities: Landscape, Display and Identity* (Manchester: Manchester University Press, 1999)

Driver, F. and Maddrell, A. (eds), 'Geographical education and citizenship', *Journal of Historical Geography*, 22 (1996), pp. 371–442

Du Bois, W. E. B., *The World and Africa: An Inquiry into the Part which Africa Has Played in World History* (New York: Viking Press, 1947)

Duncan, J. and Gregory, D. (eds), *Writes of Passage: Reading Travel Writing* (London: Routledge, 1999)

Duthie, J. L., 'Sir Henry Creswicke Rawlinson and the art of great gamesmanship', *Journal of Imperial and Commonwealth History*, 11 (1983), pp. 253–74

Duveyrier, H., 'L'Afrique nécrologique', *Bulletin de la Société de Géographie de Paris*, 6th series, 8 (1874), pp. 561–644

Dwyer, P., *General Booth's 'Submerged Tenth', or the Wrong Way to Do the Right Thing* (London: Swan Sonnenschein, 1891)

Dyos, H. J., 'The slums of Victorian London', in D. Cannadine and D. Reeder (eds), *Exploring the Urban Past: Essays in Urban History by H. J. Dyos* (Cambridge: Cambridge University Press, 1982), pp. 129–53

Edney, M., *Mapping an Empire: The Geographical Construction of British India, 1765–1843* (Chicago: Chicago University Press, 1997)

Edwards, E., 'Photographic "types": the pursuit of method', *Visual Anthropology*, 3 (1990), pp. 235–258

Elston, P., 'Livingstone and the Anglican Church', in B. Pachai (ed.), *Livingstone, Man of Africa* (London: Longman, 1973), pp. 61–85

Elwin, M., *Charles Reade: A Biography* (London: Jonathan Cape, 1931)

Emery, F., 'Geography and imperialism: the role of Sir Bartle Frere (1815–84)', *Geographical Journal*, 150 (1984), pp. 342–50

Erskine, St. Vincent, 'Journey to Umzila's, South-East Africa, in 1871–2', *Journal of the Royal Geographical Society*, 45 (1875), pp. 45–128

Evans, R., 'Rookeries and model dwellings: English housing reform and the moralities of private space', *Architectural Association Quarterly*, 10 (1978), pp. 24–35

Eyton, R., *A Rash Investment: A Sermon on the Salvation Army Scheme of Social Reform* (London: Kegan Paul, 1890)

Fancher, R., 'Francis Galton's African ethnography and its role in the development of his psychology', *British Journal of the History of Science*, 16 (1983), pp. 67–79

Fara, P., *Sympathetic Attractions: Magnetic Practices, Beliefs and Symbolism in Eighteenth-Century England* (Princeton, NJ: Princeton University Press, 1996)

Feest, C. (ed.), *Indians and Europe* (Aachen: Edition Herodot, 1987)

Fitzroy, R. and Raper, H. (eds), 'Hints to travellers', *Journal of the Royal Geographical Society*, 24 (1854), pp. 328–58

Flynn, J., *Sir Robert N. Fowler: A Memoir* (London: Hodder and Stoughton, 1893)

Foote, G. W., *Salvation Syrup, or Light on Darkest England: A Reply to General Booth* (London, 1891)

Forrest, D. W., *Francis Galton* (London: Elek, 1974)

Fox Bourne, H., 'South Africa and the Aborigines Protection Society', *Contemporary Review*, 56 (1889), pp. 346–60

Fox Bourne, H. R., *The Other Side of the Emin Pasha Relief Expedition* (London: Chatto & Windus, 1891)

Fox Bourne, H. R., *Civilisation in Congoland* (London: King, 1903)

Fraser, A. Z., *Livingstone and Newstead* (London: John Murray, 1913)

Freshfield, D., 'Preliminary hints', in Royal Geographical Society, *Hints to Travellers* (London, 1889), pp. 1–7

Friendly, A., *Beaufort of the Admiralty: The Life of Sir Francis Beaufort, 1774–1857* (London: Hutchinson, 1977)

Galbraith, J. S., *Mackinnon in East Africa, 1878–1895: A Study in the 'New Imperialism'* (Cambridge: Cambridge University Press, 1972)

Gallagher, J. and Robinson, R., 'The imperialism of free trade', *Economic History Review* 6 (1953), pp. 1–15

Galton, F., *The Art of Travel: Or, Shifts and Contrivances Available in Wild Countries* (London: John Murray, 1855)

Galton, F., *Arts of Campaigning: An Inaugural Lecture Delivered at Aldershot* (London, 1855)

Galton, F., *Catalogue of Models Illustrative of Camp Life* (London: Thomas Brettell, 1858)

Galton, F., *English Men of Science* (London, 1874)

[Galton, F.], 'Stanley's discoveries and the future of Africa', *Edinburgh Review*, 147 (1878), pp. 166–91

Galton, F., *Memories of My Life*, 3rd edn (London: Methuen, 1909)

Gardiner, A. G., *The Life of Sir William Harcourt* (London: Constable, 1923)

Garson, N., 'The Swaziland question and a road to the sea, 1887–1895', *Archives Yearbook for South African History*, 2 (1957), pp. 267–434

Garstin, W., 'Fifty years of Nile exploration', *Geographical Journal*, 33 (1909), pp. 117–147

Gascoigne, J., *Science in the Service of Empire: Joseph Banks, the British State and the Uses of Science in the Age of Revolution* (Cambridge: Cambridge University Press, 1998)

Gay, H. and Gay, J., 'Brothers in science: science and fraternal culture in nineteenth-century Britain', *History of Science*, 35 (1997), pp. 425–53

Gilbert, D., 'Introduction: a forum on Shell, the Ogoni dispute and the Royal Geographical Society (with the Institute of British Geographers)', *Ethics, Place and Environment*, 2 (1999), pp. 219–28

Gilman, S., 'Black bodies, white bodies', *Critical Inquiry*, 12 (1983), pp. 204–42

Glacken, C., *Traces on the Rhodian Shore: Nature and Culture in Western Thought from Ancient Times to the End of the Eighteenth Century* (Berkeley: University of California Press, 1967)

Godlewska, A. and Smith, N. (eds), *Geography and Empire* (Oxford: Blackwell, 1994)

Godlewska, A., 'Map, text and image: the mentality of enlightened conquerors: a new look at the *Description de l'Égypte*', *Transactions of the Institute of British Geographers*, 20 (1995), pp. 5–28

Godwin, G., *Town Swamps and Social Bridges* (London: Routledge, 1859)

Godwin, G., *Another Blow for Life* (London: Allen, 1864)

Gogwilt, C., *The Invention of the West: Joseph Conrad and the Double-Mapping of Europe and the Empire* (Stanford, Calif.: Stanford University Press, 1995)

Goldsworthy, D., *Colonial Issues in British Politics, 1945–1961* (Oxford: Oxford University Press, 1971)

Gosse, E., 'A poet among the cannibals', in E. Gosse, *Books on the Table* (London: Heinemann, 1921), pp. 63–6

Gould, P. C., *Early Green Politics: Back to Nature, Back to the Land, and Socialism in Britain, 1880–1900* (Brighton: Harvester, 1988)

Graham, P. W. and Oehlschlaeger, F. H., *Articulating the Elephant Man: Joseph Merrick and His Interpreters* (Baltimore, Md.: Johns Hopkins University Press, 1992)

Grant, J. A., 'On Mr H. M. Stanley's exploration of Lake Victoria Nyanza', *Geographical Magazine*, 3 (1876), pp. 25–8

Green, D., *From Artisans to Paupers: Economic Change and Poverty in London, 1790–1870* (Aldershot: Scolar Press, 1995)

Green, J., *Black Edwardians: Black People in Britain, 1901–1914* (London: Frank Cass, 1998)

Greenfield, B., 'The problem of the discoverer's authority in Lewis and Clark's *History*', in J. Arac and H. Ritvo (eds), *Macropolitics of Nineteenth-century Literature: Nationalism, Exoticism, Imperialism* (Philadelphia: University of Pennsylvania Press, 1991), pp. 12–36

Greenhalgh, P., *Ephemeral Vistas: The Expositions Universelles, Great Exhibitions and World's Fairs, 1851–1939* (Manchester: Manchester University Press, 1988)

Gregory, B., 'Staging British India', in J. Bratton, R. Cave, B. Gregory, H. Holder and M. Pickering (eds), *Acts of Supremacy: The British Empire and the Stage, 1790–1930* (Manchester: Manchester University Press, 1991), pp. 150–78

Gregory, D., *Geographical Imaginations* (Oxford: Blackwell, 1994)

Gregory, D., 'Imaginative geographies', *Progress in Human Geography*, 19 (1995), pp. 447–485

Greppi, C., 'On the spot: L'artista-viaggiatore e l'inventario iconografico del mondo (1772–1859)', *Geotema* 8 (1997), pp. 137–49

Griffith, J. W., *Joseph Conrad and the Anthropological Dilemma* (Oxford: Clarendon Press, 1995)

Griffithes, T. P., *From Bedford Row to Swazieland* (London: Bradbury, Agnew and Co., 1890)

Hall, B., *Fragments of Voyages and Travels* (London: Edward Moxon, 1852 edn)

Hall, C., 'Competing masculinities: Thomas Carlyle, John Stuart Mill and the case of Governor Eyre', in C. Hall, *White, Male and Middle Class* (Cambridge: Polity, 1992), pp. 255–95

Hall, R., *Stanley: An Adventurer Explored* (London: Collins, 1974)

Hallett, R. (ed.), *Records of the African Association, 1788–1831* (London: Thomas Nelson, 1964)

Hansen, P., 'The dancing lamas of Everest: cinema, orientalism and Anglo–Tibetan relations in the 1920s', *American Historical Review*, 101 (1996), pp. 712–47

Hansen, P., 'Vertical boundaries, national identities: British mountaineering on the frontiers of Europe and the Empire, 1868–1914', *Journal of Imperial and Commonwealth History*, 24 (1996), pp. 48–71

Hansen, P., 'Tenzing's two wrist-watches: the conquest of Everest and late imperial culture in Britain, 1921–1953', *Past and Present*, 157 (1997), pp. 159–77

Haraway, D., 'Teddy bear patriarchy: taxidermy in the Garden of Eden', in D. Haraway, *Primate Visions: Gender, Race and Nature in the World of Modern Science* (London: Verso, 1989), pp. 26–58

Harcourt, F., 'Disraeli's imperialism, 1866–1868: a question of timing', *Historical Journal*, 23 (1980), pp. 87–109

Hargreaves, J. D., 'Winwood Reade and the discovery of Africa', *African Affairs*, 56 (1957), pp. 306–16

Harley, B., 'Silences and secrecy: the hidden agenda of cartography in early modern Europe', *Imago Mundi*, 40 (1988), pp. 57–76

Harries, P., 'Slavery, social incorporation and surplus extraction: the nature of free and unfree labour in South-East Africa', *Journal of African History*, 22 (1981), pp. 318–30

Harrison-Barbet, A., *Thomas Holloway: Victorian Philanthropist* (Egham: Royal Holloway, 1994)

Heffernan, M., 'Geography, cartography and military intelligence: the Royal Geographical Society and the First world War', *Transactions of the Institute of British Geographers*, 21 (1996), pp. 504–33

Helly, D., 'Informed opinion on tropical Africa in Great Britain, 1860–1890', *African Affairs*, 68 (1969), pp. 195–217

Helly, D., *Livingstone's Legacy: Horace Waller and Victorian Myth-making* (Athens: Ohio University Press, 1987)

Herschel, J. (ed.), *A Manual of Scientific Enquiry: Prepared for the Use of Officers in Her Majesty's Navy; and Travellers in General* (London: John Murray, 1849)

Herschel, J., *Preliminary Discourse on the Study of Natural Philosophy* (London: Longman, 1851 edn)

Hevly, B., 'The heroic science of glacier motion', in H. Kuklick and R. Kohler (eds), *Science in the Field* (Chicago: Chicago University Press, 1996), pp. 66–86

Hobson, J. A., *The Psychology of Jingoism* (London: Grant Richards, 1901)

Hobson, J. A., *Imperialism: A Study* (London: James Nisbet, 1902)

Holder, H., 'Melodrama, realism and empire on the British stage', in J. Bratton, R. Cave, B. Gregory, H. Holder and M. Pickering (eds), *Acts of Supremacy: The British Empire and the Stage, 1790–1930* (Manchester: Manchester University Press, 1991), pp. 129–49

Honour, H., *The Image of the Black in Western Art*, vol. iv, part 1, *Slaves and Liberators* (Cambridge, Mass.: Harvard University Press, 1989)

Hudson, B., 'The new geography and the new imperialism', *Antipode*, 9 (1977), pp. 12–19

Hughes, W., *The Maniac in the Cellar: Sensation Novels of the 1860s* (Princeton, NJ: Princeton University Press, 1980)

Hulme, P., *Colonial Encounters: Europe and the Native Caribbean, 1492–1797* (London: Routledge, 1986)

Hunt, B., 'Doing science in a global empire: cable telegraphy and electrical physics in Victorian Britain', in B. Lightman (ed.), *Victorian Science in Context* (Chicago: Chicago University Press, 1997), pp. 312–33

Hunt, J., 'On the negro's place in nature', *Memoirs of the Anthropological Society of London*, 1 (1863–4), pp. 1–64

Hutcheson, J. A., *Leopold Maxse and the National Review* (New York: Garland, 1989)

Huxley, T., *Social Diseases and Worse Remedies* (London: Macmillan, 1891)

Hyndman, H. M., *General Booth's Book Refuted* (London: Social Democratic Federation, 1890)

Hyndman, H. M., *The Record of an Adventurous Life* (London: Macmillan, 1911)

Inglis, K. S., *Churches and the Working Classes in Victorian England* (London: Routledge & Kegan Paul, 1963)

Ingram, J., *The Land of Gold, Diamonds and Ivory* (London: Whittingham, 1889)

Jackson, J. R., *What to Observe; or the Traveller's Remembrancer* (London: James Madden, 1841)

Jardine, N., 'Naturphilosophie and the kingdoms of nature', in N. Jardine, J. Secord and E. Spary (eds), *Cultures of Natural History* (Cambridge: Cambridge University Press, 1996), pp. 230–45

Jardine, N. and Spary, E., 'The natures of cultural history', in N. Jardine, J. Secord and E. Spary (eds), *Cultures of Natural History* (Cambridge: Cambridge University Press, 1996), pp. 3–13

Jeal, T., *Livingstone* (London: Heinemann, 1973)

Jerdan, W., *The Autobiography of William Jerdan*, vol. iv (London: Arthur Hall, 1853)

Johnston, H., *Liberia* (London: Hutchinson, 1906)

Johnston, H., 'Livingstone as an explorer', *Geographical Journal*, 41 (1913), pp. 423–46

Jones, L. M. and Jones, I. (eds), *H. M. Stanley and Wales* (St Asaph: Stanley Exhibition Committee, 1972)

Jones, R., ' "The sight of creatures strange to our clime": London zoo and the consumption of the exotic', *Journal of Victorian Culture*, 2 (1997), pp. 1–26

Karp, I. and Lavine, S. (eds), *Exhibiting Cultures: The Poetics and Politics of Museum Display* (Washington, DC: Smithsonian Institution Press, 1991)

Kass, A. M. and Kass, E., *Perfecting the World: The Life and Times of Dr Thomas Hodgkin, 1798–1866* (Orlando: Harcourt Brace Jovanovich, 1988)

Kearns, G., 'Closed space and political practice: Frederick Jackson Turner and Halford Mackinder', *Environment and Planning D: Society and Space*, 2 (1984), pp. 23–34

Keating, P., *Into Unknown England, 1866–1913: Selections from the Social Explorers* (London: Fontana, 1976)

Keay, J. (ed.), *The Royal Geographical Society History of World Exploration* (London: Hamlyn, 1991)

Keltie, J. S., 'Mr Stanley's expedition: its conduct and results', *Fortnightly Review*, 48 (1890), pp. 66–81

Keltie, J. S., 'What Stanley has done for the map of Africa', *Contemporary Review*, January 1890, pp. 126–140

Keltie, J. S., 'Industry and commerce', in Royal Geographical Society, *Hints to Travellers* (London, 1893), pp. 411–20

Kennedy, D., 'Imperial history and post-colonial theory', *Journal of Imperial and Commonwealth History*, 24 (1996), pp. 345–63

Kern, S., *The Culture of Time and Space, 1880–1918* (Cambridge, Mass.: Harvard University Press, 1983)

Koven, S., 'The dangers of castle building: surveying the social survey', in M. Bulmer, K. Bales and K. Sklar (eds), *The Social Survey in Historical Perspective* (Cambridge: Cambridge University Press, 1991), pp. 368–76

Kügelgen, H. von and Seeberger, M., 'Humboldt und Bonpland in Enders "Urwaldatelier"', in *Alexander von Humboldt: Netzwerke des Wissens*, exhibition catalogue (Berlin: Haus der Kulturen der Welt, 1999), p. 157

Kuklick, H. and Kohler, R. (eds), *Science in the Field* (Chicago: Chicago University Press, 1996)

Kury, L., 'Les instructions de voyage dans les expéditions scientifiques français, 1750–1830', *Revue d'Histoire des Sciences*, 51 (1998), pp. 65–91

Lang, C. Y., *The Swinburne Letters*, vol. i (New Haven, Conn.: Yale University Press, 1959)

Larsen, A., *Not Since Noah: The English Scientific Zoologists and the Craft of Collecting, 1800–1840* (PhD thesis, Princeton University, 1993)

Latour, B., 'Visualisation and cognition: thinking with eyes and hands', *Knowledge and Society*, 6 (1986), pp. 1–40

Latour, B., *Science in Action: How to Follow Scientists and Engineers Through Society* (Milton Keynes: Open University Press, 1987)

Lévi-Strauss, C., *Tristes Tropiques* (London: Cape, 1973)

Lévi-Strauss, C., *Saudades do Brasil: A Photographic Memoir* (Seattle: University of Washington Press, 1994)

Light, J., 'The changing nature of nature', *Ecumene*, 4 (1997), pp. 181–95

Lightman, B. (ed.), *Victorian Science in Context* (Chicago: Chicago University Press, 1997)

Lindfors, B., 'Circus Africans', *Journal of American Culture*, 6 (1983), pp. 9–14

Livingstone, D., *Missionary Travels and Researches in South Africa* (London: John Murray, 1857)

Livingstone, D. N., 'Darwinism and Calvinism: the Belfast–Princeton connection', *Isis*, 83 (1992), pp. 408–28

Livingstone, D. N., *The Geographical Tradition* (Oxford: Blackwell, 1992)

Livingstone, D. N., 'The spaces of knowledge: contributions towards a historical geography of science', *Environment and Planning D: Society and Space*, 13 (1995), pp. 5–34

Lloyd, C., *Mr. Barrow of the Admiralty: A Life of Sir John Barrow, 1764–1848* (London: Collins, 1970)

Loch, C. S., *An Examination of General Booth's Social Scheme* (London: Swan Sonnenschein, 1891)

Lorimer, D., *Colour, Class and the Victorians* (Leicester: Leicester University Press, 1978)

Louis, W. R., 'The Berlin Congo Conference', in P. Gifford and W. R. Louis (eds), *France and Britain in Africa* (New Haven, Conn.: Yale University Press, 1971), pp. 167–220

Lowe, N. and White, R., *Wards of Court* (London: Butterworth, 1979)

Lutz, C. and Collins, L., *Reading National Geographic* (Chicago: Chicago University Press, 1993)

Mabberley, D. J., *Jupiter Botanicus: Robert Brown of the British Museum* (Braunschweig: J. Cramer, 1985)

McCook, S., ' "It may be truth, but it is not evidence": Paul du Chaillu and the legitimation of evidence in the field sciences', in H. Kuklick and R. Kohler (eds), *Science in the Field* (Chicago: Chicago University Press, 1996), pp. 177–97

MacDonald, R. H., *Sons of the Empire: The Frontier and the Boy Scout Movement, 1890–1918* (Toronto: University of Toronto Press, 1993)

MacDonnell, W., *Exeter Hall: A Theological Romance*, 10th edn (Boston: Colby and Rich, 1885)

McEwan, C., 'Gender, science and physical geography in nineteenth-century Britain', *Area*, 30 (1998), pp. 215–23

MacKay, D., 'A presiding genius of exploration: Banks, Cook and empire, 1767–1805', in R. Fisher and H. Johnston (eds), *Captain James Cook and His Times* (Vancouver: Douglas and McIntyre, 1979), pp. 21–39

MacKay, D., *In the Wake of Cook: Exploration, Science and Empire, 1780–1801* (London: Croom Helm, 1985)

MacKay, D., 'Agents of empire: the Banksian collectors and the evaluation of new lands', in D. P. Miller and P. H. Reill (eds), *Visions of Empire: Voyages, Botany and Representations of Nature* (Cambridge: Cambridge University Press, 1996), pp. 38–57

Mackenzie, J., 'The expansion of South Africa', *Contemporary Review*, 56 (1889), pp. 753–76

MacKenzie, J. M., 'David Livingstone and the worldly after-life: imperialism and nationalism in Africa', in *David Livingstone and the Victorian Encounter with Africa*, exhibition catalogue (London: National Portrait Gallery, 1996), pp. 201–19

MacKenzie, J. M., *Propaganda and Empire* (Manchester: Manchester University Press, 1984)

MacKenzie, J. M., *Orientalism: History, Theory and the Arts* (Manchester: Manchester University Press, 1995)

MacKenzie, J. M., 'The second city of the empire: Glasgow, imperial municipality', in F. Driver and D. Gilbert (eds), *Imperial Cities: Landscape, Display and Identity* (Manchester: Manchester University Press, 1999), pp. 215–37

Mackenzie, N. (ed.), *The Letters of Sidney and Beatrice Webb*, vol. i, *Apprenticeships, 1873–1892* (Cambridge: Cambridge University Press, 1978)

Mackinder, H., 'The geographical pivot of history', *Geographical Journal*, 23 (1904), pp. 421–44

MacLaren, I., 'Exploration/travel literature and the evolution of the author', *International Journal of Canadian Studies*, 5 (1992), pp. 39–68

MacLaren, I., 'From exploration to publication: the evolution of a nineteenth-century Arctic narrative', *Arctic*, 47 (1994), pp. 43–53

McLynn, F., *Stanley: The Making of an African Explorer* (London: Constable, 1989)

McLynn, F., *Stanley: Sorcerer's Apprentice* (London: Constable, 1991)

Macnair, J., *Livingstone the Liberator* (London: Collins, 1940)

Maddrell, A., 'Discourses of race and gender and the comparative method in geography school texts, 1830–1918', *Environment and Planning D: Society and Space*, 16 (1998), pp. 81–103

Maitland, A., *Speke and the Discovery of the Source of the Nile* (London: Constable, 1971)

Manchester, A., *A Modern Legal History of England and Wales, 1750–1950* (London: Butterworth, 1980)

Mangan, J. (ed.), *The Imperial Curriculum: Racial Images and Education in the British Colonial Experience* (London: Routledge, 1993)

Markham, C. R., *A History of the Abyssinian Expedition* (London, 1869)

Markham, C. R., 'From China to Peru', *Geographical Magazine*, 1 (1874), pp. 367–70

Markham, C. R., *The Fifty Years Work of the Royal Geographical Society* (London: John Murray, 1881)

Marsden, W., 'Rooting racism into the educational experience of childhood and youth in the nineteenth and twentieth centuries', *History of Education*, 19 (1990), pp. 333–53

Marshall, P. and Williams, G., *The Great Map of Mankind: British Perceptions of the World in the Age of Enlightenment* (London: Dent, 1982)

Marshall-Cornwall, J., *History of the Geographical Club* (London: privately printed, 1976)

Martineau, H., *How to Observe: Morals and Manners* (London: Charles Knight, 1838)

Martins, L., 'Mapping tropical waters', in D. Cosgrove (ed.), *Mappings* (London: Reaktion, 1999), pp. 148–68

Martins, L., *O Rio de Janeiro dos Viajantes: O Olhar Britânico* (Rio de Janeiro: Jorge Zahar Editor, 2000)

Mason, P., *Infelicities: Representations of the Exotic* (Baltimore, Md.: Johns Hopkins University Press, 1998)

Masterman, C. (ed.), *The Heart of the Empire* (London: Fisher Unwin, 1901)

Masterman, C., *From the Abyss* (London: Dent, 1902)

Masterman, C., *In Peril of Change* (London: Fisher Unwin, 1905)

Mathers, E., *Golden South Africa*, 4th edn (London: Whittingham, 1889)

Mathews, B., *Livingstone the Pathfinder*, 2nd edn (London: Oxford University Press, 1913)

Matless, D., *Landscape and Englishness* (London: Reaktion, 1998)

Matsebula, J., *A History of Swaziland*, 3rd edn (Cape Town: Longman, 1988)

Maxse, F., *The Causes of Social Revolt* (London: Longman, 1872)

Meacham, S., *Toynbee Hall and Social Reform* (New Haven, Conn.: Yale University Press, 1987)

Middleton, D. (ed.), *The Diary of A. J. Mounteney Jephson, Emin Pasha Relief Expedition, 1887–1889* (Cambridge: Cambridge University Press, 1969)

Middleton, D., 'Banks and African exploration', in R. Banks, B. Elliott, J. Hawkes, D. King-Hele and G. Lucas (eds), *Sir Joseph Banks: A Global Perspective* (London: Royal Botanic Gardens, 1994), pp. 171–6

Mill, H. R., *The Record of the Royal Geographical Society, 1830–1930* (London: Royal Geographical Society, 1930)

Miller, D. P., 'Between hostile camps: Sir Humphry Davy's presidency of the

Royal Society of London, 1820–1827', *British Journal for the History of Science*, 16 (1983), pp. 1–47

Miller, D. P., 'The revival of the physical sciences in Britain, 1815–1840', *Osiris*, 2 (1986), pp. 107–34

Miller, D. P., 'Joseph Banks, empire and "centers of calculation" in late Hanoverian London', in D. P. Miller and P. H. Reill (eds), *Visions of Empire: Voyages, Botany and Representations of Nature* (Cambridge: Cambridge University Press, 1996), pp. 21–37

Miller, D. P. and Reill, P. H. (eds), *Visions of Empire: Voyages, Botany and Representations of Nature* (Cambridge: Cambridge University Press, 1996)

Mitchell, T., *Colonising Egypt* (Cambridge: Cambridge University Press, 1988)

Mivart, St G., *On the Genesis of Species* (London: Macmillan, 1871)

Montgomery, S., 'Through a lens, brightly: the world according to *National Geographic*', *Science as Culture*, 4 (1993), pp. 4–46

Moon, H. P., *Henry Walter Bates, 1825–1892* (Leicester: Leicestershire Museums Service, 1976)

Moore, J. R., *The Post-Darwinian Controversies* (Cambridge: Cambridge University Press, 1979)

Moore, J. R., 'Darwin lies in Westminster Abbey', *Biological Journal of the Linnean Society*, 17 (1982), pp. 97–113

Moore, J. R., 'Freethought, secularism, agnosticism: the case of Charles Darwin', in G. Parsons (ed.), *Religion in Victorian Britain*, vol. i, *Traditions* (Manchester: Manchester University Press, 1988), pp. 274–319

Moore, J. R., 'Wallace's Malthusian moment: the common context revisited', in B. Lightman (ed.), *Victorian Science in Context* (Chicago: Chicago University Press, 1997), pp. 290–311

Morrell, J. and Thackray, A., *Gentlemen of Science: Early Years of the British Association for the Advancement of Science* (Oxford: Oxford University Press, 1981)

Morris, W., 'News from nowhere', in *Collected Works of William Morris*, vol. xvi (London: Longman, 1910–15)

Morton, P., *The Vital Science: Biology and the Literary Imagination* (London: Allen & Unwin, 1984)

Morus, I., Schaffer, S. and Secord, J., 'Scientific London', in C. Fox (ed.), *London: World City, 1800–1840* (New Haven, Conn.: Yale University Press, 1992), pp. 129–42

Mounteney-Jephson, A. J., *Emin Pasha and the Rebellion at the Equator* (London: Sampson Low, 1890)

Murdoch, N., 'William Booth's In Darkest England and the Way Out: a reappraisal', *Wesleyan Theological Journal*, 25 (1990)

Musselman, E., 'Swords into ploughshares: John Herschel's progressive view of astronomical and imperial governance', *British Journal for the History of Science*, 31 (1998), pp. 419–35

Nast, H., 'Women in the field', *Professional Geographer*, 46 (1996), pp. 54–66

Nicoll, D. J., *Stanley's Exploits: Or Civilising Africa* (Aberdeen: James Leatham, 1890)

Nord, D. E., 'The social explorer as anthropologist: Victorian travellers among the urban poor', in W. Sharpe and L. Wallock (eds), *Visions of the Modern City* (Baltimore, Md.: Johns Hopkins University Press, 1987), pp. 122–34

Nord, D. E., *Walking the Victorian Streets: Women, Representation and the City* (Ithaca, NY: Cornell University Press, 1995)

O' Day, R. and Englander, D., *Mr Charles Booth's Inquiry: Life and Labour of the People in London Reconsidered* (London: Hambledon, 1993)

Oliphant, L., 'African explorers', *North American Review*, 124 (1877), pp. 383–403

Oliver, R., *Sir Harry Johnston and the Scramble for Africa* (London: Chatto & Windus, 1964)

Omissi, D., 'The Hendon Air Pageant, 1920–1937', in J. MacKenzie (ed.), *Popular Imperialism and the Military* (Manchester: Manchester University Press, 1992), pp. 198–220

Ophir, A., 'The place of knowledge: a methodological survey', *Science in Context*, 4 (1991), pp. 3–21

Opie, R., *Rule Britannia: Trading on the British Image* (Harmondsworth: Penguin, 1985)

Osborne, J., 'Wilfred G. Thesiger, Sir Edward Grey and the British campaign to reform the Congo, 1905-9', *Journal of Imperial and Commonwealth History*, 27 (1999), pp. 59–80

Outram, D., 'New spaces in natural history', in N. Jardine, J. Secord and E. Spary (eds), *Cultures of Natural History* (Cambridge: Cambridge University Press, 1996), pp. 249–65

Outram, D., 'On being Perseus: new knowledge, dislocation and Enlightenment exploration', in D. Livingstone and C. Withers (eds), *Geography and Enlightenment* (Chicago: Chicago University Press, 1999), pp. 281–94

Palladino, P. and M. Worboys, M., 'Science and imperialism', *Isis*, 84 (1993), pp. 94–102

Paradis, J., 'Darwin and landscape', in J. Paradis and T. Postlewait (eds), *Victorian Science and Victorian Values* (New Brunswick: Rutgers University Press, 1985), pp. 85–110

Parke, T. H., *My Personal Experiences in Equatorial Africa* (London: Sampson Low, 1891)

Parrinder, P., *Shadows of the Future: H. G. Wells, Science Fiction and Prophecy* (Liverpool: Liverpool University Press, 1995)

Pedler, F., *The Lion and the Unicorn in Africa: A History of the Origins of the United Africa Company, 1787–1931* (London: Heinemann, 1974)

Peters, C., *New Light on Dark Africa* (London: Ward, Lock and Co., 1891)

Phillips, R., *Mapping Men and Empire: A Geography of Adventure* (London: Routledge, 1997)

Ploszajska, T., *Geographical Education, Empire and Citizenship: Geographical Teaching and Learning in English Schools, 1870–1944* (Historical Geography Research Group, 1999)

Ploszajska, T., 'Down to earth? Geography fieldwork in English schools, 1870–1944', *Environment and Planning D: Society and Space*, 16 (1998), pp. 757–74

Pollock, G., 'Vicarious excitements: *London: A Pilgrimage* by Gustave Doré and Blanchard Jerrold, 1872', *New Formations*, 4 (1988), pp. 25–50

Poole, D., *Vision, Race and Modernity: A Visual Economy of the Andean Image World* (Princeton, NJ: Princeton University Press, 1997)

Pope-Hennessy, J., *Monckton-Milnes* (London: Constable, 1951)

Pope Hennessy, J. and Dicey, E., 'Is central Africa worth having?', *Nineteenth Century*, 28 (1890), pp. 478–500

Port, M. H., *Imperial London: Civil Government Building in London, 1851–1915* (New Haven, Conn.: Yale University Press, 1995)

Porter, B., *The Lion's Share: A Short History of British Imperialism, 1850–1983*, 2nd edn (London: Longman, 1984)

Potter, B., *My Apprenticeship*, 2nd edn (London: Longman, 1945)

Poulton, E. B., *William John Burchell* (London: Spottiswoode, 1907)

Pratt, M. L., *Imperial Eyes: Travel Writing and Transculturation* (London: Routledge, 1992)

Pritchett, V. S., 'Books in general', *New Statesman and Nation*, 25 (1943), p. 323

Quaini, M., 'Alexander von Humboldt: cartografo e mitografo', in C. Greppi (ed.), *Alexander von Humboldt: L'Invenzione del Nuovo Mondo* (Florence: La Nuova Italia Editrice, 1992), pp. ix–xxix

Radford, J., 'Sterilisation versus segregation: control of the "feeble-minded", 1900–1938', *Social Science and Medicine*, 33 (1991), pp. 449–58

Rainger, R., 'Race, politics and science: the Anthropological Society of London', *Victorian Studies* (1978), pp. 51–70

Raj, K., 'La construction de l'empire de la géographie', *Annales Histoire, Sciences Sociales*, 52 (1997), pp. 1153–80

Reade, C., *A Record of the Redes of Barton Court, Berks* (Hereford: Jakeman and Carver, 1899)

Reade, C. L. and Reade, C., *Charles Reade: A Memoir* (London: Chapman & Hall, 1887)

Reade, W., *The Veil of Isis: Or, Mysteries of the Druids* (London: Skeet, 1861)

Reade, W., 'On the bush tribes of Equatorial Africa', *Anthropological Review*, 1 (1863), pp. xix–xxiii

Reade, W., *Savage Africa* (London: Smith, Elder and Co., 1863)

Reade, W., 'Efforts of missionaries among savages', *Journal of the Anthropological Society*, 3 (1865), pp. clxiii–clxviii

Reade, W., 'African martyrology', *Belgravia*, 1 (1867), pp. 46–54

Reade, W., 'English scientific societies', *The Galaxy*, 3 (1867), pp. 733–41

Reade, W., 'Heroes of central Africa', *Atlantic Monthly*, 19 (1867), 625–35

Reade, W., 'Mr. Swinburne: a sketch', *The Galaxy*, 3 (1867), pp. 682–4

Reade, W., *The Martyrdom of Man* (London: Trübner, 1872)

Reade, W., *The African Sketch-book* (London: Smith, Elder and Co., 1873)

Reade, W., *The Story of the Ashantee Campaign* (London: Smith, Elder and Co., 1874)

Reade, W., *The Outcast* (London: Chatto & Windus, 1875)

Reeder, D., 'Introduction', in *Charles Booth's Descriptive Map of London Poverty 1889* (London: London Topographical Society, 1984)

Reeder, D., 'Representations of the metropolis: descriptions of the social environment in *Life and Labour*', in D. Englander and R. O' Day (eds), *Retrieved Riches: Social Investigation in Britain* (Aldershot: Scolar, 1995), pp. 323–38

Rennie, N., *Far-fetched Facts: The Literature of Travel and the Idea of the South Seas* (Oxford: Oxford University Press, 1995)

Richards, E., 'Huxley and woman's place in science: the "woman question" and the control of Victorian anthropology', in J. R. Moore (ed.), *History, Humanity and Evolution* (Cambridge: Cambridge University Press, 1989), pp. 253–84

Richards, T., *The Commodity Culture of Victorian England: Advertising and Spectacle, 1851–1914* (Stanford, Calif.: Stanford University Press, 1990)

Rider Haggard, H., 'The fate of Swaziland', *New Review*, 2 (1890), pp. 64–75

Riffenburgh, B., *The Myth of the Explorer* (Oxford: Oxford University Press, 1994)

Ritchie, J. E., *The Life and Discoveries of David Livingstone* (London: James Sangster, 1877)

Robertson, J. M., *A History of Freethought in the Nineteenth Century* (London: Watts, 1929)

Robinson, H., 'The Swaziland question', *Fortnightly Review*, 47 (1890), pp. 283–91

Robinson, R. and Gallagher, J., *Africa and the Victorians: The Official Mind of Imperialism* (London: Macmillan, 1961)

Rockey, J., 'From vision to reality: Victorian ideal cities and model towns', *Town Planning Review*, 54 (1983), pp. 83–105

Roos, D., 'The "aims and intentions" of *Nature*', in J. Paradis and T. Postlewait (eds), *Victorian Science and Victorian Values* (New Brunswick: Rutgers University Press, 1985), pp. 159–80

Rose, G., *Feminism and Geography: The Limits of Geographical Knowledge* (Cambridge: Polity, 1993)

Rose, L., *The Erosion of Childhood: Child Oppression in Britain, 1860–1918* (London: Routledge, 1991)

Ross, E., *Love and Toil: Motherhood in Outcast London, 1870–1918* (Oxford: Oxford University Press, 1993)

Ross, M. J., *Polar Pioneers: John Ross and James Clark Ross* (Montreal: McGill-Queen's University Press, 1994)

Rotberg, R., *The Rise of Nationalism in Central Africa* (Cambridge, Mass.: Harvard University Press, 1966)

Rotberg, R. (ed.), *Africa and Its Explorers* (Cambridge, Mass.: Harvard University Press, 1970)

Rotberg, R., *Joseph Thomson and the Exploration of Africa* (London: Chatto & Windus, 1971)

Rotberg, R., *The Founder: Cecil Rhodes and the Pursuit of Power* (Oxford: Oxford University Press, 1988)

Rousseau, J.-J., *Émile: Or, On Education* (Harmondsworth: Penguin, 1981)

Roxby, R. B., *General Booth Limited: A Limelight on the 'Darkest England' Scheme* (London: Sutton, 1892)

Royal Geographical Society, *Hints for Collecting Geographical Information* (London: Clowes, 1837)

Royal Geographical Society, *Hints to Travellers*, various edns (London: Royal Geographical Society, 1865–1901)

Royal Geographical Society, *Royal Geographical Society Illustrated* (London: Scriptum Editions, 1997)

Royle, E., *Radicals, Secularists and Republicans: Popular Freethought in Britain, 1866–1915* (Manchester: Manchester University Press, 1980)

Ryan, J., *Picturing Empire: Photography and the Visualization of the British Empire* (London: Reaktion, 1997)

Ryan, S., *The Cartographic Eye: How Explorers Saw Australia* (Cambridge: Cambridge University Press, 1996)

Rydell, R., *All the World's a Fair: Visions of Empire at American International Expositions, 1876–1916* (Chicago: University of Chicago Press, 1984)

Samarin, W., *The Black Man's Burden: African Colonial Labour on the Congo and Ubangi Rivers, 1880–1900* (Boulder, Colo.: Westview, 1989)

Samuel, R., *Theatres of Memory* (London: Verso, 1994)

Samuel, R., *Island Stories: Unravelling Britain* (London: Verso, 1998)

Sandwith, H., *The Land and Landlordism* (London: Kerby and Endean, 1873)

Savours, A., 'Clements Markham', in R. Bridges and P. Hair (eds), *Compassing the Vaste Globe of the Earth: Studies in the History of the Hakluyt Society, 1846–1996* (London: Hakluyt Society, 1996), pp. 165–99

Savours, A. and McConnell, A., 'The history of the Rossbank Observatory, Tasmania', *Annals of Science*, 39 (1982), pp. 527–64

Schimlek, F., 'New ways in the missions of South Africa', in *Mariannhill and its Apostolate: Origin and Growth of the Mariannhill Missionaries* (Reimlingen: St Joseph Mission Press, 1964), pp. 65–84

Schneider, W., *An Empire for the Masses* (Westport, Conn.: Greenwood, 1982)

Schneider, W., 'Geographical reform and municipal imperialism in France, 1870–1880', in J. MacKenzie (ed.), *Imperialism and the Natural World* (Manchester: Manchester University Press, 1990), pp. 90–117

Schulten, S., 'The perils of *Reading National Geographic*', *Reviews in American History*, 23 (1995), pp. 521–7

Schults, R., *Crusader in Babylon: W. T. Stead and the Pall Mall Gazette* (Lincoln: University of Nebraska Press, 1972)

Schwarz, B., 'Conquerors of truth: reflections on postcolonial theory', in B. Schwarz (ed.), *The Expansion of England: Race, Ethnicity and Cultural History* (London: Routledge, 1996), pp. 9–31

Secord, J., 'King of Siluria: Roderick Murchison and the imperial theme in nineteenth-century British geology', *Victorian Studies*, 25 (1982), pp. 413–42

Semmel, B., *Imperialism and Social Reform: English Social Imperial Thought, 1895–1914* (London: Allen & Unwin, 1960)

Semmel, B., *The Governor Eyre Controversy* (London: Macgibbon and Kee, 1962)

Shapin, S., 'Placing the view from nowhere: historical and sociological problems in the location of science', *Transactions of the Institute of British Geographers*, 23 (1998), pp. 5–12

Shelton, A., *Fetishism: Visualising Power and Desire* (London: Lund Humphries, 1995)

Shephard, B., 'Showbiz imperialism: the case of Peter Lobengula', in J. MacKenzie (ed.), *Imperialism and Popular Culture* (Manchester: Manchester University Press, 1986), pp. 94–112

Shepperson, G., 'A West African partnership: Winwood Reade and Andrew Swanzy', *Progress: The Unilever Quarterly*, 51 (1965), pp. 41–7

Shine, H. and Shine, H. C., *The Quarterly Review under Gifford* (Chapel Hill: University of North Carolina Press, 1949)

Shyllon, F. O., *Black Slaves in Britain* (London: Oxford University Press, 1974)

Sidaway, J., 'The (re)making of the western "geographical tradition"', *Area*, 29 (1997), pp. 72–80

Simpson, D., *Dark Companions: The African Contribution to the European Exploration of East Africa* (London: Elek, 1976)

Sinha, M., Hall, C., Smyth, G. and Young, R., 'Colonial desire' (roundtable discussion), *Journal of Victorian Culture*, 2 (1997), pp. 113–52

Sklar, K., 'Hull-House maps and papers: social science as women's work in the 1890s', in M. Bulmer, K. Bales and K. Sklar (eds), *The Social Survey in Historical Perspective* (Cambridge: Cambridge University Press, 1991), pp. 111–47

Smith, B., 'Cook's posthumous reputation', in R. Fisher and H. Johnston (eds), *Captain James Cook and His Times* (Vancouver: Douglas and McIntyre, 1979), pp. 159–85

Smith, C. and Agar, J. (eds), *Making Space for Science: Territorial Themes in the Shaping of Knowledge* (Basingstoke: Macmillan, 1998)

Smith, I., *The Emin Pasha Relief Expedition, 1886–1890* (Oxford: Oxford University Press, 1972)

Smith, W. S., *The London Heretics* (London: Constable, 1967)

[Smyth, W. H.], *The Royal Geographical Society and Its Labours* (London: Clowes, 1846)

Sörlin, S., 'National and international aspects of cross-boundary science: scientific travel in the eighteenth century', in E. Crawford, T. Shinn and S. Sörlin (eds), *Denationalizing Science* (Dordrecht: Kluwer, 1993), pp. 43–72

Sorrenson, R., 'The ship as a scientific instrument in the eighteenth century', in H. Kuklick and R. Kohler (eds), *Science in the Field* (Chicago: Chicago University Press, 1996), pp. 221–36

Sparke, M., 'Displacing the field in fieldwork: masculinity, metaphor and space', in N. Duncan (ed.), *Bodyspace: Destabilizing Geographies of Gender and Sexuality* (London: Routledge, 1996), pp. 212–33

Speke, J. H., *Journal of the Discovery of the Source of the Nile* (London: Blackwood, 1863)

Spurr, D., *The Rhetoric of Empire: Colonial Discourse in Journalism, Travel-*

writing and Imperial Administration (Durham, NC: Duke University Press, 1993)

Stafford, R., *Scientist of Empire: Sir Roderick Murchison, Scientific Exploration and Victorian Imperialism* (Cambridge: Cambridge University Press, 1989)

Stagl, J., 'The methodising of travel in the sixteenth century', *History and Anthropology*, 4 (1990), pp. 303–38

Stanley, H. M., *How I Found Livingstone* (London: Sampson Low, 1872)

Stanley, H. M., 'Central Africa and the Congo basin: or, the importance of the scientific study of geography', *Journal of the Manchester Geographical Society*, 1 (1885), pp. 6–25

Stanley, H. M., *The Congo and the Founding of Its Free State* (London: Sampson Low, 1885)

Stanley, H. M., *In Darkest Africa* (London: Sampson Low, 1890)

Stanley, H. M., *Through the Dark Continent*, rev. edn (London: George Newnes, 1899)

Stanley, H. M., *The Autobiography of Henry M. Stanley*, ed. D. Stanley (London: Sampson Low, 1909)

Stasny, J., 'W. Winwood Reade's *The Martyrdom of Man*: a Darwinian history', *Philological Papers*, 13 (1961), pp. 37–49

Stedman Jones, G., *Outcast London: A Study in the Relationship between Classes in Victorian Society* (Oxford: Clarendon Press, 1971)

Steedman, C., 'The space of memory: in an archive', *History of the Human Sciences*, 11 (1998), pp. 65–83

Steffel, R., 'The Boundary Street estate', *Town Planning Review*, 47 (1976), pp. 161–73

Stengers, J. and Vansina, J., 'King Leopold's Congo, 1886–1908', in R. Oliver and G. Sanderson (eds), *The Cambridge History of Africa*, vol. vi (Cambridge: Cambridge University Press, 1985), pp. 315–58

Stephen, L., *Essays on Freethinking and Plainspeaking* (London: Longman, 1873)

Stevens, T., *Scouting for Stanley in East Africa* (London: Cassell, 1890)

Stevenson, M. (ed.), *Thomas Baines: An Artist in the Service of Science in Southern Africa* (London: Christie's, 1999)

Stewart, G., 'Tenzing's two wrist-watches: the conquest of Everest and late imperial culture in Britain, 1921–1953', *Past and Present*, 149 (1995), pp. 170–97

Stocking, G., 'What's in a name? The origins of the Royal Anthropological Institute', *Man*, 6 (1971), pp. 369–90

Stocking, G., *Victorian Anthropology* (New York: Free Press, 1987)

Stoddart, D., 'The RGS and the "new geography"', *Geographical Journal*, 146 (1980), pp. 190–202

Stoddart, D. R., *On Geography and Its History* (Oxford: Blackwell, 1986)

Stoddart, D. R., 'Darwin and the seeing eye: iconography and meaning in the Beagle years', *Earth Sciences History*, 14 (1995), pp. 3–22

Stover, L., 'Applied natural history: Wells versus Huxley', in P. Parrinder and C. Rolfe (eds), *H. G. Wells under Revision* (Selinsgrove: Susquehanna University Press, 1990), pp. 125–33

Strangford. E. (ed.), *A Selection from the Writings of Viscount Strangford on Political, Geographical and Social Subjects* (London: Bentley, 1869)

Street, B., 'British popular anthropology: exhibiting and photographing the Other', in E. Edwards (ed.), *Anthropology and Photography, 1860–1920* (New Haven, Conn.: Yale University Press, 1992), pp. 122–31

Swanzy, H., 'A trading family in the nineteenth century Gold Coast', *Transactions, Historical Society of Ghana*, 2 (1956), pp. 87–120

Temperley, H., *British Antislavery, 1833–1870* (Harlow: Longman, 1972)

Temperley, H., *White Dreams, Black Africa: The Anti-Slavery Expedition to the River Niger, 1841–2* (New Haven, Conn.: Yale University Press, 1991)

Tennant, D., *London Street Arabs* (London: Cassell, 1890)

Tennent, J., *Ceylon* (London: Longman, 1859)

Thomas, D., *Swinburne: The Poet in His World* (London: Weidenfeld and Nicolson, 1979)

Thomas, N., *Colonialism's Culture: Anthropology, Travel and Government* (Cambridge: Polity, 1994)

Thomson, J., 'Through the Masai country to Victoria Nyanza', *Proceedings of the Royal Geographical Society*, 6 (1884), pp. 690–710

Thomson, J., 'The results of European intercourse with the African', *Contemporary Review* (March 1890), pp. 339–52

Thorburn, J., *Struggles in Africa* (London: Swazieland Concessionaire, 1890)

Tolen, R., 'Colonizing and transforming the criminal tribesman: the Salvation Army in British India', *American Ethnologist*, 18 (1991), pp. 106–25

Topalov, C., 'The city as *terra incognita*: Charles Booth's poverty survey and the people of London, 1886–1891', *Planning Perspectives*, 8 (1993), pp. 395–425

Tsuzuki, C., *H. M. Hyndman and British Socialism* (Oxford: Oxford University Press, 1961)

Tuathail, G. Ó, *Critical Geopolitics: The Politics of Writing Global Space* (Minneapolis: University of Minnesota Press, 1996)

Urry, J., '*Notes and Queries on Anthropology* and the development of field methods in British anthropology, 1870–1920', *Proceedings of the Royal Anthropological Institute* (1972), pp. 45–72

Vansina, J., 'Do pygmies have a history?', *Sprache und Geschichte in Afrika*, 7 (1986), pp. 431–5

Vansina, J., *Paths in the Rainforests: Toward a History of Political Tradition in Equatorial Africa* (London: James Currey, 1990)

Walker, P., ' "I live but not yet I for Christ liveth in me": men and masculinity in the Salvation Army, 1865–1890', in M. Roper and J. Tosh (eds), *Manful Assertions: Masculinities in Britain since 1800* (London: Routledge, 1991), pp. 92–112

Walkowitz, J., *City of Dreadful Delight: Narratives of Sexual Danger in Late-Victorian London* (London: Virago, 1992)

Waller, H., 'The Universities Mission to Central Africa', *Quarterly Review*, 168 (1889), pp. 229–48

Waller, H., *Nyassaland: Great Britain's Case Against the Portuguese* (London: Stanford, 1890)

Waller, H., *Ivory, Apes and Peacocks: An African Contemplation* (London: Stanford, 1891)

Ward, D., *Poverty, Ethnicity and the American City, 1840–1925: Changing Conceptions of the Slum and the Ghetto* (Cambridge: Cambridge University Press, 1989)

Ward, T. H., *Humphry Sandwith: A Memoir* (London: Cassell, 1884)

Warren, A., 'Popular manliness: Baden-Powell, scouting and the development of manly character', in J. Mangan and J. Walvin (eds), *Manliness and Morality: Middle-class Masculinity in Britain and America, 1800–1940* (Manchester: Manchester University Press, 1987), pp. 199–217

Watts-Dunton, C., *The Home Life of Swinburne* (London: Philpot, 1922)

Wells, H. G., *The Outline of History* (London: Cassell, 1920)

Wells, H. G., *'42 to '44* (London: Secker & Warburg, 1944)

White, A., *Truth About the Salvation Army* (London: Simpkin and Marshall, 1892)

White, A., *Joseph Conrad and the Adventure Tradition: Constructing and Deconstructing the Imperial Subject* (Cambridge: Cambridge University Press, 1993)

Whyte, F., *The Life of W. T. Stead* (London: Jonathan Cape, 1925)

Wiener, J. H. (ed.), *Papers for the Millions: The New Journalism in Britain, 1850s to 1914* (New York: Greenwood, 1988)

Willan, B., 'The Anti-Slavery and Aborigines' Protection Society and the South African Natives' Land Act of 1913', *Journal of African History*, 20 (1979), pp. 83–102

Winter, A., 'The construction of orthodoxies and heterodoxies in the early Victorian life sciences', in B. Lightman (ed.), *Victorian Science in Context* (Chicago: Chicago University Press, 1997), pp. 24–50

Withers, C., 'Geography, natural history and the eighteenth-century Enlightenment: putting the world in place', *History Workshop Journal*, 39 (1995), pp. 137–63

Withers, C., 'Towards a history of geography in the public sphere', *History of Science*, 36 (1998), pp. 45–78

Withers, C., 'Voyages et crédibilité: vers une géographie de la confiance', *Géographie et Cultures*, 33 (2000), pp. 3–19

Woods, E., *A Darkness Visible: Gissing, Masterman and the Metaphors of Class, 1880–1914* (PhD thesis, Sussex University, 1988)

Yeo, E., 'The social survey in social perspective, 1830–1930', in M. Bulmer, K. Bales and K. Sklar (eds), *The Social Survey in Historical Perspective* (Cambridge: Cambridge University Press, 1991), pp. 49–65

Yeo, R., *Defining Science: William Whewell, Natural Knowledge and Public Debate in Early Victorian Britain* (Cambridge: Cambridge University Press, 1993)

Youngs, T., ' "My footsteps on these pages": the inscription of self and "race" in H. M. Stanley's *How I Found Livingstone*', *Prose Studies*, 13 (1990), pp. 230–49

Youngs, T., *Travellers in Africa: British Travelogues, 1850–1900* (Manchester: Manchester University Press, 1994)

Yule, A., 'Memoir of Sir Henry Yule', in H. Yule (ed.), *The Book of Ser Marco Polo*, 3rd edn (London: John Murray, 1903), vol. i, pp. xxvii–lxxxii

Yule, H. and Hyndman, H., *Mr Henry M. Stanley and the Royal Geographical Society* (London: Bickers, 1878)

Index

Lightning Source UK Ltd.
Milton Keynes UK
16 March 2011

169353UK00001B/5/P